For Valeria, who, as usual, took it all in her stride.

HENRY BLOFELD

Over and Out

HENRY BLOFELD

Over and Out

My Innings of a Lifetime
with Test Match Special

HODDER

First published in Great Britain in 2017 by Hodder & Stoughton
An Hachette UK company

This paperback edition published in 2018

1

A CIP catalogue record for this title is available from the British Library

B format ISBN 9781473670945
eBook ISBN 9781473670938

Typeset in Adobe Caslon Pro by Hewer Text UK Ltd, Edinburgh
Printed and bound in Great Britain by Clays Ltd, Elcograf S.p.A.

Hodder & Stoughton policy is to use papers that are natural, renewable
and recyclable products and made from wood grown in sustainable
forests. The logging and manufacturing processes are expected to
conform to the environmental regulations of the country of origin.

Hodder & Stoughton Ltd
Carmelite House
50 Victoria Embankment
London EC4Y 0DZ

www.hodder.co.uk

CONTENTS

PREFACE

'WHY are you retiring from *Test Match Special*?' is a question I have been asked countless times since I made the original announcement.

There is no simple answer to that. There is no one reason. It is a combination of factors which, taken together, have convinced me that the day has come to wave goodbye to a job I have loved, one I have been incredibly lucky to do for nearly fifty years. I have to concede that at my age – and these words are being written when I am less than two months away from my seventy-eighth birthday – commentating becomes a little harder each year. One of my eyes suffers from macular degeneration, and although the other is still in mid-season form, my sight is not quite as sharp as it was. My reflexes, too, are suffering just a touch from old age. Jumping in and out of chairs in a commentary box has always been a noisy and inexact science with me. That is not going to get any better now, and then there are my hips . . . but I don't think there is any need to go down that road.

The result of all this is that I do not find commentary quite as easy as I once did, and if it is more difficult, it becomes less fun. Then there is the evolutionary progress of commentary itself, which moves in step with the way the game changes. Everything happens more quickly today. The influence of first 50-over cricket and then T20 has happily caused Test cricket, still the gold standard of the game, to move along at a much more satisfactory speed, which better suits the world in which we live. Day/night cricket has now begun to spread to Test matches, and the twilight zone when floodlights take over from daylight causes enough problems when both eyes are fully functioning. Limited-over matches offer me less time to do the one thing that I am perhaps any good at, which is to describe the scene. In fact, the curtain came down on my one-day career at the end of the 2015 season in England. *TMS* producer Adam Mountford and I quietly agreed that I should let the limited-over stuff go quietly past the off stump.

Then there is the style of commentary. Over the years it has become much more conversational. Instead of coming in at the end of the over or when a wicket falls, summarisers nowadays are involved in an ongoing conversation with the commentator. This again inevitably restricts the time I have to describe all that I can see in front of me. Try keeping Geoffrey Boycott or Michael Vaughan quiet for a couple of balls, let alone a whole over. Far from there being any harm in this, it probably makes *TMS* even more approachable and enjoyable for the listener. There are some who say that while this is true, it also leads to an increase in trivia, but we were not bad at that anyway.

Finally a vain thought: it is probably more sensible to go when people are saying nice things about you than to wait until they all shriek, 'Why on earth is he still here?'

A little bit of all these things helped me to make up my mind. In real life, people don't often wake up, jump out of bed and shout, 'I'm off!' But that is pretty well how it happened with me. It suddenly came to me one day just after the 2017 cricket season had begun. I have at least spared the BBC from having to go through the business of sacking me – or putting me out to grass, if you prefer.

With Jonathan Agnew at the helm alongside Simon Mann, *Test Match Special* is in the safest of hands, with plenty of relatively new commentators to back them up. Ed Smith, Alison Mitchell, Charlie Dagnall and Dan Norcross are all stout performers, with two more former England players, Ebony Rainford-Brent and Isa Guha, also ready to flex their most knowledgeable muscles. Then there are the wise old owls in the corner led by Vic Marks and Geoffrey Boycott, with Michael Vaughan, Phil Tufnell and my stage partner, Graeme Swann, alongside them, to make sure the commentary guys don't slip up. These are the commentators and summarisers who will soon be taking *TMS* on to further heights.

With the future in safe hands, I can now look back lovingly and laughingly at all the many mishaps and adventures I have had in and around the commentary box. Who would have thought that one of my most memorable moments on air would be describing the tropical storm to end all tropical storms; that my most loved form of transport to an overseas tour would be a 1921 Rolls-Royce; that I would once get within an hour of playing in a Test match; that I would survive liberal doses of tear gas at the cricket in Kingston, Jamaica, and then Lahore; that I would commentate with the Maharaja of Baroda . . .? And on it goes. There were some great matches to describe, some hysterical scenes in various boxes. Above all, there were the tremendous friends with whom I was lucky enough to work. Some of them were household names, others became brief and for a short time equally notable companions. Then there was the gentleman who visited our box in the Pavilion at Lord's and promptly lay down on the floor and went to sleep.

I am old enough to have worked with all the main stars in the commentary box, with three exceptions. I never even met Howard Marshall who, before the war, pioneered the course we have all followed since. By an extraordinary chance I touched base with his granddaughter the day I announced my retirement. I also missed commentating with Rex Alston – he had retired before I began – though there was one splendid moment in August 1987 when Rex and Jim Swanton, both old men, climbed up the stairs to the commentary box at the top of the Pavilion at Lord's. It was during the Centenary match between the MCC and a Rest of the World XI. For a few overs Alston and Swanton plied their old trade.

Rex still had those lovely modulated tones with a hint of the schoolmaster he had been before he took to the airwaves. His precise voice was still wonderful to listen to but his eye now missed some of the details. It was Trevor Bailey who sat beside him and lent a helping hand when it came to identification. When he had retired as a regular commentator, Rex wrote about county cricket for the *Daily Telegraph*. He was always good fun and it was lovely to arrive on the first day of a match at the county ground in Hove or anywhere else in the south of England, which had become his parish, and to find him there. His presence guaranteed three amusing days. Reassuringly, Jim Swanton boomed away like the latter-day Bismarck we had grown to love and indeed who I had encountered briefly when I first entered the box in 1972. Jim was a hard taskmaster. Even on this celebratory occasion, he pointed his finger at what he considered to be irrelevant frivolity on the air. The original plan was for these two to be joined in the commentary box by John Arlott, who had agreed to fly over from Alderney. In the end he was unable to travel and we had to make do with a telephone conversation, when those unmistakable tones were still – well, unmistakable.

Another famous commentator I never worked with, although I was lucky enough to meet him, was Charles Fortune, who was, loosely speaking, South Africa's equivalent of John Arlott. He was born in 1906 in Wiltshire and emigrated to South Africa in 1935. Fortune had a beguilingly inconsequential tone and a tendency to be lured into extravagant descriptions of the local scenery. Alan McGilvray, his Australian counterpart, whose form of commentary could hardly have been more different, wrote of Fortune, 'He would lose track of the game every so often, and he didn't often worry about such minor details as the score. But the words flowed from his mouth like a cascade of flowers, colourful and sweet-smelling and rich in warmth and character.' Which was unusually poetic for McGilvray. Another idiosyncrasy of Fortune's was his refusal to complete the knot with his necktie. The main, front bit of the tie simply hung down loose over where the knot should have been. It gave him a lopsided look. I well remember the withering and unrepeatable reply he gave to someone who, one day in Port Elizabeth, tried to put him right over this. He was a dear man and a great lover and purveyor of the English language.

Like these great names, most of the people I have encountered working for *Test Match Special* have been memorable characters in their own right. I have tried to illustrate this simply by sharing with the reader stories about them in which I was involved or for which I had a front-row seat in the stalls. Minor disputes take place in all walks of professional life, but in this regard *Test Match Special* was a special place to work. In all the years I have been with the programme, there might have been the odd rumble, but this was always safely away from the box, where professionalism ruled. Any differences were soon forgotten and the blend of commentary seldom suffered from clashing personalities.

Since I announced that I was going to retire from *TMS*, one thing that has staggered me is all the warmth, kindness and support I have received. It has all been hugely heart-warming and I never expected it to happen as it has. I have been asked to appear on a great many shows, both on radio and television, from Piers Morgan and Andrew Marr down to umpteen local BBC radio stations up and down the country. I have also taken part in a number of game shows, and at Lord's I was honoured to be asked to ring the five-minute bell before the start on the Saturday of the Test against South Africa. Nottingham City Council has even named a bus after me, which I launched at a neighbouring bus stop during the lunch interval on the first day of the Test this year against South Africa at Trent Bridge.

I hope readers will enjoy themselves in the following pages almost as much as I did at the time. I hope, too, that you will be able to see what a wonderful life I have been lucky enough to have. This is a very personal book. I am writing it without any intention of telling readers the right way or the wrong way to commentate – as if I knew. It is a chronicle of enjoyment, for I have been left with nothing but wonderful memories of the commentary box and all those I have worked with.

Henry Blofeld
London, August 2017

1

LETTING THE CAT
OUT OF THE BAG

I DON'T think it had ever really occurred to me that one day I would have to retire from *Test Match Special*. Although I was seventy-seven, I was still doing five or six Test matches a year – three or four at home and a couple on tour. I was getting by, I like to think, and my inability to determine, with anything approaching accuracy, the name of the fielder at third man had, I hope, become more of a joke than anything else. Then, in December 2016, I went out to India to commentate for *TMS* on the Tests in Bombay and Madras. In both matches England lost their last five second-innings wickets for 16 and were massively beaten. I would like to think my commentary was a touch surer than England's batting, but maybe not by much.

On 20 December, the fourth and, as it happened, final day in Madras, I was on the air when England's batsmen seemed almost to throw their hands in. A slog drive from Moeen Ali off Ravi Jadeja had ended up in Ravi Ashwin's hands at deep mid off. I got that right. Liam Dawson, in his first Test, was now facing leg-spinner Amit Mishra. We were at the bowler's

1

end and Mishra was running away from us. For Dawson, he had about five men round the bat, including a short mid off and a short extra cover. He ran in to bowl, his arm came over and I saw the ball leave his hand and Dawson start to shuffle across his stumps. Then, for a moment I shall never forget, everything went blank. I could see nothing, although the crowd were cheering their heads off, which told me a wicket had fallen. When my vision cleared, I saw Dawson taking his first step towards the pavilion and the close fielders on the off side jumping about in celebration.

I took a punt: 'And Dawson has been caught there at short extra.'

Sunny Gavaskar, sitting beside me in the summariser's chair, now entered the conversation: 'No, Henry, he was bowled.'

Get out of that one. I struggled on but it must have sounded dreadful. The memory of that moment has never left me. It was my worst experience at the microphone.

An eye specialist told me later there is a logical explanation for what happened and it was a chance in a million. Which was little help. The incident played on my mind relentlessly. Then, in the middle of the night, just as the England season was beginning in April 2017, I suddenly realised the time had come. As the problem had happened to me once, it could obviously happen again, and at my age things like that do not get better; they only get worse. I did not want to make a fool of myself and, even more important, I did not want the programme which was responsible for the wonderful life I have led to be made to look stupid too.

When I put it to my wife, Valeria, the next morning and asked her advice, she told me she understood, but insisted that it had to be my decision. Within an hour I had rung up Ralph Brünjes, my agent, and told him that I was retiring. By then, the BBC had bravely asked me to commentate on three Test matches for *TMS* during 2017. The first and the last were at Lord's, against South Africa and the West Indies. The second was against South Africa at Trent Bridge, always my favourite Test match ground. I could hardly have asked for a better way to go.

I also told my great friend Richard Kay, a man of repute, charm and influence at the *Daily Mail*. It was his paper which finally broke the story on Friday, 23 June. It would all have come out rather sooner if it had not been for the political shenanigans surrounding T. May, J. Corbyn, Brexit and the accompanying general election. They had not left much room for anything else. I must admit I was more than a touch nervous as to what the reaction would be.

The night before the story broke I spent the evening at home with Valeria. We talked about my years with *TMS*. I went through my memories of some of those I had worked with over the years: their foibles, their strengths, their characteristics at the microphone and so on. I told Valeria I was sad I had never met Howard Marshall, the man who before the war had really put cricket commentary on the map. Marshall's commentary in that wonderful voice as he described Len Hutton breaking Don Bradman's record Test score of 334, against Australia at The Oval in 1938, is immediately recognisable as the early version of what we do today. It lacks the modern flourishes and the laughter, but the format is there. Marshall was extremely good-looking, with a private life to match. He was much married and had one spectacular divorce. It was his private life to which Lord Reith objected, and the BBC did not go back to him after the war. Nevertheless, he was an important figure in the story of cricket commentary. I was sad that I had never met him and that I had never had any contact with his family. I had also been unable to find out anything about him as a man, apart from the impersonal Google facts.

I spent a moment or two that evening thinking about what it must have been like for him starting from scratch. He was the man who showed those of us who came later the path we should follow. Marshall was really the Christopher Columbus of cricket commentary. The problems he faced must have been considerable. The game's administrators at the time were deeply hostile, regarding this wireless intrusion as newfangled nonsense and a tiresome and unnecessary interference, and they were not prepared to give it house room. So much so that when he was at Lord's for the Australian Test in 1934, Marshall had to run to a basement flat in Lisson Grove to do his reports. He was about to start one when the little girl in the flat upstairs began her piano lesson.

*   *   *

I went to bed on the Thursday evening wondering if anyone would be in the least interested in my retirement. In the grand scheme of things I was surely an irrelevance. The Friday had hardly dawned before the telephone started to ring. Ralph Brünjes was an early caller and asked me, first up, how I was doing. It is the sort of unnecessary rhetorical question which never brings the best out in me, although I know it is always asked from the best possible motives. In any case, it was far too early for me to have any idea of how I was. At my age there is a whole inventory to be gone through.

He told me there was a marvellous piece opposite the leader page in the *Daily Mail*. He said he had already spoken to Ben Gallop, the BBC's head of radio sport, who had been charming. Ralph was relatively new to the agent's game and had not orchestrated a retirement before. He, like me, was slightly unsure of his ground that morning. I told him I had already had a message from Adam Mountford, the *TMS* producer, asking me to ring him back as soon as possible. I decided to get up first so that I could at least face the world on a clean-shaven footing.

Ralph soon arrived at my house, arms full of *Daily Mail*s. He was sure the telephone would ring non-stop and he wanted to be there to take charge. I found myself vaguely pondering the past, the present and the future. Up until that moment, I had been thinking of retirement as a sort of surreal game that was going to be played in a few days' time. Now it dawned on me that the whistle had gone. I did not know what I should be feeling. There was no ghastly moment of realising that I had burned my boats for ever and, oh help. Far from it. My immediate reaction was a feeling of relief, not only that it was out in the open, but that I was also no longer going to have to justify my place in the commentary box. And, of course, although I am nearly a hundred, there is so much else to do. But first I still had to commentate on three more Test matches. I was well aware of how important it was to be somewhere near my best for these final matches: to try and go out with a bang.

I could not have enjoyed my first day of official retirement more. It was incredibly hectic. Sitting at home after breakfast, I first recorded telephone interviews for the BBC six o'clock news that evening and then the ten o'clock news. There were lots of calls from local BBC radio stations wanting to talk to me. Ralph took over the calls and planned times for the interviews. Various friends who had read the news in the *Daily Mail* had also picked up the telephone. It was then the turn of the *Daily Telegraph* for a quick talk with Patrick Sawer. He wrote a lovely piece. My next job was an interview on the telephone with ITV and then I had the friendliest of chats with Radio Cornwall. After that it was Radio Norfolk, rapidly followed by Radio Merseyside. They all asked me why I had decided to retire and what my best moment had been on air. That was easy, because I had taken the last wicket at Headingley in 1981, when Bob Willis removed Ray Bright's middle stump. I was struck by the warm and friendly tones of all those who had talked to me. I am ashamed to say that I was beginning to feel rather important.

In between fielding other calls, we had a quick bite of something to eat. Valeria had already broken the record for making cups of coffee. Her Italian inventiveness now came to the fore as she managed to produce a salad which was both attractive and considerably more than just edible. I have never been a great lover of rabbit food, but she manages to do something special with it. Anyway, body and soul had been stitched together adequately enough when, soon after three o'clock, a taxi arrived to take us to Channel 4. We were in the inevitable queue on the Embankment by Chelsea Old Church when Ralph's telephone rang. It was his office to tell him they had on the line a lady who wanted to speak to me. Miraculous to say, she was apparently a relation of Howard Marshall. Ralph handed me his telephone and a moment later I was talking to Howard Marshall's granddaughter. I could hardly believe it.

Her name was Mandy Peate. She told me that, having seen the news of my retirement, she wanted to make contact because some of her grandfather's things had come to her after he had died. They included a picture of Lord's which he had painted in 1934, the year in which Hedley Verity, taking 15–104 on a drying pitch, had bowled England to victory over Australia. England had won by an innings and 38 runs, a result which prompted the BBC to send Howard Marshall to report on the next Test, at Old Trafford. Mandy Peate told me she would like to give me the picture. She had never even met me. It was unbelievably kind and an amazing coincidence, coming as it did the day after Valeria and I had talked about Howard Marshall. I promised to get in touch with her when all the fuss had died down. When Mandy and her husband, John, came round to see us about a month later she presented me with his evocative picture, which he had painted from the top of the Lord's Pavilion. It features the old Tavern and Mound Stand, with the famous tall chimney on the other side of St John's Wood Road, with all the ramshackle buildings around it, as well as some of the famous grass. Every time I look at it I get a thrill, because it has filled in the last remaining gap in my *Test Match Special* story. Mandy also had a collection of photographs, several of which showed Howard Marshall at a surprisingly sleek, earlyish BBC microphone. She kindly had a number of the pictures copied for me.

It was only a few days after Mandy and her husband came to see us that I discovered in one of my bookshelves a somewhat battered old book published in 1933. It was an anthology of cricket stories put together by Howard Marshall himself. He had written a fascinating introduction in which he tried to define what cricket should mean to us all and what it meant to him. Here was the first serious commentator, who at that time had barely dipped his toes in the waters of any sort of cricket writing:

To these important qualities of zest and enjoyment, I would add, a little diffidently perhaps, a plea for the judicious use

of sentiment. The sights and sounds of the English coun-
tryside; the smell of freshly-cut grass and the distant whirr
of the mower; the slow rhythm of play in sunlit fields; the
lengthening shadows and the cawing rooks, all these must
be added to the sum of things which form the ultimate
character of cricket.

As the head public-relations man for pigeons, seagulls, helicopters and all the other beyond-the-boundary attractions
that form part of the picture of a day's cricket, I rest my case.

After that first day, the tempo quietened. I was up early the
next morning to be interviewed on Radio 4's *Saturday Live*. I
had another early start on the Sunday to help review the
papers for *The Andrew Marr Show*. I was with two rather
earnest political experts, Fraser Nelson, the editor of *The
Spectator*, and Ellie Mae O'Hagan from the Corbyn camp. I
did not come into any of that. I talked about Prince Harry
letting everything hang out and saying that none of the young
royals wanted the top job. I said, rather pompously, that it was
probably better if they kept their feelings to themselves.

My principal amusement the next day was an appearance
on Radio 5 Live's *Tuffers and Vaughan* show on the Monday
evening. In my naïveté, I expected them both to be there in
the studio when I arrived at London's Broadcasting House
armed with lots of messages. I was shown into an empty
studio and given a microphone. On the television screen in

front of me I saw intermittent shots of a smiling Vaughany in a studio in Manchester, while. Phil Tufnell was sitting in another in Guildford – though he still managed to look as if he was bouncing in to bowl. It was terrific fun and we had several good long-range laughs.

The next morning I really was up at some ridiculous hour, for Piers Morgan and *Good Morning Britain*. In the afternoon I was going to help with the commentary at a game at Latymer Upper School's ground in Wood Lane to raise money for the victims of the unbelievably awful fire at nearby Grenfell Tower which had claimed so many lives. The stark black shell of the building stood a few hundred yards away as a painful reminder of what had happened. Lashings, a team of former international cricketers, were taking on a side from the combined Houses of Lords and Commons. Two of the Lashings players, West Indian Tino Best and England's Monty Panesar, were also in the studio to talk to Morgan about the game. To start with, he asked me a few questions about my reasons for retiring, before bringing in the other two and talking about the Grenfell Tower match. Piers had just spent five minutes rightly laying into the government and Kensington and Chelsea Council for refusing to be repre-sented in the discussion he had just orchestrated about the reasons for the fire and the immediate response to it on the ground. I still cannot think of any other disaster in my adult life that affected me as this has done. It does not bear think-ing about what those wretched people, including many children, went through in their last few minutes. That empty black shell wags a not-to-be-ignored finger at all those in any way responsible for what happened. It poured down throughout our game of cricket, but both teams were happy to ignore that. The rain somehow served to underline the sheer horror of the circumstances. I am delighted to say, too, that we raised a significant amount of money.

The first two Test matches of the summer were late in coming because the 50-over Champions Trophy competition had been played in June. Whatever one's views of one-day cricket, surely everyone will have rejoiced that this competition saw India and Pakistan playing each other twice. It seems unlikely the two countries will be able to play each other any time soon in their own backyards. Terrorism and politics have combined to make that almost impossible. But here they were, first in the preliminary round at Edgbaston, where India cantered to victory by 124 runs, and then, by a wonderful chance, in the final. By that stage Pakistan had convincingly beaten England in the semi-final in Cardiff. They were running into form at the right time. This was confirmed, to the immense delight of their supporters, in the final at The Oval, when they beat India by the extraordinary margin of 180 runs. It was a frustrating summer for Indian cricket. A few weeks later their women's team reached the final of the World Cup, but having looked as if they were going to walk it, they lost to England by nine runs in the most thrilling finish.

My own one-day commentary career had ground to a halt two years before in an hotel suite at the Ageas Bowl in Southampton. I can assure you that it was not because I behaved badly in the bedroom. Opposite the pavilion there is a Hilton Hotel which forms part of the stadium. At international matches the hotel is requisitioned for cricketing matters. We had been given a luxurious suite as a commentary box. This contained a succulent-looking double bed, which sparked much lively banter. It also enabled Tuffers to recover from a late night. New Zealand beat England by three wickets in that match. It was the first time I had commentated with Isa Guha, who had been a considerable medium-paced bowling force in the England women's side. In 2014 she had become the first woman to be used by *TMS* as a summariser. It's a job she does well. She has a good voice and certainly knows her cricket. I remember leaving the ground that day wondering if I was not getting too old for one-day cricket. Looking back on it, this was another stage in the process of age taking over. Maybe I needed that double bed more than Tuffers, or Michael Vaughan, who usurped his position in the bed as the day progressed.

2

RINGING
THE BELL

THE week after announcing my retirement from *TMS*, I was in the commentary box at Lord's for the first Test match against South Africa. My impending retirement concentrated the mind in curious ways. In the few days before the game, I found myself wondering how my life would have turned out if I had never bicycled into a bus in 1957 when I was still at Eton. If I had looked where I was going, would I have ended up in the commentary box and enjoyed such a wonderful life? Would I have been as lucky as I have been? Perhaps playing cricket might have provided an exciting alternative. I have always doubted this, and those who suggested that it might have done are only really basing their assessment of my pre-accident cricketing abilities on one week early in August 1956 when I discovered my bat had a middle as well as an edge. These are all unanswerable questions.

It must have taken me a long time to throw off the effects of the nasty head injuries I suffered. I have been told that brain bruising takes about ten years to work its way out. My head took the brunt of that bus and I don't think I ever understood the full extent of my injuries. I was only seventeen, and when I came out of hospital and started to live life again, all I wanted to do was to get on with it. I realise, looking back now, that I was under a considerable handicap, but it only occurred to me then in a few isolated instances. My first nasty shock was quick in coming.

I was desperate to go back to Eton for the last few days of my last half (as a term was called). As captain of the cricket XI I had been quite a toff and I wanted to play a part in all the activities that leaving boys get up to in those last few days. My house had got through to the semi-finals of the house cricket competition and I was determined to play. The doctors were happy that, within reason, I should do whatever I felt I could do. The match took place on Agar's Plough. My house, Mr Forrest's, were playing against Mr Wykes's boys. The captain of their side was someone I had first met when I was ten or eleven and who remained one of my greatest friends. Edward Scott and I had played boys' cricket in west Norfolk. Edward was a fast bowler and he told me later that having to bowl at me as I was then in that house match had made him more nervous than me. He was worried about hurting me. At the time, I goaded him, saying I could cope with anything he could produce at his gentle medium pace.

When we batted I managed to see the ball and I was able to defend well enough, but I had always been a bit of a dasher. I now found it much harder to play my strokes. I had got a few and had hung around for a while when Edward brought himself on to bowl. I had no fear of any sort as he ran in and I think I survived his first over without too much difficulty. Then, two or three overs later, it happened. I saw the ball was short – there was nothing wrong with my eyes – and I wanted to hook. I loved to play the hook and it was a stroke which had brought me many runs. I had always been quick-footed but now I found my feet were stuck in cement. I could not move them, even an inch. The signal from my brain to my legs did not get through. I was left waving my bat helplessly, and I suppose I was lucky the ball did not hit me. Edward came down, apologising profusely for bowling me a short one. I told him not to worry, but it was a dreadful moment. I had to face up to it that I was no longer the person who had bicycled into that bus. The irony was that we were playing the game not much more than a hundred yards from where I had had the accident, in the Datchet Lane.

The miracle was that I was playing at all, but even after that ball I was still reluctant to see it like that. To start with, I was confident that my reflexes would pull themselves together soon enough. In August I played some Minor Counties matches for Norfolk, which I should never have done, but I was so determined to show that all was well. Of course, I hardly got a run, but that did not stop me from trying. By then, I knew I was going up to Cambridge that October. As the start of term approached, it began to occur to me that I was going into a new world where most of my fellow undergraduates would have done national service. That would give them a two-year advantage. When you are eighteen, the difference between eighteen and twenty seems more than just two years. Another handicap was that I was in the middle of the unnerving process of learning that the only thing I had ever been any good at, cricket, was no longer working for me. But I did not grasp this in such clear-cut terms. I soldiered on blithely with a vague belief that all would be well in the end. After all, the Cambridge cricket season didn't begin until the following April, which was still a long way off. There was time for things to change. Or so my muddled thinking had it. No one was anxious to put me right either, because they did not want to dent my confidence. My life moved along, therefore, in a cheerful fog.

When the spring arrived I found in the nets at Fenner's, the Cambridge University cricket ground, that while it was not as bad as it might have been, it was a great deal worse than it had once been. I opened the batting in a few games for the university without much success. In my first innings in first-class cricket, I popped a short one in a gentle loop to forward short leg. The memory of that stroke haunts me now as acutely as it did then. Before the blasted bus I would have hooked it for four – or so my thinking went. It was actually my wicketkeeping that was affected most. My reflexes were behaving like idiots, which made me look like one too. My total lack of success in that year's exams also pointed at the bus. When I returned to King's College for my second year that autumn, the senior tutor showed me some of the things I had written down in my exams. I could not believe it. A great deal of it was gibberish; there is no other word for it. As it had been only a college exam rather than a university exam, they took a deep breath and had me back for another year.

Now, six decades later, my footsteps took me once again to the *Test Match Special* commentary box at Lord's. For a few years I had been growing a little nervous as Test matches approached. I was finding the job harder and I was not altogether sure the box still felt like home. Now that I had told the world I was heading off into the sunset, I could hardly have felt more relaxed and everyone was delightful – from the gatekeepers on the East Gate and the stewards by the lift up to the Media Centre, to the girl who poured my coffee and gave me too much milk, and everyone in the box. It was a sort of antepenultimate homecoming and I loved every moment of it.

Of course, sentiment relentlessly pursued me. For a moment I was back in 1948, sitting on the family rug in front of Q Stand, now the Allen Stand, eating strawberries. I actually touched the ball after Don Bradman had pulled it for four. Seven years later I was traipsing off the ground, mystified by the thunderous applause, bowled first ball in my first Eton and Harrow match, only to discover, a few minutes later, I had been the third victim of a hat-trick. A minute or two, but really a year, later I was leaving the ground raising a tentative and rather shy bat, having slogged 104 not out for the Public Schools against the Combined Services. As I walked up the steps into the Pavilion, an elderly member shook my hand and told me it was the hundredth hundred he had seen at Lord's. I was rather bewildered and did not exactly sparkle in reply.

Three years later, in 1959, I was back at Lord's again, having scraped into a pretty average Cambridge side, the eleventh choice I think, as the exceedingly average post-bus-accident opening batsman that I had become. We were taking on the MCC and Denis Compton was playing for them in one of his last first-class games. He made 71 extraordinary runs in an innings which was unrivalled for sheer imaginative improvisation and beauty. I only once saw this innings equalled, when I kept wicket for the Arabs, a touring side formed by Jim Swanton, behind Everton Weekes on a drying pitch after a violent storm at Kensington Oval in Barbados, when the ball did everything but talk. In cricketing terms, both Compton and Weekes were by then old men; if they were still that good, what they were like in their prime, goodness only knows. In Cambridge's second innings I managed to score my only first-class hundred, and I hope I can take the moment when Denis Compton came up and congratulated me into however many worlds lie ahead of us. Then, of necessity, we come briefly, but perhaps not briefly enough, to my only University match, when I made two and one and Oxford came first. That, suitably, was my last playing appearance at Lord's.

As I now looked out over the ground, my mind could see once again the coaches standing in front of the old Tavern for the Eton v Harrow match, when, in 1955, there must have been at least ten thousand people in the ground. I thought back, too, to my first match at Lord's for *TMS*, a one-day international between England and Australia in 1972. We sat in the original *TMS* box at the back of the Warner Stand looking over the head of third man, a worrying angle. This was the first ever official one-day series. I remembered, too, taking my first wife, when we were engaged, to Lord's to watch England play South Africa in 1960. As we arrived at our seats in the Grandstand she noticed a small diamond had fallen out of her engagement ring. We were on our way to the jewellers before the end of the first over. Brian Statham, whom I had faced at Fenner's two years earlier in a stand with my first Cambridge captain, Ted Dexter, took six wickets that day. I saw none of them.

As you can see, this first Test match against South Africa at the beginning of July 2017 was a moment when memories and ghosts ganged up on me from all directions. It made me realise how incredibly lucky I have been, and I enjoyed doing the commentary enormously. I took Joe Root to his hundred. Twelve months earlier I had taken him to 200 at Old Trafford against Pakistan. My greatest thrill came when I was asked by the MCC to ring the bell before the start of play on the third day, the Saturday. This is a privilege given to former Test cricketers and very few others. The bell has to be rung with great precision at 10.55, exactly five minutes before the start.

Aggers knew I was going to be asked before anyone had told me. He had spent the first day exhorting me to save my most outlandish clothes for the Saturday. I always like to be colourful for Test matches. I blame my wife, who, being Italian, and having spent years in the fashion world, has an eye for these things.

When the day arrived, my shoes and linen trousers were yellow, my shirt orange, with a green jacket and a spotted yellow bow tie. Adam Mountford had planned that I should go out to the middle at the start of the programme. I would be chatting with Aggers about ringing the bell and my memories of Lord's. Michael Vaughan, Vic Marks and Ed Smith came and went, all making their inimitable contributions, and, as always, we were shepherded by Henry Moeran, Adam Mountford's assistant. After fifteen minutes, I was collected by someone from the MCC. As I followed him up the main Pavilion steps, the members gave me a lovely round of applause. I was then led along the back of the seats to the steps leading up to the balcony of what is now known as the Bowlers' Bar, but which used to be the professionals' changing rooms. The bell hung beguilingly down over the balcony rails.

We were joined by the Secretary and Chief Executive of the MCC, Derek Brewer, who is also soon retiring. He was the master of ceremonies and he took me through the drill. At five to eleven, an MCC chap with a clock set to Greenwich Mean Time would say 'go'. There was a reassuring authority about his grey hair. By then, I would be gripping the short rope which hung down from the bell, ready to swing it when the moment arrived. Vaughany was my chief coach and had persuaded me that I had to give it a real biff. He also suggested that as it was the five-minute bell, I should go on for five minutes. Derek Brewer cautioned me against this, telling me that no less a man than former umpire Dickie Bird had got it into his mind that this was the way forward. One hell of a cacophony was the result, until restraining hands won the day.

There were now masses of MCC members standing all around me and looking up from below. When the ground announcer told the assembled multitude that I was about to ring the bell, I received another round of applause, which, although lovely, was slightly embarrassing as, after all, I was only ringing a bell. By now, Aggers and Vaughany were on the grass just in front of us describing events for our listeners. The clock chap just behind me was now clearly under starter's orders. I was gripping the rope tightly with both hands. Vaughany had recommended the two-handed interlocking grip. I was ready for blast-off. The clock chap gave me an authoritative 'go'. And off I went. I gave it everything and the interlocking grip did not let me down. There was no holding me. After six massive swings of the rope and six thunderous rings, some neighbouring hands went up to protect their ears, while others shot forward to hold me in check. Now that the bell had been well and truly rung, I was escorted up to the committee dining room. I was interviewed in front of a camera by one of the MCC staff, and I talked about my principal memories of Lord's. Then I was escorted under the Grandstand back to the Media Centre and our commentary box. What a splendid adventure it had been.

England beat South Africa in four days by 211 runs. It was a great triumph for Joe Root in his first Test as England's captain. He had made 190 in England's first innings and it seemed an auspicious start. This Test was the last time I would commentate for the BBC with Simon Mann, who has become such an outstanding and reliable commentator and friend. He bade me farewell in glowing terms in his last commentary spell, before Geoffrey Boycott wisely changed the subject. This Test match had been going on alongside Wimbledon, and it was a busy time for the Mann family. One of the Wimbledon ball-girls, mostly on the Centre Court, was Simon's fifteen-year-old daughter, Isobel. On her own initiative, she had applied for the job and been through six months of endless training sessions during which many were sent packing. She passed them all with high marks. Now she was fielding the balls – I daresay with greater athleticism than her father had ever been able to muster – for Roger Federer, Novak Djokovic, Andy Murray and the rest. She was loving it and doing the job brilliantly. I talked about this briefly on air and Simon later reminded me that I had announced her birth fifteen years earlier, also on *Test Match Special*.

There were only four days before most of us met up again, at Trent Bridge for the second Test. In recent years, when

England have won the first Test of a series they have almost invariably lost the second. We were assured that was not going to happen again. It was a thrill to do my penultimate Test match commentary at Trent Bridge. The old Trent Bridge attendants, all of whom have become such friends over the years, were as welcoming as ever and told me they were sad I was hanging up my microphone.

When I arrived, Adam Mountford told me I would be starting off the commentary in the box that morning. He added that I would have to go out with Charlie Dagnall during the lunch interval, but without telling me what for. I was delighted that Charlie was in the team. He and his young daughter, Bea, had become good friends over the last two or three years. I was keen to share a match with him. Another newcomer was James Taylor. His playing career had been ended cruelly early when the doctors discovered he had a heart problem. Now he was helping out dear old Pat Murphy, who for such a long time has been making sure that Radio 5 Live's Test match output is up to scratch. A lady who has been a regular visitor to Trent Bridge now managed to find an early way through the new combination lock on the door intended to control our privacy. She brought with her an excellent chocolate cake, with my name inscribed on the icing, so she can be forgiven. It kept me going, this cake, for the whole match.

I did two commentary spells that first morning, but no sooner had the players gone into lunch than I was spirited away into the lift by Charlie, all wired up with a roving microphone.

I knew something connected with my retirement was going to happen, but I had no idea what. We went through a gate into the Radcliffe Road and turned towards the lights and the traffic island. It suddenly came to me that we were going to one of John Arlott's favourite watering holes, the Trent Bridge Inn, which is in that corner of the ground. Wine was likely to be involved, which was a pity as I was on a teetotal stint. But no. We walked on past the pub entrance and round the bend at the road junction. What now? I couldn't think of anything. Then, at the first bus stop in the Loughborough Road, I saw a gleaming new green double-decker.

Charlie must have followed my gaze, for he said, 'You should know where we are going now.'

Rather uncertainly, I said, 'The bus?'

He nodded. In another couple of paces I could make out the sign at the top of the back of the bus: 'Blowers, my dear old thing.'

There was quite a gathering round the bus to greet me. The Nottingham City Council had, over the years, appreciated my interest in their buses trundling up and down the Loughborough Road and, more occasionally, down the Bridgford Road. I shook hands with the besuited head of the City Council. I was shown another white inscription painted across the front of the bonnet, which said 'Henry Blofeld OBE'. It was amazing, wonderful and unbelievable. They had named a bus after me. In case anyone is anxious to hop on board, it is a number six bus and its route takes it, appropriately enough, down the Bridgford Road past Trent Bridge. Funnily enough, on these journeys it stops outside Graeme Swann's house and Swanny, I know, jumps on board whenever he can. I was then interviewed by Charlie, whose busmanship was impressive, and the whole thing was broadcast during the tea interval. We had a tremendous laugh and I felt greatly honoured. Masses of photographs and more laughter and much hand-shaking followed before we had to scarper and pay attention to the afternoon session.

That was not quite the end of it, though. Soon after our return, the Nottinghamshire chairman, Richard Tennant, came into the box, followed by two or three others and another gentleman with a chain of office round his neck. The chairman dropped his hand on my shoulder and presented me with a lovely large cake with a photograph of me which somehow had been transferred onto the magnificent green icing. Modern technology, I suppose. Then the bechained chap stepped forward. I took a plunge and said I imagined he was the Lord Mayor. He was swift to deny the accusation and told me he was the Sheriff of Nottingham. I said something to him about Robin Hood and I think Friar Tuck also got a mention. Then he presented me with another huge cake covered in thick white icing which bore a glowing tribute to me. I can never thank the City of Nottingham enough, but I had to break off when I was sharply interrupted by the need to do another bit of commentary.

I was overwhelmed by the generosity and warmth of everyone I met. The icing on the cake, if I am allowed the pun, came two days later when an old friend, from the Nottinghamshire committee, who is a year or three ahead of me, walked round the ground from the pavilion. He came up to wish me well before the start of play.

On the third morning, Adam Mountford even asked me to go out to the middle and start the programme, which must surely have been against his better judgement. This is something I love doing. Vaughany, Ed Smith and Graeme Swann, who was summarising for this match, all took turns to be there. Charlie Dagnall, who was down to take over from me after a quarter of an hour, was also hovering.

It was a pity that England lost the match by 340 runs without ever looking much like doing anything else. As I walked back to the car park afterwards I felt sad that my working days at Trent Bridge were over, but exhilarated that I had been able to commentate one last time at this lovely ground. As at Lord's, my mind was full of some personal playing memories of the ground. I first played there for Norfolk against Notts Second XI in the Minor Counties Championship in 1956. When I reported this fact on air, not a minute had gone by before the miraculous Andrew Samson, our scorer, told listeners that I had made 13 and 27. All I can remember of the match was the vast scoreboard in the corner of the ground where the council office block now stands. It was the first one in the country to have the names of all the individual players on it. There was something rather

magnificent about seeing the light go up against your name
every time you fielded the ball. There was at least one awful
occasion when I looked up too soon, to see the lights flicker
against my name. I took my eye off the ball and it went straight
through my legs for four.

I played one first-class match there too, for Cambridge
against Nottinghamshire in 1959. Reg Simpson was captain
of the county side, and to try and raise interest in this game,
which was played over the weekend, he enlisted the services
of the immortal Australian allrounder Keith Miller. He had
retired after Australia's tour to England in 1956 and Lord
Beaverbrook had signed him up for the *Daily Express*. His
presence certainly improved the crowd on the Saturday and
we were thrilled to be playing against such a famous cricketer.
He always seemed to be in high good humour. He talked to
us all as if we had been friends for years and his hair gleamed
most satisfyingly with Brylcreem.

We batted first. I opened the innings with David Kirby,
who went on to captain Leicestershire in the dying days of
the amateur captain. Keith Miller, playing one of his last two
or three first-class games, opened the bowling, and in his first
over he turned his wrist over and bowled a couple of quick
leg-breaks. I did not make many runs, but what a great experience it was. We were bowled out for not very many during
the last session of the day. We then took two Nottinghamshire
wickets, which brought in Keith. He was a few not out at the
end of the day. He had brought up from London with him a

beautiful girl who had recently been selected as Miss Victoria, and you felt the judges had got it right. She sat patiently all day in the ladies' stand on the Saturday before disappearing off with Keith for the weekend – no Sunday play in those days.

On the Monday morning, about fifteen minutes before the start, Reg Simpson came down to our dressing room, which was, as it is now, immediately under the home dressing room. He wanted to know if we had seen Keith. We told him we had not and he left. About three minutes later there was a loud bump against the door, which flew open, revealing a dishevelled Keith Miller.

'Now, boys, I can't get up there,' he said, pointing in the direction of the home dressing room. 'Be good blokes and lend me some kit.'

There was not much time and we helped him undress. I had the luck to be one of those who helped remove his shirt, which was stuck to his skin and covered in small red patches. When we eventually got it off, it seemed as if something rather more significant than a light skirmish had recently taken place on his back. For us, it was all part of life's rich learning curve. The power of Miss Victoria's fingernails was impressive.

Oh yes, Keith made a hundred in Nottinghamshire's second innings. When he was 65 he swung and skied an off-break from Alan Hurd to deep midwicket. I circled underneath the ball for a long time before making a real mess of the catch. Forty years later I found I still had the scorecard of that game.

I sent it to Keith, asking him to sign it. When he sent it back, he had scrawled across the card, 'Well dropped, Henry. Keith Miller.' Nothing wrong with his memory, either.

The old stories are often the best and at Trent Bridge in that second Test against South Africa, Aggers trotted out an old gem. As a schoolboy, he had gone to the famous cricket school in Wandsworth in south-west London owned by the former England and Surrey fast bowler Alf Gover. Aggers told listeners how fond he was of Gover. He then told the story from the private tour taken to India in 1936–37 by Lord Tennyson, who had captained England three times against Australia in 1921. Gover was on the tour and opened the bowling when they played a first-class match in Poona. Gover had marked out his long run at the end furthest from the pavilion. The Indian opening batsman took guard, looked round the field and took his stance. Gover started in and he had only gone about six paces when he felt something like a red-hot knife go through his tummy. He knew the score and kept on running. He went past the umpire, past the stumps, past the striker and then the wicket-keeper. He ran straight into the pavilion, into the dressing room and into the lavatory. He had been sitting there for a couple of minutes when there was a great banging on the door and a furious voice shouted, 'Give us back our ball!' Gover looked down and found he still had the new ball in his trouser pocket.

I took over from Aggers and could not resist telling the other Gover story from that tour. The side was staying at a maharaja's palace. One night everything had been set up for His Lordship to shoot a tiger. He asked Gover, who was a good friend, to go with him. They were taken to a clearing in the jungle where there was a hide which the maharaja often used. It was some way off the ground and they climbed up by the ladder and settled themselves in for a long wait. As was the custom, a live goat was tied to a stake in the clearing as bait to attract the tiger. They waited more than an hour and a half in complete silence, watching the clearing and the goat, which suddenly became agitated. His Lordship was now on red alert and the tiger soon appeared. It circled the goat, which was protesting loudly. His Lordship, who had a clear field of fire, raised his gun and fired. The tiger, unharmed, sprinted off into the bush while the goat slumped to the ground at the foot of the pole. At which point Gover said from the back in a loud and startled voice, 'Good Lord, My Lord, you've shot the goat.'

M.C.C. v Cambridge University

Played at Lord's Cricket Ground on 8, 9, 10 July 1959

Umpires: BL Muncer, HP Sharp

Toss: Cambridge University

CAMBRIDGE UNIVERSITY

D Kirby	c Stevenson b Kimmins	89	c Melluish b Wait		2
HC Blofeld	c Cook b Kimmins	3	st Melluish b Cook		138
MJL Willard	b Goonesena	81	c Kimmins b Wait		87
DJ Green†	c Kimmins b Wait	29	not out		8
RM Prideaux	c Goonesena b Kimmins	11	run out		44
NSK Reddy	not out	28	not out		10
JR Bernard	c & b Compton	40			
CB Howland*	not out	21			
A Wheelhouse					
AM Hurd					
S Douglas-Pennant					
Extras	(b 1, lb 14, nb 1)	16	(b 18, lb 3)		21
Total	(106 overs)	318	(72 overs)		310

M.C.C

PE Richardson	lbw b Wheelhouse	9	c Green b Bernard		1
WHH Sutcliffe	c Howland b D-Pennant	14	c Green b Bernard		98
GW Cook	run out	0	c Reddy b Bernard		24
DCS Compton	c Prideaux b Hurd	71	c Hurd b Bernard		36
G Goonesena	run out	9	c Green b Willard		22
MH Stevenson	c Reddy b Hurd	13	b Willard		122
JGW Davies †	lbw b D-Pennant	0	c sub b D-Pennant		43
SEA Kimmins	c Kirby b D-Pennant	29	b Hurd		30
DK Fasken	c Kirby b Bernard	12	c Howland b D-Pennant		1
MEL Melluish*	run out	3	c Howland b Hurd		10
OJ Wait	not out	6	not out		4
Extras	(b 5, lb 3)	8	(b 11, lb 1, w 1)		13
Total	(42 overs)	174	(108 overs)		404

M.C.C	O	M	R	W	O	M	R	W
OJ Wait	17.0	4	49	1	18.0	1	63	2
SEA Kimmins	25.0	8	74	3	13.0	2	50	0
DK Fasken	17.0	6	74	0	16.0	3	68	0
G Goonesena	28.0	4	96	1	11.0	1	42	0
JGW Davies	5.0	2	9	0	5.0	1	17	0
DCS Compton	12.0	2	40	1	5.0	1	20	0
GW Cook	2.0	1	1	0	4.0	0	29	1

CAMBRIDGE	O	M	R	W	O	M	R	W
S D-Pennant	15.0	2	66	3	26.0	2	116	2
A Wheelhouse	9.0	2	52	1				
AM Hurd	14.0	6	36	2	32.0	8	85	2
JR Bernard	4.0	1	12	1	28.0	6	101	4
MJL Willard					13.1	0	56	2
D Kirby					8.0	2	25	0
HC Blofeld					1	0	8	0

Fall of wickets:

	Cam	MCC	Cam	MCC
1st	4	9	8	2
2nd	165	12	160	40
3rd	196	50	269	87
4th	226	100	292	133
5th	228	107	-	231
6th	283	107	-	235
7th	-	121	-	336
8th	-	152	-	345
9th	-	167	-	400
10th	-	174	-	404
	-		-	

Result: Cambridge University won by 50 runs

3

TESTING TIMES
IN THE CITY

I WONDER where the world would be without the Ashes. I cannot think of any other single thing that has had such a lasting effect on my life. I made contact with the Ashes in 1948 when I went to Lord's for the first time to see the third day's play in the second Test against Australia. I watched Don Bradman make 89. I was instantly grabbed by the sinister thrill of that dark green baggy cap: sinister because Australia came out on top more often than not.

Bradman. What a name. I can picture him now, a small man dwarfed by that huge, well-worn cap. Even though I was not yet nine, I can still see his walk to the wicket. There was a sprightly, almost springy, determination about his purposeful stride out to the middle. It was thrilling and irresistibly magnetic. I had been absorbed by his prodigious run-scoring feats and at the time I was upset that he did not make a hundred. I went on to devour a little green book called *Bradman* by the Australian journalist and commentator A.G. Moyes, which told the story of the Don's life. I remember that my mother, with me in tow, had gone into Norwich to change the library books, and I came across Moyes's book on a shelf of well-worn books discarded by the library and up for sale at bargain prices. It cost me half a crown. I still have the book with my name inscribed in my childish handwriting inside the front cover. It became my most valued possession. I took it everywhere. And yes, I have to own up: I probably slept with an Australian captain under my pillow. For an Englishman, there surely could not be a worse start to life than that. The 'Boots Booklovers' Library' label is stuck on the outside of the front cover. There is a healthy black cross over it too, to show it has not been stolen. I keep it inside a book-case sitting next to a dog-eared Bible I also had as a boy. There is no doubt which of them I considered to be more important then. Even now, the Bible has a fight on its hands to hold its own.

The main effect of that first visit to Lord's was to turn me instantly into a passionate devotee of cricket commentary on the wireless. I couldn't get enough of it. (As small boys, we were not even aware of the existence of television.) Before long, Arlott, Alston and Swanton had assumed a God-like status for me. I was irretrievably hooked and have remained so ever since. I remember that I was at Sunningdale, my prep school, when Freddie Brown's side went to Australia for the 1950–51 tour. Pauline, the new under-matron, let me sit on a stool to listen to the commentary in the tiny, narrow room where matron dispensed medicine. It was half past six in the morning. It was dark. We were going over live to Australia for commentary on the first day of the first Test in Brisbane. Imagine the excitement.

The first voice I heard belonged to 'Johnny' Moyes, the chap who had actually written my new bible. England had had a brilliant first day. They had bowled Australia out for 228 on a good batting pitch. The Australian accents of the commentators seemed magical as they conveyed this stirring news. The frequent breaks in transmission were infuriating. I relive those moments, almost ball by ball, as I write. Sadly for England, the Brisbane weather then took a hand. When play restarted two days later under a scorching sun, the pitch had become the sticky dog to end all sticky dogs. England declared their first innings at 68–7. Australia then declared their second at 32–7, leaving England to make 193 to win. They were bowled out for 122, although Len Hutton, held back in the hope the pitch would ease, went in at number eight. He made 62 not out in one of the great innings played on such a treacherous pitch. England's defeat was agony to listen to through the snap, crackle and pop of the airwaves, but even so, I could not get enough of it.

What eventually happened in my life afterwards was a sort of logical progression. Ferdinand Mount, the well-known political commentator, was a contemporary at Sunningdale. In his charming autobiography, *Cold Cream*, he was extremely kind when recounting a memory from his time there:

Another little epiphany took place ... just between the sightscreen and the pavilion ... From further down the bench a strange fluent burbling came to my ears. It was a commentary on the game but one which imparted an almost foreign excitement to the desultory proceedings out in the middle ... It came from a freckled, beaky-nosed boy with hair the colour of dark tan shoe polish. So enchanting was the sound that I remember turning back to front so that I was facing into the privet hedge ... and the effect of the commentary was even more mesmerising if you weren't actually watching the game. This was the first time, I think, that I became conscious how in certain departments art could be superior to life. Fifty years later Henry Blofeld is plummier, more measured ... Yet he has undeniably trained on.

I had forgotten all about this until I read Ferdie's excellent book. With the advantage of hindsight, I now think I can vaguely remember doing such a commentary. I must have been aping the commentators on the wireless at the time. I have no memory, though, of thinking then that I wanted one day to become one myself, which I know is what happened to Christopher Martin-Jenkins when he was at school. And I can only think that for some reason I was off games when I did that commentary at Sunningdale, otherwise I would have been in the thick of it out in the middle. Later, at Eton, I was so involved with playing the game that I am sure I never had a moment to think about commentating, which at that stage would certainly have seemed a second-best option. I know that I had no such thoughts when I joyfully left the City in 1962 to try my hand at writing about the game.

Now, the City. I cannot imagine my family unleashed me on the financial world in the genuine belief that it was my destiny. It was certainly not my chosen path, for I was never consulted at any stage on what the best course of action might be. The truth is more likely to be that when I was virtually sent down from Cambridge after only two years, in something approaching disgrace, my parents had no clue what to do with me. When Uncle Mark suggested I start off under his auspices in the City, it must have been a straw they clutched at with both hands. One thing was quite certain: my views on the subject were of no importance. I was simply told what was happening. There was no discussion. Mind you, I don't altogether blame my parents, for there was a singular lack of alternatives. If I had been asked, I don't think I would have had anything constructive to suggest.

At least those two and a half years in the City concentrated my mind to the extent that at the end of them I knew what I *didn't* want to do – which I suppose was consolation of a sort, even though I hated every moment. I can remember all too clearly, at the end of September in 1959, walking in a three-piece suit with a rolled umbrella from St Paul's Underground Station to 1 Aldermanbury Square, London, EC2, where Messrs Robert Benson Lonsdale plied their trade. I was not looking forward to my first day and had no idea what to expect. The general manager, Mr Paine, was tall and angular in the way of a limp and bespectacled sock that suddenly felt it should make an effort. Small talk was not his strength and he spoke to me like only a fairly indulgent schoolmaster. He took me down a floor and introduced me to the manager of the general office, a Mr Lewis, with balding fair hair, who smiled benevolently through friendly teeth. He had been briefed and before long spoke to me about cricket, a subject which I doubt had ever grabbed Mr Paine. At that point Mr Paine left us like a man who had suddenly realised he was late for his next appointment.

Mr Lewis walked me halfway down the long general office and introduced me to Mr Sutherland. I received the briefest of smiles from beneath a toothpick moustache. Mr Sutherland was a man who was large enough to have raised a good many eyebrows if he had tried to join the Light Infantry. He had a soft voice, a mild manner and a great love of tea, to go with a sensational appetite. I never discovered his first name, or if I did, I have forgotten it. We worked together for four weeks, filling the vast clients' ledgers with details of share purchases and sales. He steered me skilfully from rock to rock, although I'm sure I was an inconvenience he could have done without. Mr Sutherland was a dedicated ledger enthusiast. He handled these two massive tomes as if they were elderly bibles. In no time at all, I had discovered that they were unlikely ever to quicken my pulse.

I found myself, rather incongruously, pondering these memories of the City as I walked down the Radcliffe Road from the car park to the *TMS* box that first morning at Trent Bridge in July 2017. The sun was shining and most people were smiling, as they always seem to be at this splendid ground. I suggested the third floor to the delightful elderly lift attendant. He was determined it should be the second or maybe the fourth. When he had discovered it was neither, he decanted me at the third with the air of a man who, with sublime skill, had suddenly pulled off an extraordinary conjuring trick. It was a long way from EC2.

When I arrived, the commentary box was already buzzing. As always, we had good fun as Aggers and co started the programme off out in the middle. We had all the usual first morning questions. Were the teams the same as the scorecard? Of course not. Kagiso (unpronounceable) Rabada was suspended for one match. Who would replace him? Duanne Olivier was most likely. Not pronounced like Laurence; more like 'Ollie Fear'. Rehearsals with Andrew Samson. Was my Ollie Fear any good? What would you do if you won the toss? What was the forecast? Would they play both spinners? Too chilly for the ball to swing? Had the pork pies come yet? What were the numbers for the new combination lock on our door? There was much anticipatory to-ing and fro-ing. I hadn't been there anything like half an hour and already 1 Aldermanbury Square, London, EC2 seemed an outrageously tedious and mercifully distant alternative.

Across the desk from Mr Sutherland sat a younger, more frisky, wavy-haired Mr Langley. He checked the brokers' contracts when they came down from the dealing room. This was one of the hubs of the business, situated above us on the fourth floor. It was presided over, excitingly and entertainingly, by the wonderful grey-haired Count Vladimir Kleinmichel. The Count, a white Russian, was getting on a bit and, with a certain amount of drama, manoeuvred himself about the place with the help of a recalcitrant stick. In 1917, with some of his family, he had managed to escape from the Bolshevik revolution after walking hundreds of miles to the frontier. Here was someone who actually came close to making this dreary business seem fun. I have a memory of him smoking an evil-smelling brand of cigarette – Russian, no doubt. He had a fruity Russian accent, an engaging laugh which was perhaps more of an elongated chuckle, and plenty of strong grey hair, some of it sprouting from unlikely places. Vladimir, as he liked everyone including upstart trainees to call him, was a friend to everyone.

The nearest we got to a foreign accent that morning at Trent Bridge was the mild South African twang of their former captain, Graeme Smith. No newcomer can ever have entered into the spirit of *Test Match Special* so well. He 'got' us and the programme from the moment he had uttered his very first syllable in the *TMS* box at the Wanderers in Johannesburg just over eighteen months earlier. Smith is a huge and delightful man with a sense of humour to match. Unlike some visiting commentators, he never gloated when his side were having the better of things, as they were to do at Trent Bridge.

South Africa won the toss and chose to bat. In the middle Aggers handed over to Daggers and came back to the box to start the commentary at eleven o'clock. After twenty minutes I took over from Aggers. Anderson and Broad continued to bowl too short on a pitch which should have helped them. I found the words were coming out of my mouth as I wanted – which I suppose, as I was in my forty-sixth year as a commentator, shouldn't have come as a surprise. Yet whenever I settled into the chair for my first spell of any match I was never entirely certain of what was going to happen. When I looked over to my left at the hieroglyphic scrawl that is Andrew Samson's scoresheet, I was certain that Mr Sutherland and the clients' ledger would never have matched this.

Yet Mr Langley himself most certainly did provide a flicker of both humour and fun. He was constantly on the telephone to stockbrokers on official and unofficial business and he laughed a lot. He loved to have rather more than the occasional flutter and he did not often get it wrong. For me, buying and selling shares was the only part of the whole process of working in the City that held any sort of appeal. I'm afraid Mr Langley led me down what was to become something of a rocky path. To start with, however, I had an extraordinary piece of luck. One weekend I drove back to Hoveton in Norfolk and my mother told me that she had been given a good stock-market tip by no less a person than Gwen, her village hairdresser. A more unlikely source would be hard to imagine. Gwen had heard from a relation who was working in the Far East that a rubber stock called Jugra Land & Carey was a snip because it was about to be taken over, or so the rumour had it. I bounced into the general office the following Monday morning with this breathtaking news. It was greeted with either raised eyebrows or sympathetic smiles and sometimes both. I felt I had a point to prove, so I held my breath and bought two hundred shares. Over the next few days the price rose to the extent that Mr Langley, who I had by now discovered liked to be called Derek, also bought a swag of Jugra Land & Carey. The shares continued their upward progress and one or two others in the office jumped aboard. The following week the *Financial Times* delivered the goods: the company had indeed been taken over. The general office had never witnessed such scenes of celebration. Second cups of tea were the order of the morning. This was my only significant success in the City of London. I was the office hero. For about a day and a half I was treated as though my name was Henry de Rothschild. There was not the slightest chance it would last. My subsequent suggestions went unerringly in the opposite direction. My status soon returned to that of an upstart office boy.

Although my location changed from time to time, the effect was the same: infinite boredom. I even changed offices, for after Robert Benson Lonsdale (RBL) had joined forces with Kleinworts, RBL shovelled me off with deafening sighs of relief to the Kleinwort offices in Fenchurch Street. Perhaps they hoped the banking side of things would be more my scene. It was not. I suspect they simply wanted to get rid of me. Early in my sojourn there I had gone for the first time to the Royal Ascot meeting. Knowing nothing about racing, I pursued Lester Piggott relentlessly – I had heard of him – and in the two days we were there he rode seven or even eight winners. Making money on the horses was obviously a piece of cake. Back in the City I located a nearby betting shop by Monument underground station. Alas, I soon discovered, just as I had done with stocks and shares, that there was also a downside to this pursuit. I was, by the way, being paid the princely sum of three hundred and sixty pounds a year, but, can you believe it, with Luncheon Vouchers at the rate of 2s 6d a day thrown in on top.

I have told the story of this brief adventure into the world of megabucks so that readers can understand the enthusiasm with which I greeted the world of journalism. It was at the end of May in 1962 when, out of the blue, I was offered two days' work by *The Times* no less. The sports editor had had his card marked about me by their normally reliable cricket correspondent, John Woodcock. They asked me to go to the Bat and Ball Ground at Gravesend for two days to watch Kent play Somerset. I had to write an account of 500 words on each day's play. To my astonishment they printed them all. They did the same the following week when I was sent down to Portsmouth. Again, I had told my office I was ill. The following week *The Times* offered me four days' cricket and the next morning I could hardly wait to ring up Mr Paine and tell him he had seen the last of me. He didn't much like it, which was surprising. He asked me what I meant. I told him my career in the City of London had sadly come to an end and there was no prospect of it continuing. He must have been glad to get rid of me, but I don't think he liked being preempted and he made all sorts of unfriendly noises down the telephone. It may have been unorthodox, but I was free.

I had only been a journalist for about eighteen months when I went on my first overseas tour as a freelance reporter, covering England's trip to India in 1963–64. It gave me an early glimpse of what I hoped my life would become. There was no turning back after that. Of course, the tours were the jewels at the end of the road and in their different ways they were all tremendous fun. For me, India was the best adventure of all, but an Ashes tour of Australia has to be the ultimate cricketing experience, and I first went there in October 1968. I began this chapter with my unchauvinistic passion for Don Bradman, and now here he was in Adelaide in person. One look at the small coil of iron and steel camouflaged with flesh, blood and bones was enough to tell you that this man had reigned supreme in his own particular kingdom: he played fifty-two Test matches, only in Australia and England, and finished with a batting average of 99.94. Shaking him by one of the hands that scored all those runs was quite a moment. So much was encapsulated in that small, yet colossal figure. There was a glint in his eye Hercules would have envied, a canny awareness James Bond would have recognised and a determination Napoleon would have appreciated. Nothing could shake him from his views; all this explains why Bradman was admired more than he was loved. You disagreed with him or ignored him at your peril.

If meeting the Don was my most thrilling moment in Australia, my most amazing came three decades later. England were playing a Test match at the Gabba in Brisbane, where they have a well-established habit of losing. It was the first Test of the 1998–99 series. England had been set to score 348 to win and after losing six wickets for 161, they were saved by one of the most remarkable thunderstorms in cricket's history. The *TMS* box was perched high in the stand at the Vulture Street End. As the final afternoon wore on, the storm clouds were gathering ominously in the far distance towards the coast. A tropical storm was coming. It was simply a question of whether it would arrive in time to save England. It came nearer and nearer, the light grew worse and worse, but still the rain would not come. The umpires were Darrell Hair of Australia, who always seemed to draw attention to himself, and the less demonstrative Kandiah Thirugnansampandapillai Francis. When it came to filling in landing cards on aeroplanes, Francis's parents had certainly dealt him a raw hand with a second name like that. The two umpires kept meeting to discuss the light. It looked as if the players would need miner's lamps on their caps before they were prepared to admit it was too bad for play to go on.

I was at the microphone with Vic Marks beside me. It was as though night had suddenly decided to come early. It was three o'clock in the afternoon and the cars had their headlights on. All round it was closing in fast. We were looking towards the Stanley Street End and the sky was being lit up by vivid, almost scary sheets of lightning. To our right, in the middle distance, stood the now-closed Boggo Road Jail, such a solid landmark in that part of Brisbane. By now it was hard to see even a vague outline of the prison. Obstinately, almost obtusely, it still refused to rain, and in spite of the lightning there was no thunder. I remarked on this to Vic and the second after he had agreed, there was the most earth-shattering roar of thunder I have ever heard. At that moment the umpires were having yet another chat. The players had gathered in groups. As the roar ended, they began to walk towards the pavilion, which suggested the umpires had finally given the weather best. They had not gone three steps before the brisk walk turned into a fierce sprint as the heavens opened in a torrent that was remarkable even for Brisbane. The players were completely soaked in the few seconds it took them to reach the stand. A meteorological hell now broke loose. It was close to being pitch dark. The rain was clattering down with so much noise that even the thunder was being given a run for its money. I have never seen a sight like it. If someone had said to me the world was going to end in the next ten minutes, I would have felt he had a good point.

By this stage, Vic and I had been joined in the box by Thommo, otherwise known as Jeff Thomson. A landscape gardener by trade, he is the most delightful and charming of men. You would never guess he was one of the most violently hostile fast bowlers of all time. I was at the Gabba in 1974 when Thommo and Dennis Lillee burst on the scene. They were sharing the new ball for Australia and breaking English bones for the first time. Their combined pace and hostility is as frightening to think about now as it was to watch all that time ago.

As he sat down beside Vic and me, Thommo's first remark was, 'It's looking a bit black over Boggo Road Jail.'

Vic's considered assessment was that, 'It doesn't get as bad as this in Tiverton.'

There was a lot of truth in that too. There was something primeval about the build-up and the ferocity of that storm. I was completely taken over by it. I continued to talk and describe a scene which grew increasingly eerie and surreal. The fact that the storm had saved England from losing a Test match was irrelevant. This was an outburst of nature, a tsunami of rain, which was relevant only to itself. It is at the top of the list of remarkable things I have experienced in all my years in the *TMS* commentary box. I did not hear my description again until I was writing this chapter nearly twenty years later. I could hardly believe what I heard. At the time it was broadcast, an excerpt was selected for the weekly radio programme *Pick of the Week*, which was extremely good news. How lucky

I was, too, to have first Victor and then Jeff Thomson in the box with me. There are others who might have regarded this storm simply as an interruption to the cricket.

I am glad Victor has popped up early in this book. He is the perfect example of one of the reasons I think *Test Match Special* has been both valuable and unique among sporting programmes. He came to us almost by chance in India in 1984–85 and has become, as you will see later on, one of the main, if understated, pillars on which our present house has been built.

4

A SACK OF SAWDUST IN SYDNEY

THERE is nothing more invidious than when old commentators start to dissect the way their colleagues do the job. The great temptation is to think that because someone doesn't do it in the same way as you, it must therefore be bad. Which is nonsense. *Test Match Special* has always been home to a fascinating and irresistible mix of people with their own idiosyncratic approaches to the job. When it comes to commentary, there are many ways of bringing home the bacon.

This was perfectly illustrated by our two best-known commentators: John Arlott and Brian Johnston. I had the great luck to work with both when I first joined *TMS* in 1972. Arlott purred like the finely tuned piece of vocal machinery that he was. Without effort, he would pluck one linguistic gem after another out of thin air, sitting slightly hunched at the microphone. He was not a sprinter. His movements were methodical; his diction, like his smile, slow and controlled; his walk deliberate. When he looked round at his summariser at the end of the over, it was with the air of an amiable bear who was not in too much of a hurry. Johnston could hardly have been more different. He was forever like a bottle of champagne which had just been shaken up, ready to froth furiously over the top. Fun bubbled out of him and when you heard his voice, you could be sure a laugh was just round the corner. Looking back, it was as if, from the moment I first met him in a commentary box, his whole life was being steered towards the famous 'leg over' moment nineteen years later at The Oval that somehow came to define it. Both Arlott and Johnston, in their very different ways, were instantly recognisable, and listeners knew at once they would be in for a treat.

The flavour of the box, even now, is the flavour of Brian Johnston more than anyone else. The present style is a direct legacy of all that he brought to us in 1970 and developed over the next twenty-four years. He turned *TMS* into a programme that does much more than simply tell the unfolding story of a game of cricket. No one else would have decided to offer Alan McGilvray, our eminent Australian colleague, a large slice of chocolate cake and then, just as he had taken his first considerable bite, ask him a question. The result was that the window in our box at Edgbaston received a thick coating of chocolate cake as a spluttering McGilvray tried to answer. McGilvray was not known for his sense of humour and it took him a while to see the funny side. Our nicknames were Brian's doing too. He had answered to 'Johnners' ever since he was up at Oxford in the thirties, when it was the fashion to give everyone a nickname, prefer-ably one ending in '-ers'.

He had commentated for BBC television from 1946 to 1969, when he was suddenly sacked for an incredible reason. They considered him to be too funny, if you can believe it. He also will not have much enjoyed the strict disciplines of tele-vision commentary and was not the best at keeping to them. He was then snapped up by *TMS* and proceeded to introduce the radio box first to nicknames and soon afterwards to choc-olate cakes, as well as Jones, laughter and uproarious enter-tainment. John Arlott became 'Arlo', Jim Swanton had to make do with 'Swanny', and McGilvray became 'McGillers', which never seemed to please him that much. It was at a civic reception in Lancaster that Johnners once saw Don Mosey across the room and decided he had a distinctly Aldermanic look. He immediately became 'the Alderman'. Mosey had been born in Yorkshire before decamping to Lancashire, which is not all that different from having a sex-change oper-ation. He took a serious view of most things, rumbled rather than chuckled, and described himself as a 'bowler's commen-tator', whatever that may have meant. Johnners also dubbed Bill Frindall 'the Bearded Wonder', which soon became Bearders, and in so doing turned our scorer into a larger-than-life figure. Inevitably, I became 'Blowers', just as Jonathan Agnew was later unable to avoid 'Aggers'. Chris Martin-Jenkins went through a spell of 'Jenkers', but before long 'CMJ' prevailed.

Initials provided some of the other nicknames too, thanks to our producer's habit of using initials when he drew up his daily commentating rota. In 1989, Neville Oliver was the visiting Australian commentator for that summer's Ashes series. On the rota, alongside each of his commentary spells, Peter Baxter had written 'NO'. On the first morning of the first Test, at Headingley, Johnners came to the end of his spell and checked the sheet to see who he had to hand over to. He saw the letters 'NO' and hadn't a clue who they belonged to, and so he said, 'Now, after a word from you, Fred, it will be Doctor No to carry on the commentary.' Neville was 'Doctor No' from that moment on. Tony (A.R.) Lewis was known, I suspect not entirely to his liking, as 'Arl', and on it went. Things have changed in the last few years and although the old, Johnners-inspired nicknames linger on, there has been no attempt to turn Charlie Dagnall into 'the Compact Disc', Ed Smith into 'Smithers' or Alison Mitchell into 'Before Lunch' (A.M.). They will be thankful.

John Arlott's face was usually an impressive red, and more often than not he sweated profusely whatever the temperature outside. On entering the box, his first move was to open a window. There were those who felt the chill more easily than Arlott. Brian Johnston and Don Mosey were two, and they were keen to shut it. In the end, after a certain amount of muttering, Arlott usually got his way – until he had finished his spell, at any rate. With about half an hour's play left, Jim Swanton would make an entrance to the box that should have been accompanied by a trumpet voluntary, to put the finishing touches to his close-of-play summary. He liked to begin this by reading out the full scorecard, and so he insisted that the day's last commentator should avoid the scorecard during the final twenty-minute spell. If anyone failed to comply with his wishes – as Alan Gibson, a trifle mischievously, invariably did – Swanton was never slow to erupt, which provided the rest of us with great amusement. Gibson was a commentator more in the mould of Arlott than anyone else. He had great descriptive powers, a lovely rich voice, a riotous imagination, a delightfully waspish sense of humour and a thirst he found difficult to control. Swanton really did not enjoy being upended by Gibson, and I still wonder if he realised Gibson was doing it on purpose. Jim was also quick to complain if the producer had not provided a large whisky and soda with ice alongside his notes when he sat down at the microphone. On one occasion Michael Tuke-Hastings, Peter Baxter's predecessor, as producer failed to supply the ice. He whispered to Swanton that the bar had run out. Quick as a flash, and in all seriousness, Swanton came back with, 'Errr . . . Michael, did you tell them who it was for?'

In those days alcohol was no stranger to the box. It was not until well into the nineties that a more cautious approach turned us into a teetotal bastion of political correctness. After that we restricted ourselves to pulling the corks after the close of play, and still do so occasionally today if an obliging listener sends a bottle or two our way. In my early years with *TMS*,

however, it was guaranteed that at around midday, from somewhere in the box would come that magical explosion made by
the cork as it leaves a bottle of champagne. Peter Baxter never
enjoyed hearing this sound and reacted as though he had been
stung by a wasp, for I fear he thought it told listeners a story.
I am glad to say that since he has retired, he has mended his
ways. When this explosion occurred, Trevor Bailey, who never
wasted words, was always quick to intervene and lay the ghost
to rest with a resounding 'Ah, the medicine!' This took the
sting out of it – I am still not sure why – and a brief smile
would flicker across our producer's face.

You can see from the names and the dates that these stories
come from the days when the programme may have come
across as a sort of exclusive public-school old boys' club.
Cricket commentary, thanks to Howard Marshall, had made
a sensible start before the last war and when it was over, those
pioneers who remained regrouped into what was officially to
become *Test Match Special* in 1957, when it became ball-by-
ball. In those days when the shadow of Lord Reith still
loomed large, broadcasters were chosen only if they
pronounced the English language as he expected them to. The
public schools were inevitably the main recruiting fields, with
the notable exception of the lovely rich, claret-marinated
Hampshire tones of John Arlott. Both Arlott and Johnston
originally arrived at the BBC in unusual circumstances as
willing and enthusiastic amateurs. When Johnners was looking for a job after the war, Stewart MacPherson, a brilliant

broadcaster himself, suggested to him that he might like one at the BBC. Johnners said, yes, he might. A little later, John Betjeman read some of the poetry Arlott had written while a policeman in Southampton. Betjeman sent them on to a friend at the BBC and the upshot was that Arlott, in 1946, was employed as Literary Producer to the Eastern Service. Since those distant days, the recruitment policy of the BBC has changed just a trifle.

In 1974, Peter Baxter took over the production from Michael Tuke-Hastings. Tuke-Hastings, a Scot trained in the Reithian ways of the BBC, never much liked cricket, which had made it a somewhat curious appointment. Nonetheless, he had looked after it well and in 1974 Peter Baxter inherited a vibrant programme. Good gardener that he was, Peter successfully watered, weeded, pruned and propagated what he had been given. He had also been handed a bunch of new commentators – CMJ, Mosey and me – and he had to knock us into shape, although, as I remember it, Mosey was not for knocking into shape. Peter's greatest piece of luck was that he had at his elbow Brian Johnston, who moved and guided things along in his own inimitable way.

When Johnners had arrived in 1970, *Test Match Special* was perhaps a little too strait-laced and almost *Movietone News*-ish. Although he was the instrument of change and made things much more lively, no one was more protective of *TMS* than Johnners. A few years before he died, the programme was in trouble. We had to be shifted from Radio

3 Long Wave, which had been our home for some years, and none of the other networks were particularly keen to have us. Would we disappear? There were even Early Day Motions in the House of Commons pleading for us to be saved. The *TMS* team was covering a Test match at Old Trafford when Johnners virtually summoned the then mildly unlikely head of sport, 'Slim' Wilkinson – his shape made one ponder over his nickname – to come up and tell us what was going on. Four or five of us were staying just south of Manchester, at the Swan at Bucklow Hill. We met before dinner and Wilkinson was far from convincing when he tried to reassure us. In no time at all, Johnners had near enough lost his temper. It was the only time I saw this happen. He did not mince his words and a machine gun on a good day would have been proud of his delivery. Our boss was dumbfounded and out of his depth. Johnners extracted a promise from him to keep the team fully informed of everything that was said by the powers that be about the future of *TMS*. He urged Wilkinson to fight for all he was worth to save us, and Wilkinson, who by this stage was not putting up much of a defence, readily agreed. While in one way the meeting was good fun, it was also alarming because a wishy-washy Wilkinson had failed to assure us that *TMS* was going to be saved. Later, Johnners often spoke about that meeting with wry humour tinged with sadness that it had been necessary at all, rather than with relish at having won the day. I think he had even surprised himself at the way he worked our boss

over. In addition to all his other qualities, Johnners occasionally showed a fierce determination and when he did, as we saw that evening at the Swan, he took no prisoners.

Peter Baxter – warm and sympathetic until things went wrong, when a certain amount of iron entered his usually genial soul – pulled the strings behind us for thirty-four years. In his early days, with two such experienced performers as Arlott and Johnston at the helm, any production problems on the commentary front came from the newcomers. He suddenly found, for example, that he had to cope with the increasingly regular appearance of pigeons, seagulls, aeroplanes, helicopters and other forms of passing aerial entertainment. To some extent this was his own fault, because early in my career he had said to me one evening, 'Look, Blowers, there's no need to stick exclusively to the cricket. You can afford occasionally to look over the boundary.' He may have come to regret these words as much as any he ever uttered.

In those days I did not often commentate on more than one Test match a year. There were simply too many commentators available, and to make it even more difficult to fit in newcomers, Arlott and Johnston were automatic choices for every Test match, as was our visiting commentator for the series, the likes of Alan McGilvray (Australia), Tony Cozier (West Indies) or Alan Richards (New Zealand). The situation was eased when John Arlott became cricket correspondent of the *Guardian*. From then on he did only three spells of commentary a day, finishing soon after lunch, which meant there was a greater need for a fourth commentator. Even so, CMJ, the Alderman and I were still kept on a tight leash. The main problem with doing just the occasional Test was that I never really got into the rhythm of commentating in the way I did when I had three or more matches in a row. I imagine that went for the other two as well. I am not sure that having to keep too many commentators in practice all at once makes for better commentary.

Of course, I was keen to cover as much Test cricket as I could and Baxter often asked me along to man the number two position. This was usually in a tiny box close to the main commentary box where, with the aid of a stopwatch, I would do the reports during the day for various sports bulletins across the networks, as well as for the main news and anything else that cropped up. I shared these tiny rabbit hutches with whoever was doing the reports for the World Service. This was a great deal better than not being at the Test match, even if it was not quite the real thing.

Stopwatch broadcasting could be extremely hazardous, and at times it would drive me nearly mad. I would sit for most of the day with my headphones on and every so often a voice would speak to me down the line: 'This is Radio 4. We want thirty seconds for the sports desk after the one o'clock news.' They would tell me which item I was following and give me the feed of the news bulletin in my ear.

When I started out, I found that successfully squeezing even two hours' play into thirty seconds required an element of verbal contortionism. It sometimes happened that when the previous report was finishing a frantic voice would come down the line saying, 'Keep it to twenty seconds.' More contortionism at my end, but before I could think what I was going to leave out, I heard the presenter start to hand over to me – and, after clicking the stopwatch, off I went. I did what I could without, I hope, gabbling too much and finished with the score. To start with, it was as if every insert was life-threatening. There were a number of occasions when I clicked the stopwatch only to find that I hadn't pressed it all the way down. When I was in full flow, I would glance at the stopwatch to see how I was getting along. To my horror the hands would still be stationary and my heart would stop. Panic set in and I had to try to remember what the required twenty, thirty or forty-five seconds felt like. Phew! When I stopped talking after giving the score, I would wait anxiously to see if anyone was going to give me the most fearful rollocking for going a few seconds over. They often did. I had no excuse, but I could not admit to not having started the stopwatch, because that would have showed what an idiot I was.

Outside of Test matches, Peter would often send me to a county match to do inserts through the day for the weekend and holiday sports programmes. This was also stopwatch reporting, with an occasional five-minute burst of commentary thrown in to keep me honest. I loved it when we were joined by the World Service programme and I would have a more than lively chat with the presenter, a delightful Irishman called Paddy Feeny. Feeny was huge fun with a wonderful and imaginative sense of humour and a splendid chuckling laugh. We would talk about the most extraordinary things. When on one occasion we touched on the joys of ecclesiastical architecture and the sound of church bells – prompted, I think, by a six at Taunton hit into a neighbouring churchyard – I could not help wondering what they were making of it in the Gobi Desert. It is one of my great sadnesses that, having got on so well with Paddy Feeny on air for such a long time, I was never able to meet him face to face.

I came to realise that, as far as my future was concerned, the most important aspect of stopwatch broadcasting was getting the timing right. It didn't matter if I had made the greatest report ever – if it lasted for a minute and I had been asked for forty-five seconds, I would be roundly pilloried. If, on the other hand, I did a lousy report but got out after forty-three seconds, the people running the programme would be delighted. In the same way, if a newspaper asked me for a report of 400 words and I gave them a gem which ran for 560 words, I would be in for it. A poor report of 395 or 403 words would be gratefully received. Brilliance was apparently a matter of timing and length and had little to do with content.

It was difficult enough to do all this from a well-ordered BBC box, but sometimes I had to work in far less enviable circumstances. I think the most taxing situation of this kind I ever found myself in was at the Sydney Cricket Ground in the eighties. Australia were playing the West Indies and I was asked to do a live piece by telephone towards the end of a one-day match. I was not able to borrow a telephone from anyone in the press box, and there were, of course, no mobiles in those days. I scurried around trying to see if I could borrow a telephone in one of the catering outlets, but no luck. I had walked behind the Bradman/Noble Stand to see if I could find any public telephones when I ran into the head groundsman. I asked him if he knew of one I might use for my report in about an hour's time. He did. He had one in his 'shed', which was, as I remember it, a narrow window-less room at the back of the stand in which he kept a good deal of his equipment. He was delighted for me to use it. So far, so good. Ten minutes before I was due to broadcast, I made my way to this airless hole. The telephone was on the wall by the door. I was surprised at how quickly I was able to put through a reverse-charge call to Broadcasting House in London, but the report was not going to be easy to deliver. The only thing I could sit on with the telephone up to my ear was a large, wobbly sack of sawdust. I waited with the telephone in one hand and my stopwatch in the other, with my notes resting on my knee. Miraculously, I got through to the right studio. When the time came for the minute-long report, it seemed that nothing could go wrong. I was about ten seconds into it when the door beside me was shoved open and two men, talking loudly, barged in. My notes immediately blew off my knee and the sack of sawdust gave a dramatic lurch to the left as one of the men stumbled into it, almost pushing me to the ground. The next forty seconds were among the more interesting of my broadcasting life, but somehow I got through it. At least my stopwatch had kept going.

On a number of occasions, there were tours overseas that did not involve England but which I was covering for various newspapers. As they didn't have to pay expenses, the BBC were quick to sign me up to do daily reports for them. Before I left England, I would go round to Broadcasting House by Oxford Circus and from Peter Baxter's office I would pick up a Uher, a German-made tape recorder on which I was able to record interviews of broadcastable quality. A Uher was the most unwieldy and ghastly piece of equipment you could imagine. It was about the size of an old-fashioned, pre-war wireless set and it fitted into an oblong leather bag with a grip handle. It weighed a ton. Uhers caused me many serious problems at airports, as security invariably took an extremely dim view of them. Every time I took one through a scanner it was as if I had won the jackpot, with bells and sirens going off all over the place. Of course, I had masses of paperwork from the BBC saying what it was and what I was going to use it for. Nonetheless, even in those pre-9/11 days, a Uher almost had security men reaching for their pistols. The stories that resulted from lugging them around India and Pakistan, which

I did any number of times, are almost worth a book on their own. Letters of explanation from the BBC cut very little ice in Jullundur, Sahiwal or Faisalabad. They caused much perplexed shaking of heads followed by lengthy inaction. On one tour I missed an aeroplane as I tried, at great length, to persuade security that a Uher was not an offensive weapon. The Uhers also had an uncanny knack of failing to record important interviews that I was never going to get the chance of doing again. There were far too many occasions when I pressed the appropriate button to play back a recording I had just made only to be confronted by that evil hissing sound of nothingness – though the fact that I had usually managed to press the wrong button before starting the recording might have had something to do with it. On top of that, there was always the chance that I might drop the wretched thing on my toes. If I have the luck to live to a serious old age, it will be no thanks to Uhers.

Under Baxter's shrewd command, *Test Match Special* began to let its hair down, bit by bit and not in any great rush. The delivery of cakes increased, to everyone's enjoyment and delight, although John Arlott would have much preferred liquid to solid refreshment. There was one memorable occasion during a Test match at Lord's when he got his wish. Johnners had gleefully read out the cards that had come with the last delivery of cakes. Arlott then succeeded Johnners at the microphone and said, 'Of course, I would also like to thank those people who have sent us such a plentiful array of cakes.' And then, almost as an afterthought, he added, 'But I do wish they would send us something useful, like champagne.' Later that day, a tentative knock on the door produced a gentleman from Fortnum & Mason, the royal grocers, bearing a whole case of champagne. The following day we suggested that a tin of caviar would also go down a treat, but, alas, that heartfelt appeal fell on stony ground.

John Arlott retired at the end of the 1980 season, leaving an immense gap in the *TMS* ranks. I doubt that there will ever be a commentator of his like again. One can't help wondering whether Arlott, with his leisurely style, his voice, his delivery and his remarkable descriptive powers, would have settled comfortably into a Twenty20 setting, or for that matter into any commentary situation at the present time. Being the supreme broadcaster that he was, I have no doubt that he would have coped with T20, but would he have enjoyed it? More important, would the product have been the incomparable Arlott we knew and loved? Arlott and T20 are surely contradictory products. We still miss him, but like most commentators Arlott was a product of his time. As the game changes, so commentating styles must change too, to keep pace with the game. If a young man arrived today for a trial commentary sounding like Arlott, what chances would he have of making the cut, at a time when it sometimes seems that conformity rather than individuality is the order of the day? This is not the least of the reasons why the time has come for me to be writing this book.

The next severe shock came in January 1994. I distinctly remember being in Norfolk and hearing the early-morning news bulletin on Radio 4 that ended with the announcement of Brian Johnston's death. For me, it was a Kennedy-assassination moment, something I will never forget. It left me feeling completely hollow. The previous December, he had had a heart attack in the back of a taxi taking him from his home in St John's Wood to Paddington station on the way to Bristol, where he was to make a speech. Johnners had seemed immortal. He personified *TMS* and all its joys and idiosyncrasies. Arlott's retirement had taken away the greatest commentator of them all; Johnners's death robbed *TMS* of its guiding spirit.

At the time, I was not actually part of the *TMS* team, because my career had gone off in a new direction. We now had all the modern trappings: coloured clothing for ODIs, black sightscreens, restrictions on defensive field placing and the rest, had arrived on the field of play. Off it, Australia's Channel Nine used as many as eighteen cameras, if not more, and the coverage itself was more dramatic. David Hill, who had been the genius behind that, was running the sports coverage as Rupert Murdoch's new satellite network, Sky Television, tried to gain its first foothold in the UK. They had won the rights to televise the Sunday League and Hill asked me if I would join their commentary team. The BBC and Sky were mortal enemies, but the BBC held their collective nose and allowed me to cover the Sunday League for Sky, because in 1990 no Test cricket was being played on Sundays.

I joined such sporting luminaries as Tony Greig, who had been loaned by Packer to Murdoch and was never consumed by self-doubt, and Bob Willis. I must have got some sort of pass mark for that summer's work, because early in 1991 I was summoned to join Hill and Greig for lunch at a minuscule, posh, upmarket restaurant called Joe's at the top of Draycott Avenue in trendy London SW3. Sky had recently teamed up with satellite rival British Satellite Broadcasting, and they now had close on a hundred days' cricket after doing a deal with the old Test and County Cricket Board that allowed them to share the rights to the Test matches with the BBC. Sky wanted to sign me up for the full season, which would mean leaving *TMS*. To back this up, they made me an offer my bank manager never came near to refusing. I was hugely optimistic about it all. I was sure a brave new world lay ahead of me – what could possibly go wrong?

It was a chaotic summer as I drove frantically round England, usually with Bob Willis in the passenger seat. Our most memorable moment came on the drive back from a one-day game in Hartlepool. We came tootling down the A1 that evening and had got to Hatfield at about half past ten when I was pulled over by a police car. Two young policemen told me I had been weaving all over the place – they always seem to trot that one out – and were certain I was drunk, or at least thought I was well over the limit. They were sure they were onto a good thing, but I was in the happy position of not having had a drink for twenty-four hours. I asked for very precise instructions on how to blow, which seemed to strengthen their firm belief that they were onto a winner. I blew furiously into the breathalyser, and to their obvious dismay did not register a thing. The chap holding it said loudly that something must be wrong and shook it vigorously. He then went back to his car and returned with a new breathalyser. I wasn't sure that was strictly according to the rulebook but, being certain of my safety, I had begun to find it amusing. We went through the same process, with the same result, and once more they couldn't believe it. For them both, this was their Devon Loch moment. They had seen their horse leading by a mile, only to stumble and fall in the run-in to the finishing post. With as much bemused and irritated grace as they could muster, they told me to be on my way.

As we drove off, I said to Bob, who had been sitting quietly in the passenger seat through the whole thing, 'You know, I think they thought I was drunk.'

With a benign smile, he replied, 'Of course they did, Blowers: they had never heard anyone speak like you before.'

In spite of my televisual incompetence, I enjoyed this new experience with Sky enormously. On each day of Test cricket, there was one nice little touch. Before the start of play, I would sit at a table on the outfield and have a tea party with Geoffrey Boycott. There was a white tablecloth, cups and saucers, teapot, sugar bowl and, if I remember rightly, a strainer too. We stirred our tea and discussed what was likely to happen that day and what had gone wrong the day before. Believe it or not, we had some good chuckles, but sadly it was for just one year. The following winter Hill decided that he would use only former Test players as commentators for Test matches, although unfortunately he forgot to tell me. The following year, 1992, I did about a dozen Sunday League games for Sky and my bank manager became restless. Still no word from Hill, who avoided every attempt I made to talk to him on the telephone. In 1993 I did not do a single match for Sky. Understandably, by that stage the BBC had taken the view that by leaving *TMS* amid such a fanfare and going to the enemy, I was beyond the pale. My broadcasting career had, therefore, ground ignominiously to a halt.

In the summer of 1994 I was in a gloomy state. I had effectively driven my career into a brick wall. That season South Africa were making their first tour of England since being brought back into Test cricket after the abolition of apartheid. The summer had started with three Tests against New Zealand, but apparently it was felt that the *TMS* coverage of that New Zealand series had been a trifle flat and certainly Johnners had been badly missed. Peter Baxter, who had always tried to fight my corner, had had talks about reinstating me.

Unfortunately, one of his bosses, the number two in the department, was of the opinion that going back was never a good thing to do. That seemed to settle it.

There was obviously considerable interest in the first visit of a South African side since 1965. It was important, therefore, that *TMS* should get it right. After further discussion and argument, the BBC finally held their nose once more and decided to have me back. A telephone call from Peter Baxter gave me the news and I do not think I have ever felt happier or more relieved. But I had to get it right. I am sure that when the first day arrived – it took for ever to come – I was even more nervous than I had been before my first Test at Old Trafford in 1974. For a minute or two after I had sat down at the microphone on that first morning at Lord's, it felt strange, almost as if I didn't quite belong. That might have been because I was acutely aware that there were one or two people listening who would have been more than happy if it had not worked for me. In a perverse way I think it made me even more determined to succeed. I had to show them.

Very soon, thank goodness, it was as if I had never been away. I loved every moment, and there was one piece of the commentary I shall not forget. This was the first time Jonty Rhodes's amazing fielding had been seen in England. He was an extraordinary blur at cover point. He never stopped moving for a single second and I found myself constantly talking about him. He was athletic, entertaining, highly amusing and, in his way, unique. The crowd were with him too. There seemed to be a constant twinkle in his eyes under that floppy fair hair that bounced all over the place as he set off here, there and everywhere like a streamlined and rather unruly jack-in-a-box. He was such fun. In the middle of one spell I decided to commentate for an over only on Rhodes and nothing else, other than to keep things in context. Fanie de Villiers was bowling to Graeme Hick and Rhodes's antics hardly gave me the chance to mention either. Rhodes on his own was pure theatre.

This was the match in which the England captain, Michael Atherton, was discovered to have dirt in his pocket which gave rise to a suspicion he was using it to tamper with the ball. He maintained that he was using the dirt to keep his fingers dry. He was fined £2,000 by the England manager, Ray Illingworth, for giving incomplete information in response to questions from the match referee, the charming Australian Peter Burge who gave him a dressing down. The final irony came when Atherton fled after the match to an hotel in the Lake District to chill out. One of the first people he bumped into was fellow guest Peter Burge, who was also taking a break. Burge, a dear man, was lovely and cuddly, and you would never for a moment suspect that he had once, in 1964, hooked Fred Trueman into oblivion at Headingley. History does not relate if he and Atherton dined together and, if they did, what they drank and how the conversation went.

After Brian Johnston left us, the change in *Test Match Special* was at first imperceptible. We soldiered on as before and, although it seems awful to say so, I was conscious that I owed my return to the colours of *TMS* to Johnners's sad departure and, of course, to Peter Baxter's persistence. I like to think we did our best to keep the programme going as Johnners would have liked.

TMS had already seen plenty of changes to the game, of course. Back in the sixties, one-day county cricket had tentatively stepped onto the scene with the Gillette Cup, which immediately established a strong foothold. Nine years later, in 1972, when England played Australia, we had the first official series of one-day matches – I can still see the Bearded Wonder, sitting beside me like an irritated schoolmaster, reaching for his ruler to rap me over the knuckles for not referring to them as 'ODIs'. The 40-over Sunday League was up and running in 1969; three years later another part league, part knock-out competition was sponsored by Benson & Hedges. By the 1990s, one-day cricket was well established and *TMS* covered the various competitions in England and, of course, the one-day internationals. It required a different form of commentary, because one-day cricket has an entirely different pace to Test cricket.

In the Test coverage, our new, young cricket correspondent, Jonathan Agnew, had not only injected a lovely soothing new voice into it all, but had also introduced a more conversational approach to the business of commentary, going beyond anything Johnners had done. Aggers and his summariser, particularly if it was Vic Marks, were now engaged for most of the time in a continual conversation.

In the old days, the commentator described the action and the summariser came in at the end of each over, or in the middle of the over if something dramatic had happened. Having been brought up in this way, I still tended to use my summariser like this. The main reason was that it had become an ingrained habit. I also stuck to it because the long gaps between balls when fast bowlers are on gave me the chance to describe the scene all round me, which I so loved doing. That was where red double-decker buses and all those pigeons and seagulls had their moments. One of the justifications for this antiquated self-indulgence was that these things, and cakes too, were still as important for one part of our audience as the technical criticisms and intricacies of cricket were for another. I suppose I might have been guilty of whistling to keep up my courage. Now that I have gone, I daresay we will not hear quite so much about all the extraneous things that have given me such fun over the years.

After I had done my trial commentary at the Oval in 1968, I was summoned to Broadcasting House by Henry Riddell, the Assistant Head of Outside Broadcasts. He was a huge man with a rather jerky walk which suggested that every step he took would be a self-contained adventure. He was wearing a dinner jacket even though it was mid-afternoon, and he assured me he had known Lord Reith personally. When we listened to my two recordings in his office, he stressed afterwards the importance of painting the picture. 'Position yourself for the audience. Then tell them all you can see from where you are sitting, so they are able to place you exactly and their imagination can come into play. Only then are you likely to receive the ultimate compliment for a radio commentator, which is when a listener says, "You made me feel that I was there."'

I rest my case, but I am getting ahead of myself. As we approached the new millennium, *Test Match Special* was in good shape. The gradual process of change had begun and, although admirably controlled, was going to get faster.

5

'YES, WE'VE GOT
A FREAKER'

LOOKING back at the seventies, it sometimes seems that in almost every Test I commentated on something happened to make it particularly memorable. We had some remarkable characters in the box then, of course – or is this simply distance lending enchantment? I do not think so, because we were more of a free-range bunch than we are today. The inmates of the box were not afraid to go off in their own direction, and no one tried to pull them back. It was even encouraged. Conformity did not sit easily with the great big rumble which had gathered pace in the sixties and then lingered on like a rolling thunderstorm.

It is hardly surprising that the first Test match on which I ever commentated for *Test Match Special*, England v India at Old Trafford in 1974, should be indelibly carved into my memory. I was more nervous than I had been before those two one-day internationals against Australia two years before. This time I was going to be joining John Arlott, Brian Johnston, Christopher Martin-Jenkins, Trevor Bailey, Jim

Swanton and the Maharaja of Baroda, even if some may have thought the last two were the same person.

The maharaja was a member of the Indian Board of Control and had managed their team on a previous tour of England. He was the most genial and amusing of men who had played a bit of cricket himself and knew the game well. Robert Hudson, Head of Sport at the BBC, along with our newish producer, Peter Baxter had made the unusual decision to use the Maharaja as a summariser. They had an interesting introductory meeting in Hudson's office at Broadcasting House. It had just about finished when Hudson asked the maharaja how he would like us to refer to him on air. He thought for a moment and then came back strongly with, 'Lieutenant-Colonel, His Highness, Fatehsingh Gaekwad, the former Maharaja of Baroda.'

After allowing this to sink in for a moment, Hudson spoke again with just a touch of incredulity in his voice: 'Every time?'

'The first two or three times,' came the immediate reply, 'and then you may call me "Prince".'

We did indeed call him 'Prince', and everyone thought we had a dog in the box. Off air his friends called him 'Jackie'. I don't know how this originally came about. Maybe he had thought he should anglicise himself. He was good fun and always ready for a laugh, even though some of his cricketing thoughts had Trevor Bailey shaking his head in incredulous disbelief.

I can still feel my nerves as I drove my dark green Ford Cortina – once referred to by an angry bus driver in The

Strand as a 'wretched sardine can' – to Bucklow Hill, where we were billeted as usual at the Swan Hotel. There were five of us at dinner that night. Arlott's first instruction to the wine waiter, who took an irritatingly long time to turn up, was, 'We'll have two of the white and four of the red to start with, and then we will include you in our toast to absent friends.'

The wine waiter apparently did not do irony and was clearly unaware of who he was talking to. He came back with·a sprightly 'Glasses, sir?'

'No, my good man, bottles,' was Arlott's snappy rejoinder.

I didn't get much sleep that first night. Breakfast in a daze was followed by an anxious drive to Old Trafford through Altrincham – no motorways then – and much shuffling around outside the commentary box, precariously perched in those days at the top of the scoreboard at the Stretford End. The toss was recorded and the countdown to the start of the programme began. I even found myself thinking, 'There's no way out now.'

Johnners had started things off and I was the third commentator on. The time seemed to go so very slowly until John Arlott handed over: 'And after a word from the Prince, it will be Henry Blofeld for the first time in a Test match.' And off I went. The rest of the day passed in a blur. Keith Fletcher made a hundred and Tony Greig played some good shots.

There were two amusing Brian Johnston moments later in the match which were both a trifle unnerving for a newcomer. During India's first innings, with Johnners on air, Greig was bowling to Sunny Gavaskar. He played forward to successive balls and both were fielded by Mike Hendrick at mid on. The first time, he threw it on to Greig, who 'polishes the ball on his right thigh as he walks back to his mark'. History then repeated itself and this time, with Greig walking back to his mark, we heard from Johnners, 'And now, to ring the changes, Greig polishes his left ball.' The small wooden box was still shaking at the end of the over when he passed the commentary over to me. I somehow kept myself together and got through the next over, despite Bill Frindall's extravagant snorts, but it was a close-run thing.

The second memorable moment was caused by the rain, which must have robbed the match of almost a full day. By this time it had become the custom for the commentators to chat through the rain breaks. Believe it or not, I was really worried about this. Johnners and Arlott were so terrific at it, I couldn't see that I would have anything to add. I was scared stiff. On the first day I got away with it. The rain breaks were short and there were none when I should have been commentating. After lunch on the second day, though, there was no escape. It began to pour during the lunch interval and Johnners, in top form, started the afternoon chat session. I tiptoed into the box hoping no one would notice me. Of course Johnners did and in no time I was sitting in his chair. By then, I had come up with a few things to say and I couldn't wait to get them out. I believe I spoke non-stop for nearly ten minutes. After that, I ran out of steam and looked to my right for help. To my horror,

I saw that both chairs were empty. There should have been at least one other commentator to lend a hand. All I could see was a note in Johnners's handwriting lying on the green baize in front of me which said, 'Keep going until 6.30 and don't forget to hand back to the studio.' I panicked and tried to stutter on. It was dreadful. I could not think of anything to say. It seemed to go on for hours, though I think they only let me stew in my own juice for about two minutes. Then they all came tumbling back into the box, laughing their heads off. I can't see this happening today, but it taught me a lesson about playing a team game, for a while anyway.

In spite of the weather, England just had time to win the match. It was a game which was later made memorable by Geoffrey Boycott's decision to take a break from Test cricket. At Old Trafford, he had made ten in the first innings before he was lbw to Abid Ali. When he ran in to bowl, Abid Ali looked a bit like a moustached captain in the Indian army. He bowled, appropriately enough, at about military medium. In the second innings, Boycott was caught behind off Eknath Solkar's left-arm spin for six. Whether it was these indignities that made up his mind to go into hibernation or whether it was a more deep-seated problem or simply a reaction to Mike Denness holding the England captaincy remains a mystery. He obviously would not have been in the right frame of mind to deal with the considerable pace of Jeff Thomson and Dennis Lillee the following winter in Australia. The even sharper West Indian menace of Andy Roberts, Michael Holding and co soon afterwards would have been an even greater problem. However, this break enabled him to confront his talents and eventually come back to be just as effective for England as before.

By the start of the seventies the one-day game was poking its head round the corner and, in 1975, England staged the first World Cup. The West Indies beat Australia in the final late in the evening at Lord's on Midsummer's Day. When the Australians stayed on afterwards for four Test matches, I was given the opportunity to do my first Lord's Test at the end of July, which is surely another reason I remember it so well. The others in the box were Arlott, Johnston, McGilvray, Bailey and Trueman. I had done a couple of Tests the year before, but even so, when I walked into the box to join that august company I still felt as if it was my first day at a new school. The *TMS* box had by then moved from the Warner Stand to the top turret of the Pavilion directly over the committee dining room. We were still not right behind the bowler's arm, but we were a great deal nearer to it. We had lots of friends around us who were members of MCC, sitting on the top deck of the Pavilion. Most of them had their radio earpieces in and kept us on our toes. We were also well within range of Nancy, who presided for so many years over the players and the committee dining rooms. She cheerfully supplied Johnners with his daily lunchtime diet of well-cooked lamb sandwiches in brown bread. It was a wonderful vantage point.

One highlight of the match for me came an hour before the start of the second day. I met John Arlott at the members' entrance at the back of the Pavilion. He was carrying two large leather briefcases. I offered to give him a hand with them and after a substantial sharpener in the members' bar delivered by Maisie, wallowing, as always, in her pink hair, we climbed three flights of stairs. The briefcases grew heavier with each step. Once in the box, Arlott waited until everyone else had clocked in and then stepped forward like a member of the Magic Circle about to perform his favourite trick. He should have been wearing a top hat. Lo and behold, each briefcase revealed five bottles of claret and not cricket books as I had imagined.

'With any luck that little lot should see us through to the lunch interval,' were his immortal words as he stood back with a victorious grin. They were actually required for a function that evening.

The game produced the dullest of draws. For the record, England batted first and made 315 and Australia replied with 268. Tony Greig, perhaps a shade defensively, then carried on England's second innings until they had reached 436–7. Australia batted through for a comfortable draw, but for me, it was the most amazing experience as one subplot followed another.

I had seen Tony Greig make a brilliant 156 against Lancashire in his first game for Sussex. I was his greatest fan, although his aggressive manner, not helped by his bruising South African accent, did not make him universally popular.

This was his first Test as England's captain. He made a brilliant, robust and combative 96 in the first innings. Here is John Arlott's take on him as he came out to bat: 'Here he is ... that slightly pigeon-toed walk, long-legged ... coming out to bat with England, once more, in crisis'. He reached 48 and turned Lillee to fine leg. Johnners told the story: 'Greig has got his fifty. A lucky England captain. By that I mean he captains his first Test, he wins the toss, he comes in and with all his skill he plays an absolutely wonderful innings.' When Greig was eventually out, Trevor Bailey let his hair down with unaccustomed relish: 'You simply could not ask for more, it was absolutely first class.'

We had the joy, too, of describing David Steele in his first Test match. Grey-haired, studious and bespectacled, he made 50 in one innings, 45 in the second. Arlott had a word about him too: 'His hair is prematurely grey, showing quite strikingly under the cap. He plays in glasses; a good sticker with some punishing strokes.' When his time came the mysterious Steele, looking more like a conjuror than Arlott, eventually emerged from the Pavilion having gone down one flight of stairs too many to the gents loo in the basement where he struggled to find the exit door. A search party was sent to find him. Clive Taylor hit the jackpot the next morning in the *Sun*, memorably describing him as 'looking like a bank clerk going to war' as he walked out late and a trifle myopically to the wicket. Jeff Thomson put it rather differently when he said to one of his colleagues, 'Jeeeesus, mate. What have we got here:

Howard Marshall, perched on the top balcony of the Pavilion at Lord's, describing events while England play Australia in 1938.

The incomparable Don Bradman, aged 39, on Australia's 1948 tour of England.

The flamboyant and irresistible Keith Miller, watched over by keeper Billy Griffith, bats for the Australians against the Duke of Norfolk's XI in 1956.

Above: My first tour of India in 1963–4.

Denis Compton cuts one past W. C. Blofeld at slip. M.C.C. v. Cambridge University.

Right: An ageing Denis Compton in one of his last first-class matches, MCC v Cambridge University at Lord's in 1959. A misidentified Blofeld sprawls in the gully.

Fred Trueman had probably the best bowling action of all time – and a wry humour to go with it.

Brian Johnston attempts to hook in 'Let's Go Somewhere', a feature of *In Town Tonight* in February 1950. Dirty pads and caught at long leg?!

The Brabourne Stadium, Bombay, January 1964. Five journalists: me,
Crawford White, S.K. Gurunathan at the back; Clive Taylor and Ian
Todd in front.

John Arlott purring along effortlessly with a tousled and pithy Fred Trueman
during the 1979 World Cup at Trent Bridge.

Keith Miller's last lunch in London, in 2004, with hosts Johnny Woodcock, me and Colin Ingleby-Mackenzie.

This says it all. 'Tiger', the Nawab of Pataudi, had style, class, humour and a patrician confidence.

Too close for comfort. This must be the nearest a Blofeld has come to Ian Fleming's Jamaican home, Goldeneye. But relax, it's Henry Calthorpe, not Ernst Stavro.

John Edrich, aged 39, Brian Close's youthful opening partner, is uprooted by Wayne Daniel, England v West Indies, Old Trafford, 1976.

Captain Mike Brearley and Derek Underwood celebrate England's victory over Australia at Headingley in 1977.

Brian Close, aged 45, takes this short one from Michael Holding on the chest, Old Trafford, 1976.

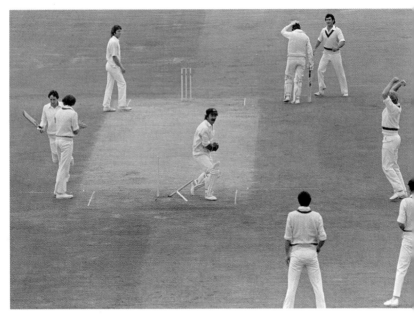

Derek Randall run out in his first Test innings on his home ground of Trent Bridge in 1977. At the other end, the culprit, Geoffrey Boycott, holds his head in anguish.

John Arlott enjoys a last joke on air in his final commentary spell, during the Centenary Test at Lord's in 1980.

With firmness, skill, quiet control and chess-like precision, Mike Brearley setting his field at Headingley in 1981.

This stroke encapsulates his innings. Ian Botham swings Ray Bright for four during his 149 not out at Headingley in 1981.

Ian Botham has just taken Australia's first second-innings wicket. He had Graeme Wood caught behind.

The predators are ready as Willis bowls. Mike Gatting is about to catch Graham Yallop at short leg. Australia 58–4.

Willis (8–43) has just removed Ray Bright's middle stump, England have won by 18 runs, pandemonium breaks loose.

Groucho ----ing Marx?' When Thomson bounced him, Steele stood up fearlessly and straight and never once flinched. Some bank clerk, some war.

There was an outstanding 99 from Australia's Ross Edwards, one of the game's more brilliant cover points and all-round good eggs. He became Bob Woolmer's first Test wicket when he played round a straight ball. We were all sorry he had not reached a hundred, and no one more so than Johnners, who described his dismissal: 'Woolmer bowls . . . Oh my goodness, he's out . . . Yes, yorked lbw on 99! Oh dear me, how awful.' England were then held up by Lillee. Ever the showman, he irritated the Poms to screaming point, just as he had set out to do, with his affected antics at the crease. No one enjoyed describing Lillee more than Arlott. Two years later, in 1977, Arlott joined the Australian commentary team for the Centenary Test match in Melbourne. Lillee was bowling magnificently in England's first innings and we heard, 'And Lillee, setting a field of immense hostility,' a phrase which had a lovely Arlottian ring to it. Now, in this Test at Lord's, Lillee was bowling as usual in a shirt that was more like a nightshirt. It was at least two sizes too big for him. Open to the navel, with the medallions round his neck glittering in the sun as he ran in to bowl. In accordance with the fashion of the time, he was wearing drainpipe-thin trousers. Arlott was on the case: 'It's Lillee again from the Nursery End, the shirt big enough for two men – if they could get into the trousers.'

As you can see, Arlott had a splendid game, almost a

benefit match – and off the field too. On the second day he was given lunch by his publisher. This meant that his normal lunchtime ration of two bottles of claret 'of a very good year', will have become four and just possibly five, as the publisher was paying. When he returned to the box twenty minutes after lunch he was, I think it's fair to say, mellow. In the box he found the Managing Director of BBC Radio, Ian Trethowan, later to become the Director-General. So when he came to face the microphone twenty minutes later, he was not only mellow, he was also showing off, which can be a dangerous combination.

He then had the greatest piece of luck any commentator has ever had at Lord's. He had to describe the ground's first ever streaker. A chubby cook in the Merchant Navy, improbably named Michael Angelow, came running out from the Tavern Stand dressed only in short socks and trainers. Trevor Bailey was the first to spot him. He knew there was a collective word for people who did this sort of thing, but he couldn't quite remember it. After a short pause Trevor said, with some emphasis, 'Ah, a freaker.'

Arlott was happy to run with that. 'Yes,' he said, 'we've got a freaker down the wicket now. Not very shapely ... and it's masculine ... and I would think it's seen the last of its cricket for the day.' He described him jumping the stumps at both ends. And then, 'Now he's had his load. He's being embraced by a blond policeman ... and this may be his last public appearance. But what a splendid one ... and so warm ... He is now being marched down in the final exhibition, past at least eight thousand people in the Mound Stand, some of whom, perhaps, have never seen anything quite like this before.' The future Director-General laughed louder and longer than anyone.

England's second innings revolved around a typically patient knock of 175 from John Edrich, which led to worthy if not extravagant commentary. Greig set Australia to score 484 to win and although they batted well, the match ran out of time. It was a question of going through the motions towards the end. During Australia's second innings on this last day, I was taught a painful lesson by Trevor Bailey. In the closing stages, Greg Chappell was batting well within himself. He was facing Peter Lever – he with the long run-up and 'Plank' for a nickname – and suddenly unwound a heavenly off drive for four. 'You won't see many better strokes than that,' I was quick to say. 'Those of us who are lucky enough to get to heaven and see the ultimate coaching book will surely find more photographs of Greg Chappell playing that stroke than anyone else. I am sure Trevor will agree.'

Without a moment's pause, Trevor came back with, 'Well, of course, the stroke that Greg Chappell is best known for is the on drive.'

Ouch! Never lead your summariser, especially if he is Trevor Bailey.

That was my one Test in 1975. The following year I managed to get selected for the third Test against the West Indies at Old

Trafford. The commentary team was the same except that McGilvray was back in Australia and Tony Cozier was our West Indian commentator. Tony, a white Bajan, was an extraordinary performer with one exceptional gift. Commentating on radio could hardly be more different from television. On radio, there is no picture to distract the listener. The commentator has to paint the picture and can talk about anything he wants. He has a 360 degree angle of vision. On television the commentator must not talk about things the viewer cannot see on the screen. Also, he does not tell the viewer the bowler is coming in to bowl, for he can see that for himself. It is his job to explain the picture, to interpret what is going on and to make the picture more understandable for the viewer. On radio, the commentator is doing the job the camera does for the television audience. Generally speaking, radio commentators talk far too much when they turn their hand to television. They also tend to talk about things viewers cannot see in front of them, which makes producers scream. Tony Cozier, on the other hand, moved seamlessly from one box to the other. Sometimes barely more than a minute would elapse between putting his microphone down in the television box and picking up the next one in the neighbouring radio box. He was marvellous at both jobs and the only commentator I have ever listened to who had the ability to adapt himself so cleanly, so skilfully and so quickly from one discipline to the other. He had a lovely light sense of humour too, a cheerful, almost naive-looking face, a wonderful Bajan voice and it was always a joy to work with him. His comments were so even handed.

This was the series before which there was a reckless and distasteful intervention by Tony Greig that had a considerable effect on all that followed. England's captain was a born optimist, sometimes well past the point of good sense. Before the West Indians arrived, he had declared that it was his intention to beat the West Indians, but in terms that were considerably less than ideal.

'If they get on top,' Greig told a BBC Television audience, 'they're magnificent cricketers. If they're down, they grovel. And I intend to make them grovel.'

No one could have conveyed the West Indian point of view more succinctly than Tony Cozier when he said in a broadcast soon afterwards, 'To have a white South African – albeit captaining England – using a word like "grovel" certainly raised the hackles of the West Indies team. It committed them even more fiercely to winning the series.'

That word came back to haunt England's captain. It came with the clear implication of servility, which made it close to being unacceptable even before Greig's South African background was taken into account. It was that country's hideous policy of apartheid which had led to their sporting isolation. There were those who felt there might even have been a degree of malicious intent in those words. I would settle for unthinking exuberance. What is certain is that it was a word guaranteed to cause a good deal of West Indian fury. Of course, it was hugely counterproductive, because the best way for Clive Lloyd's side to get level with Greig was to annihilate him as a player. With a fast-bowling attack that included Michael Holding, Andy Roberts and Wayne Daniel, to say nothing of Vanburn Holder and Bernard Julien, the odds were in their favour. 'Grovel' was a word that hung over this series like a pernicious cloud and short-pitched fast bowling proliferated.

Greig got what he asked for. In the Headingley Test he played two courageous innings, making 116 and 76 not out. His other seven innings produced only 49 runs and Roberts and Holding made a meal of him. Although I doubt he would ever have admitted it, he must have come to regret what he had said as he watched Holding and company race in to bowl over the next few weeks. Holding was not fit for the first Test at Trent Bridge and with Roberts out of sorts, England got away with a draw. The second Test at Lord's was also drawn, with Holding back but feeling his way. Roberts took five wickets in each innings and his hostility made his intentions clear. Right at the end of the last day of that match, when the West Indies, needing 323 to win, were 210–2 with eleven overs left, Clive Lloyd claimed the extra half hour. When he himself was fourth out at 233 with six and a half overs left, he wanted to come off. Greig again tested the West Indies' sense of humour by insisting on continuing. He took one more wicket himself and only came off when three balls remained to be bowled. This undoubtedly tightened the notch a fraction and an explosion seemed imminent.

The England selection for this series had been unusual too.

Persuaded, no doubt, by the demands of the captain, the selectors decided to turn back the years and pick Brian Close at the age of forty-five, twenty-seven years after he had first played for England. Close was a sort of antiquated Aunt Sally. In 1963 at Lord's, he had taken on another pair of West Indian fast bowlers, Wes Hall and Charlie Griffith, mostly with his body. Greig was expecting him to do it again, even though he was at a pensionable age for a cricketer. He went in fourth in the first two Tests and just about got away with it. Now, at Old Trafford, Greig pushed him up the order to open the batting with John Edrich, who was only six years younger and had been recalled for this match. This was only eighteen months after the forty-two-year-old Colin Cowdrey had been sent out to Australia as a reinforcement when Lillee and Thomson burst on the scene and caused mayhem. That didn't work either.

If anything, the appearance of these two middle-aged openers would have made Roberts and Holding press even harder on the accelerator. They may have found it insulting to their intelligence. It would have made them even more reluctant to pitch the ball up. It was never going to work. Close and Edrich made ten between them in the first innings at Old Trafford and an extremely courageous 44 in the second. But it was terrifying to watch. Even Close must have been near to being battered into submission by the continuous bombardment, although he would never have admitted it. It was cruel but effective, and the West Indies won by a small matter of 425 runs. One of the umpires was Bill Alley, the Australian all-rounder, a great character who had played for many years for Somerset. Before the match, he had let it be known in no uncertain terms that he was not going to toler-ate too many bouncers. When it came to it, he hardly said a thing. His partner, Lloyd Budd, standing in his first Test, could hardly have been expected to take a firm line if his more experienced colleague had shirked the issue. There was only one side grovelling at Old Trafford and that was not the West Indies.

It was an extraordinary Test to commentate on, especially at the moments it became blatantly physical and unpleasant. There were obviously glaring issues that could not safely be talked about on the air, which made it more difficult. I remem-ber Brian Johnston going pale as he watched the assault on Close and Edrich. Arlott, too, was more forthright than usual in his disapproval of short-pitched bowling. I am getting ahead of myself as far as the actual match was concerned. It was a considerable achievement by England's bowlers to dismiss the West Indies on the first day for 211. The game had been given a remarkable and, for *TMS*, a pertinent start. Mike Selvey, playing in his first Test, at medium fast, had taken the first three West Indian wickets for six in twenty balls. His victims were Roy Fredericks, Viv Richards and Alvin Kallicharran, and you can't get much better than that. Selvey only played three Test matches, but he became a redoubtable and perceptive summariser for *TMS*. Then, when

Peter Baxter retired as the producer in 2007, changes were made and Selvey was unlucky enough to be dropped. His eminently sensible contributions were much missed. In the West Indies first innings, England's only serious obstacle was Gordon Greenidge, who made 134 in the first innings – an extraordinary 63.5 per cent of the West Indies total of 211 – and 101 in the second innings. He became the second West Indian to score two hundreds in a Test in England. The great George Headley had been the first to do it, at Lord's in 1939. But I fear the batsmen, especially England's two aging heroes, would have known only too well what lay just around the corner.

Brian Close and John Edrich received a great and prolonged reception when they emerged from the pavilion. Close would have been sticking out his chin, for he knew no other way. Edrich, who always sold his wicket dearly, would have been less sanguine about his immediate future as Roberts and Holding, looking even more predatory than usual, marked out their runs. It was terrifying to watch and shameful that the two umpires, Bill Alley and Lloyd Budd, did not do more to protect the elderly. This was the last time that either Close or Edrich played for England – maybe, after this, they were grateful.

In all the years I have been watching cricket I don't think I have seen anything as frightening as Roberts, Holding and Daniel on that first evening. I was on the air when Holding was bowling to Close. You will get some idea of what it was like in the middle from the way I talked about these few balls.

'Holding walks slowly back into the distance . . . Now here he is. He certainly runs in at absolutely breakneck speed. He's in, past Alley . . .

'That's another short one. Close backs away and it flies past his shirt buttons . . . Well, that's two in a row.

'And I'm quite certain, in a way, although Close can't exactly be enjoying this, there's part of him will be relishing it . . . He loves a fight . . . And no one is better equipped to take these fast bowlers on, even at the age of forty-five.

'Here's Holding again . . . Another short one. And now Close takes that one on the body . . . He buckles at the knees and John Edrich comes down the wicket to talk to him.

'Dear Brian Close is still not rubbing anything . . . He looks quite unconcerned talking to Edrich and patting down the pitch . . . As he was hit on the side he moved slightly over to the off side, and that's why he lost his balance, don't you think, Fred?'

'I dunno,' was the basso-profundo reply. 'I think it hurt the old boy. It was a nasty one and you can see where they are patting down the pitch. It wasn't all that short. It came up a bit, didn't it.'

'And still Close has not rubbed any part of him.' This was me again. 'What an amazing man he is.

'Here's Holding in again . . . It's another short one and Close backs away . . . And now I think Bill Alley is going to step in . . . He does; he warns Holding. He gives him his first warning, and quite rightly so too, I would say. He's bowled Close four short balls in that over.'

There is no more genial and more pleasant a man than Michael Holding. But he is every inch his own man and no one is truer to his convictions. If Greig had not used that word 'grovel', I have always strongly doubted that we would have seen what we did when Close and Edrich came out to bat that evening at Old Trafford. I don't blame Holding. It was up to the umpires to step in before they did. It was always likely to be a combustible moment, but Alley's brave words in the build-up were shown to be nothing if not hot air.

My choice of these Test matches in the seventies shows, more than anything, how lucky I was to be selected for these extraordinary games. The fourth of them was played in 1977 at Trent Bridge, by which time Tony Greig had become an important recruiting agent for Kerry Packer's World Series Cricket. Not surprisingly he was replaced as England captain, although he was kept in the side as a player. Mike Brearley took over the leadership for an Ashes series that was played in a surreal atmosphere. There were players on both sides whose primary allegiance was now to Packer. For them, this series was not much more than a warm-up act. World Series Cricket was scheduled to start in Australia later in the year and it hung over proceedings like a dark cloud. Packer had signed up almost forty of the best players in the world. They were all of them the staunchest defenders of their new faith. The Ashes series was now played as if the minds of some of the participants were elsewhere.

This match saw the return of Geoffrey Boycott to England colours after he had taken that voluntary break for three years and thirty Tests. Tony Greig had made an attempt to persuade him to change his mind the year before against the West Indies. The thought then of Close and Boycott, not always the greatest of friends, opening the England innings could not help but raise a smile or two. Now, for the third Test, Boycott announced that he was prepared to come back. It was a coincidence that this was also Ian Botham's first Test match. What could have been more appropriate, therefore, than the Queen's visit to the ground on the first day?

England arrived at Trent Bridge one Test to the good, having won the second at Old Trafford. At that time, our small but delightful commentary box was on the first-floor balcony of the pavilion alongside the official scorer's box. By the time Bill Frindall had spread himself in the left-hand corner of the box and an ample summariser had stationed himself in the other, the commentator had to perch himself like an apprehensive wren somewhere in between. The substantial Arlott saw to it, of course, that he had a wren on either side of him. This box may have been small and uncomfortable, but it was wonderfully intimate. We were so close to the play that you almost felt you were in the slip cordon. On a cold day with the windows shut, Fred Trueman's pipe became a good deal more than just a health hazard. Cigarette smoke did not exactly jolly things along either, for Don Mosey, Alan McGilvray and I all smoked in the seventies.

One other great joy for us was that the Nottinghamshire committee gave us honorary membership of the committee room throughout all matches at Trent Bridge. The great and the good gathered there and it was therefore easy to lure them up to our box for a chat on air. There was also a loo leading off the short passage to the committee room itself, which was a great bonus. I remember it being placed strictly out of bounds, along with the committee room itself, on the day of the Queen's visit, for, unaware, I tried to force an entry. Normally, whenever I had finished a spell of commentary, unless Peter Baxter needed me for something else, I went straight down to the committee room. The wine was eminently acceptable. Strangely, I do not remember John Arlott heading there in search of liquid sustenance. This was almost certainly because he had made alternative arrangements. Perish the thought that the committee's wine was not up to his standard. He had a great liking for the famous Trent Bridge Inn, which stands in the far corner of the ground backing onto the bridge over the Trent. He found it a splendid watering hole, although it gave him a good walk to get there.

Australia won the toss and batted. They had reached 131–2 well into the afternoon when Brearley brought back the twenty-one-year-old debutant Ian Botham. Johnners was on air as he ran in to bowl his third ball: 'Now Botham runs up and bowls this to [Greg] Chappell ... and he's out. He's bowled him. The off stump leaning back there, Fred.'

Fred did not go overboard: 'That's a classical case of did the drinks interval break the batsman's concentration?'

I was on again towards the end of the innings: 'Botham, in now to bowl to Thomson, he bowls. Thomson swings and he's caught behind ... He slashed at it and Botham has taken his fifth wicket.' It was the first of twenty-seven five-wicket hauls for England.

The next morning England were 34–2 when Derek Randall came out to join Boycott in his first Test on his home ground. John Arlott takes up the story: 'Thomson comes in, bowls to Boycott, who pushes that ... there must be a run there ... oh ... how tragic, how tragic, how tragic.' He welcomed the World Service with the news that Randall 'has just this minute been sacrificially run out ... Let's leave the applause for Randall from a Trent Bridge crowd as he comes in, very crestfallen and very unlucky. Almost with tears in his eyes, he looks very disconsolate.'

A wonderful innings by Alan Knott got Boycott going again and they put on 215 for the sixth wicket. I had the luck to take them both to their hundred. 'You can almost hear the prover-bial pin drop as Thomson starts in again ... Knott on 99 wait-ing for him ... He bowls it short ... Knott cuts ... there's his hundred ... the crowd rise all round the boundary boards.' And then, 'Thomson to bowl to Boycott ... Will he get his hundred? Thomson's up to the wicket ... Boycott cuts ... there it is. What a triumph for Geoffrey Boycott ... and I don't think anyone here underestimates the measure of what he has achieved.'

I was on at the end too: 'Just three runs needed to win. [Kerry] O'Keeffe bowls to Randall . . . Randall on-drives and that's the winning runs . . . England have won this third Test by seven wickets. Boycott's got his arm round Randall. Randall's laughing, Randall's clapping Boycott, Boycott's raising his bat, both very happy in their different ways.'

In the next Test, at Headingley, Boycott scored his hundredth first-class hundred. Fred Trueman led up to it: 'There are people holding their hearts when he plays a shot. The one he hit in the air over there, there was two chaps at the side of me who nearly passed out.'

CMJ saw him over the line: 'Chappell [Greg] turns, goes in again. Boycott 96 not out. He bowls to him . . . it's a half volley . . . he drives it down the ground . . . and there it is . . . he's done it . . . and the crowd cannot resist coming onto the pitch any longer.'

Love him or hate him, and there will always be people who will do both, Geoffrey Boycott was an extraordinary batsman who was as determined then as he is now in the commentary box.

England v Australia

(3rd Test)

Played at Trent Bridge, Nottingham on 28, 29, 30, July and 1, 2 August 1977

Umpires: Dickie Bird, David Constant

Toss: Australia

AUSTRALIA

RB McCosker	c Brearley b Hendrick	51	c Brearley b Willis		107
IC Davis	c Botham b Underwood	33	c Greig b Willis		9
GS Chappell*	b Botham	19	b Hendrick		27
DW Hookes	c Hendrick c Willis	17	lbw b Hendrick		42
KD Walters	c Hendrick b Botham	11	c Randall b Greig		28
RD Robinson	c Brearley b Greig	11	lbw b Underwood		34
RW Marsh†	lbw b Botham	0	c Greig b Willis		0
KJ O'Keeffe	not out	48	not out		21
MHN Walker	c Hendrick b Botham	0	b Willis		17
JR Thomson	c Knott b Botham	21	b Willis		0
LS Pascoe	c Greig b Hendrick	20	c Hendrick b Underwood		0
Extras	(b 4, lb 2, nb 6)	12	(b 1, lb 5, nb 17, w 1)		24
Total	(82.2 overs)	243	(127 overs)		309

ENGLAND

JM Brearley*	c Hookes b Pascoe	15	b Walker		81
G Boycott	c McCosker b Thomson	107	not out		80
RA Woolmer	lbw b Pascoe	0			
DW Randall	run out	13	not out		19
AW Greig	b Thomson	11	b Walker		0
G Miller	c Robinson b Pascoe	13			
APE Knott †	c Davis b Thomson	135	c O'Keeffe b Walker		2
IT Botham	b Walker	25			
DL Underwood	b Pascoe	7			
M Hendrick	b Walker	1			
RGD Willis	not out	2			
Extras	(b 9, lb 7, nb 16, w 3)	35	(b 2, ln 2, nb 2, w 1)		7
Total	(124.2 overs)	364	(for 3 wkts) (81.2 overs)		189

ENGLAND	O	M	R	W		O	M	R	W		Fall of wickets:			
RGD Willis	15.0	0	58	1		26.0	6	88	5			Aus	Eng	Aus	Eng
M Hendrick	21.2	6	46	2		32.0	14	56	2	1st	79	34	18	154
IT Botham	20.0	5	74	5		25.0	5	60	0	2nd	101	34	60	156
AW Greig	15.0	4	35	1		9.0	2	24	1	3rd	131	52	154	158
DL Underwood	11.0	5	18	1		27.0	15	49	2	4th	133	64	204	-
G Miller						5.0	2	5	0	5th	153	82	240	-
RA Woolmer						3.0	0	3	0	6th	153	297	240	-
										7th	153	326	270	
AUSTRALIA	O	M	R	W		O	M	R	W	8th	155	357	307	-
JR Thomson	31.0	6	103	3		16.0	6	34	0	9th	196	357	308	-
LS Pascoe	32.0	10	80	4		22.0	6	43	0	10th	243	364	309	-
MHN Walker	39.2	12	79	2		24.0	8	40	3					
GS Chappell	8.0	0	19	0										
KJ O'Keeffe	11.0	4	43	0		19.2	2	65	0					
KD Walters	3.0	0	5	0										

Result: England won by 7 wickets

6

TOPLESS BLONDE
AT THE OVAL

I HAVE always been hopeless at television commentary. Having learned the job with radio, I found it impossible to adapt in the way that Tony Cozier seemed to manage so easily, and I regularly left those brave television producers who tried to corral me heading for an early grave. I have often thought that if I had tackled television commentary first, it might have been the other way round. The golden rule when it comes to television is not to talk about things the viewer cannot see on the screen. When I was on television, however, if ever I saw something amusing happening at third man, in the crowd or wherever, I could not resist it. The producer, meanwhile, was showing his viewers a close-up of, say, the batsman and was expecting me to say something intelligent and interesting about his technique or his haircut. My descriptive adventures meant that the cameras had to abandon the batsman to try and locate what I was talking about. By the time they had got there, I had usually moved on to something else and the chaos became even more confused. I think too, as a commentator, I have always found it difficult to appreciate the value of silence, which is often essential on television. On the other hand, if you stop talking for too long on radio, people may think you have gone home and switch off.

The embarrassing thing is, I did actually begin my broadcasting career in television. In the sixties the independent television companies occasionally dipped their toes into county cricket. It was in 1964 that I was rung up by Crawford White, the most charming and mildly avuncular cricket correspondent of the *Daily Express*. He was a tall, good-looking man who hailed from Yorkshire. In the press box he wrote every piece as if he feared it was going to be his last. The agony of compilation was invariably accompanied by a tuneless hum which had some of the qualities of an agitated bumblebee. Away from the cricket he was adventurous and charming. He asked me if I would be interested in covering a county match in London for ITV. I was delighted and became part of their commentary team for a couple of matches, at Lord's and The Oval. Crawford himself was one of the commentators and contributed nobly to my first on-air broadcasting gaffe.

We were at The Oval and it was a cloudless day in July. There was nothing remarkable about the cricket, which meandered on for three days. I cannot remember who Surrey were playing. Although this was my first job behind a microphone, my instinct, when I was on air, was already to have a look round the ground for anything out of the ordinary or amusing. I don't think the producer then was as strict as his successors were to become in my later forays into this medium. We were sitting in the old television box high up in the pavilion. I found myself looking across at the now extinct Cricketers pub on the other side of the road going round the east side of The Oval. Next door to it there was a short row of two-storey red-brick houses with balconies on the first floor which provided an excellent view of the cricket. I noticed movement on one of these balconies and through my binoculars I saw behind the railings two deckchairs occupied by sunbathing cricket-watchers. I relayed this information to our viewers and in a moment the cameras had followed me and the balcony was on our screens. One of the occupants of the chairs now stood up, with glass in hand, and stretched, bare from the waist upwards. I said something like, 'That chap's sensibly taken off his shirt in order to brush up his suntan. What a great time he's having. I wonder what he's drinking,' and looked back at the cricket.

At this point, Crawford, who had been keenly following events on the balcony, picked up his microphone and I heard him say in his quiet, measured, but now anxious tones, 'Be careful. Henry. That's the most beautiful man I've ever seen.'

My eyes raced back to the monitor and by the time I got there the producer had gone back to the cricket. I had to wait until the end of my spell before discovering that the 'chap' who got up and stretched was actually an ample blonde who was indeed brushing up her suntan, because she was topless. One of the papers the next morning had a catchy little headline: 'TV commentator stumped by blonde.' That was the end of my commentary career with ITV. I am not sure the two events were connected. If they were, it suggests a massive sense-of-humour failure.

One man who enjoyed my gaffe enormously was our scorer, the great Lancashire and England wicketkeeper George Duckworth. By then, there was quite a lot of George, even though he was a short man. He was the greatest of fun, with a wonderful sense of humour. After the war he became scorer and baggage-man for the England side when they toured overseas. He was one of the game's great characters. He scored for us in both the games I covered for ITV and although they were the only times I met him, we became good friends. It was very sad when he died early in 1966 at the age of only sixty-four.

One of my great friends in the sixties was Frank Keating, whom I had met while working as a holiday relief on the *Guardian* sports desk. Frank, a brilliant writer and the most innovative of thinkers, kept himself busy on many fronts. He worked for a time for the independent television company Associated Rediffusion, who held the midweek ITV franchise in the south of the country. In the mid-sixties Frank had hit upon the idea of a series of sporting programmes embracing all the summer sports. Apparently my topless escapade had been forgotten – or perhaps they felt the memory of it might encourage listeners. Before I was signed up for two days' cricket on the programme, I had a studio test and it turned out to be one of the most nerve-wracking broadcasting moments I have been through. I went to the Rediffusion building at the bottom of Southampton Row. In a big studio with masses of people sitting behind me, I had to commentate on a few minutes of the football World Cup final at Wembley in 1966. I had done lots of homework and now I sat in an uncomfortable upright chair clutching a microphone, frightened out of my mind. It called for strong nerves.

'Are you ready?' somebody asked.

I suppose I said yes. The lights went out and suddenly on the screen in front of me was Nobby Stiles on the move and off I went. I gabbled away for about ten minutes and I thought I was dreadful. When it ended, there was a deafening silence, broken by Frank putting his arm round my shoulder and saying, 'Well done, my dear. That was terrific.' Which it certainly was not. Two days later I was summoned to a meeting with Grahame Turner, who was Rediffusion's head of sport. He was a man with a tough, no-nonsense approach to everything. He told me I had been selected, implying too that it had been a close-run thing. Frank must have fought my corner for all he was worth.

The series was called *Spring Out* and was introduced by the soap opera king Desmond Carrington, who played Dr Chris Anderson in *Emergency – Ward 10*. We televised the match from the old television commentary box in the Warner Stand at Lord's. Colin Cowdrey was another commentator, and the incredibly smooth Carrington chipped in occasionally. I don't think he knew anything about cricket, but it didn't matter because it was not that sort of programme. We had lots of heart-throbby stuff from him and a blonde lady who popped up on his arm from time to time. She was another soap star and she had a rather toothy grin. I made some youthful and enthusiastic squeaks, I hope in the right places, but there was little to suggest that much of my life was going to be spent behind a microphone. Certainly, no one rushed to offer me more of the same.

Lots of new faces were used for that series. Two others who were making first appearances in front of or behind the cameras were Anne Robinson, who even then was the strongest link of us all, and Barry Davies, who was to become such a superb football commentator. Barry could turn his hand to anything and still does, given half a chance. At the final inquest on that series, I daresay, as far as I was concerned, Frank just about got away with it in that soothing voice of his, which was so good at producing a disarming shrug of the shoulders.

I have already touched on the bitter split within world cricket caused by the television takeover of the game in Australia by Kerry Packer. His World Series Cricket had begun in 1977–78. The following season in Australia, the Ashes were again up for grabs and England were captained by Mike Brearley. Almost all Australia's best players had signed for Packer, amid a fierce rolling of drums. England were effectively up against an Australian second XI, while Packer's cricket, with the top forty players in the world on board, were carrying on in direct competition. Packer's PR machine was at full throttle and his Channel Nine television network was also revving up, under the innovative direction of David Hill. They were up against the relatively antiquated ABC, who had been covering all international cricket in Australia for years until these arrivistes challenged their position. ABC still had the rights to the Ashes series, and so they had to roll up their sleeves and give of their best. They decided to use a few more cameras and also came up with a new interview slot. That is how the delightful Peter Meares, who worked for ABC in Brisbane, ended up interviewing me each day during the tea interval. It appeared to go reasonably well and led to a most unusual diversion.

The battle between World Series and the Australian Cricket Board continued through the entire Australian summer. Both sides spent their time insulting the other and claiming victory, which seemed to be sliding slowly but irresistibly towards World Series. The quality of their output, both on the field and in the country's living rooms, was simply better. But, nonetheless, the Establishment's supporters were loyal and big crowds still turned up for the Ashes series. The fourth official Test began on 6 January 1979 at the Sydney Cricket Ground, with England 2–1 up in the series. On the first day there were getting on for 40,000 people in the ground. We all settled down in the press box to watch the morning's play. Just before lunch, Phil Tresidder, who worked for one of the local newspapers, asked me if I had seen the message pinned to the new floodlight pylon on the famous Hill. The Trustees of the SCG had by now been forced by the New South Wales government to allow Packer to use the ground. He had, as a result, installed floodlights which rose above the ground on huge black columns like space-age mushrooms. I picked up my binoculars and saw the sheet pinned to this column. In red paint it proclaimed, in bold letters, 'THE BESPECTACLED HENRY BLOWFLY STAND'. (I wore tinted glasses in those days.) It took me a moment to realise I was the object of this slogan. Of course, much leg-pulling went on, but I was rather chuffed to get a mention in this way. The next day there were two sheets on the pylon. The one below the original read, again in large letters, 'HENRY COME ON OVER AND HAVE A PINT'. I could not refuse that one.

After lunch I took off my tie and headed over there. Waving my press pass, I went through the gate onto the grassy banks of the Paddington Hill just to the left of the Noble Stand where the press lived, and began to walk about a third of the way round the ground, trying to find a path through the crowd. Derek Randall was in the exceedingly boring process of making the slowest ever hundred in a Test between England and Australia. It took him 406 minutes. The crowd found my arrival on the Paddington Hill altogether more jolly. My lengthy progress through the spectators, past the old scoreboard and onto the Hill was greeted with loud cheering. Even the players turned round to see what was going on. I was embarrassed by the fuss. However, I eventually arrived at the floodlight column amid terrific cheers. Quite a number of students from Sydney University had laid claim to the area around it and it was they who had stuck up those red-lettered sheets. I was submerged by all these lovely youngsters who pumped my hand and offered me cans of cold beer. They were in great spirits and we talked and laughed for several minutes. Then, a beautiful dark-haired lady came up to me, kissed me warmly on the cheek and told me she wanted to marry me. I told her it was the best offer I had had that day and it certainly merited a discussion. Actually, I really thought I was on to a winner. She poured a jug of cold water all over me, though, when she added, 'The man I am really after is Geoffrey Boycott.' I could not quite follow her thinking, because when Boycott had opened England's second innings that morning, he had been lbw to the very first ball. It had been a slow and amiable loosener from Rodney Hogg. It was, incidentally, the only time Boycott had been out first ball in 193 Test innings. Unaccountably, this appeared to have won him the sympathy vote at Sydney University. Undaunted, I polished off two or three cans of beer before starting back to the other end of the ground for my teatime interview with Peter Meares.

I got much ribbing when I returned to the press box, not least from Jack Fingleton, who had opened the batting for Australia before the war. He was now a journalist and could never resist the chance to have a dig at anyone, especially a

Pom. He asked me how I had got on with the chaps on the Hill. When I told him, he drawled back at me, 'Blofeld, why don't you take those marbles out of your mouth.' Oh dear.

The next day another sheet read, 'OUR HENRY CAN EVEN OUTDRINK KEITH MILLER'. Miller did not sue. The day after that we had 'OUR HENRY IS TO CRICKET WHAT TONY GREIG IS TO LIMBO DANCING'. I never quite worked that one out. When the match ended, with an England victory by 93 runs, all the students brought the 'BESPECTACLED HENRY BLOWFLY' sheet across the ground and presented it to me on the outfield. Two days later they came round to my hotel and we had a party. What fun it all was, and somehow it seemed to sum up the wonderful sense of spontaneity that is one of the joys of Australia.

My next outing in front of the cameras was in New Zealand. This came about as a result of my going there after England's tour to Australia in 1978–79 to watch them play Pakistan. I did the odd piece to camera for TVNZ, for which I think I got a pass mark. This led to me being asked back each year in the eighties to join their commentary team. Those few years were tremendous fun. We were a varied bunch in the box. John Morrison, the former New Zealand opening batsman, who could not have been better suited to his nickname 'Mystery', was a joy. He had an open, wide-eyed face with dark hair and a lovely all-purpose smile. This could be used to greet a long-lost friend or, without the slightest change, it would do duty as a sarcastic rebuke. You had to spot which it was. Mystery was always promising an after-hours sortie. He was delightfully friendly on air and was always a joy to be with, even if you could not be sure, deep down, what he was really thinking. In a precise voice, Glenn Turner, probably New Zealand's best ever opening batsman, talked excellent cricket sense, mainly from a New Zealand point of view. Then there was Peter Sharp, who had captained Canterbury in the old Plunket Shield. He commentated just as he had scored his runs, which was carefully, but accurately. Two former players joined us in the mid-eighties, Martin Crowe, a truly great batsman, and Ian Smith, a fine wicketkeeper who could bat much more than just a bit and scored his share of pugnacious Test hundreds.

Like all other networks, TVNZ was creeping towards a cast made up only of former Test players. Another recruit was the former All Black Grahame Thorne, who with the rugby ball in his hands ran like a hare on the wing. He was small with an elusive jink. A man of many parts, his life stumbled through a few crises, although he always emerged with a smile on his face. I once spent what was surely an unforgettable afternoon with him in the tasting room at Cloudy Bay in Blenheim, but unfortunately I can remember none of it. We were with Kevin Judd, the vineyard's famous winemaker, who first made the sauvignon blanc which brought Cloudy Bay its fame. We were now tasting his new pinot noir. I don't remember getting to the tasting room, let alone leaving, and I am

sure Thorney doesn't either. I can though, I think, vouch for
the pinot being delicious. Thorney was once elected as a
member of parliament for the Liberal Party by the voters of
Onehunga, a suburb of Auckland. Our intrepid television
team was completed by Grant Nisbett, a big man who was
primarily a rugby commentator. He had a lovely rich voice, a
good sense of humour and just occasionally a formidable
thirst. Peter Williams was the presenter as well as a commentator. His voice electrified the young ladies of New Zealand,
even if his domestic status did not allow him to take full
advantage of it. He was, sadly, one of those who seemed to
attract problems for which there was usually no solution. He
constantly walked about with a worried expression.

Our producer, Doc Williams, so called because his initials
were 'D.O.C.', was a large, friendly man who from time to
time blew a pretty considerable gasket. When that happened
it was sensible not to be around. He had been a cricketer
himself and as a young man had had trials as an off-spinner
for Glamorgan, for whom he had played a handful of games.
He was under the testing captaincy of that all-pervading
Welshman Wilf Wooller, who ran Glamorgan's cricket seem-
ingly for ever and as a not particularly benevolent despot.
Maybe a little of Wooller rubbed off on Doc. I enjoyed working under him and he allowed me a greater licence to go my
own way than any other television producer I worked with.
TVNZ was as full of politics as any TV organisation, and I
don't think Doc was much good at political games, which

probably led to his eventual downfall. I remember him being unwilling to change his mind about almost anything – the Wooller touch again.

During the mid-eighties my television career took another direction when Pakistan Television (PTV) asked me to commentate on the one-day international matches played in Sharjah in the United Arab Emirates. The cricket stadium in Sharjah was the handiwork of a Pakistani emigré, Abdul Rahman Bukhatir, a trader who had made more money than you can shake a stick at by shipping goods across the Arabian Gulf to India. He wanted at first to stage one-day international cricket, inspired maybe by Kerry Packer's example in Australia. His aim was to centre it around the involvement of India and Pakistan. That rivalry of course runs deep; the political climate is seldom right for them to play in India and it was a no-brainer to want to bring them together in Sharjah. Sri Lanka were also popular, with the other Test-playing countries taking turns to provide the fourth side for their competitions before Bangladesh came on the cricketing scene.

I was amazed by the ground when I first saw it. Here, in the middle of the desert, was a green oasis. The stands were only half built then, but now it has grown up and Test matches are held there. In the early days, Bukhatir sat in pomp in his box at the Pavilion End, just below the commentary area. He was usually surrounded by a galaxy of beautiful Bollywood film stars whom he had specially flown in for the occasion. A number of cricketing dignitaries would also be present. It was a rich mix. Sharjah itself was officially alcohol-free, which I heard was a stipulation made by the ruler of Saudi Arabia when he made Sharjah a significant loan. Nonetheless, there were ways and means, I can assure you. Although as a precaution on my first visits I stayed in Dubai, which was a short distance down a road known, not unreasonably, as 'Kamikaze Causeway'.

Bukhatir employed the former Pakistan batsman Asif Iqbal to organise the cricket at Sharjah. The PTV commentary team was led by the legendary Iftikhar Ahmed, a considerable businessman who had prospered mostly across the Atlantic. A regular with PTV, he loved cricket and spent his holidays watching Pakistan play. There was just a touch of the matinee idol in Ifty's appearance, as well as his suggestive walk. As a commentator, he was inclined to back both ends to the middle, but he had a good appreciation of the beauty of the game and of the skill that was needed to play it successfully at this level. He had an easy, relaxed voice. There was always an assortment of former Pakistan Test players with us. One of them I remember particularly well was the smooth Saleem Altaf, known by one and all as 'Bobby', although I never found out why. There was usually an Indian equivalent and also an anchorman from PTV in Karachi. The commentary was passionate, excitable, with words spoken at top speed, often gloriously inaccurate, but always jolly, although I don't think politics was ever far below the surface. With India and Pakistan involved, that made it an explosive mixture.

There were times in commentary when I used to concentrate more on the Bollywood film stars than the cricket. They sat only a few yards in front of us and it was impossible to ignore them. The girls were amazing and I described them in some detail in my commentary. There were, however, some more intimate details which it was not good news to be too explicit about in front of a largely Muslim audience. I found a way round this which has lived on to delight and amuse me. The Bollywood film industry was full of ladies who had delicious boobs of every size. I thought I ought to try and convey this to our listeners, who must have numbered countless millions on the Subcontinent. I noticed these ladies also wore earrings of different shapes and sizes. The idea suddenly came to me. When an actress arrived or left carrying all before her, as it were, I described her with discretion to our listeners. Then I added that she had a wonderful pair of large and robust earrings. When the lady was of modest proportions, I described her earrings as being small, delicate and fetching. Then there were the medium-sized danglers, and on it went. Even today when I go to India or maybe just walk round Lord's, people will come up to me and say, 'I remember the earrings in Sharjah. Why don't you still talk about them?' I doubt that many, if any, had a clue what I was up to. Still, even if I was the only person who fully understood, it gave me a great laugh. I love it that the memory lingers on – and not for the right reasons either.

I am afraid that annual cricketing jamboree in Sharjah has left behind a nasty taste. There is much to suggest that match-fixing was rife in these tournaments. It is even said that Sharjah was where it all began. There were any number of surprise results there over the years. Many accusing fingers have been pointed and with some justification. All those in control shrieked their innocence, maybe a trifle too manically for their own good. No less a commentator than *TMS*'s Jonathan Agnew, who has seen his share of games in Sharjah, was convinced that at least two of the matches he watched were fixed. Aggers was by no means the only one to cast aspersions. Sir Paul Condon, the former Commissioner of the Metropolitan Police in London who was appointed as head of the International Cricket Council's anti-corruption squad, made a visit to Sharjah. It would have been interesting to see his report. Rumour had it that he was far from convinced of the innocence of those involved. The other important operatives in this saga were – and, who knows, maybe still are – the big names involved in running the illegal bookmaking industry in India. Some of these people lived in the UAE and so, for them, cricket in Sharjah was a home fixture. The vast amount of money which is bet in India on all aspects of a game of cricket makes it certain that the ungodly and the match-fixing they foster will never go away – at least until the betting industry in the Subcontinent is legalised. Which is the remotest of possibilities. Sadly, I never heard of odds being laid on the size of earrings. If they ever were, you can be sure the college of plastic surgeons would have been jumping up and down.

*   *   *

It was towards the end of the eighties when I did a fair amount of television for Trans World International, the television arm of Mark McCormack's International Management Group. The company was run at this time by Bill Sinrich, a hard-headed American journalist who took no prisoners. He had, at best, a questionable bedside manner if things were not going his way. I had a number of adventures in India and Pakistan under TWI's banner. Their biggest up-and-coming commentary star was the irrepressible Geoffrey Boycott. His views then were forthright, but not yet as implacable and unforgiving as they were to become, although they were already making strides in that direction.

My most memorable television adventure with TWI came in the West Indies. When South Africa were readmitted to Test cricket after the abolition of apartheid they visited the West Indies for the first time in April 1992. They played two one-day internationals in Jamaica and one in Trinidad before moving on to Barbados for a one-off Test match. TWI held the rights to televise international cricket in the West Indies and Bill Sinrich asked me to be part of their commentary team. This was a great moment in sporting history. The West Indies easily won the three one-day games. While we were in Jamaica, Michael Manley, the Prime Minister, agreed to be interviewed by us. Sinrich asked me to do the interview. We drove round to his house and chatted away for about half an hour, and he could not have been more friendly. He was clear-thinking, relaxed and highly intelligent, and was delighted to welcome the South Africans to Jamaica. Of course, he regarded the abolition of apartheid as a great and overdue victory, which it was.

After a brief stay in Trinidad, we moved on to Barbados for an remarkable Test match. It was a close contest, and although the West Indies won by 52 runs, it looked for a while as if South Africa might become the first visiting side to win in Barbados for fifty-seven years. The only sad aspect about the match was the local boycott. Ironically, it had nothing to do with the South Africans or apartheid. It happened because the Bajan public were upset by the way they perceived they were being treated by the West Indian Test selectors. Their particular grudge was that the selectors had not picked their own Bajan seam bowler, Anderson Cummins, to play in this match. As a result, only just over 6,000 people watched the entire match and there were only 300 there on a dramatic and exciting last day. In all other ways, this short tour was a triumph. Sadly, the empty stands at Kensington Oval gave this hugely important Test match an eerie feeling. It is not easy in the commentary box to create sustained excitement against a background of empty stands. I can only say that feelings must have run extremely deep if they kept the Bajans away from what turned out to be such a an extraordinary game of cricket.

It was not all that long after this that I met Mark Mascarenhas who had founded his own television company, WorldTel TV. He was as plausible as anyone I ever met. He was also to become Sachin Tendulkar's agent, and he will have had to fight a great many competitors to land that one. He and I got on famously and I proceeded to make what turned out to be one of the worst decisions of my life. Having said that, he and I had become such friends that I am pretty sure I would do the same thing again. I allowed him to persuade me to jump ship when I was getting on well with Sinrich and TWI. He wanted me to help him meet the authorities in the various cricketing countries so that he could use his great charm on them to help him buy their television rights. I went to India with him when, after a day in Pune, full of meetings, offers, counter offers, frantic long-distance telephone calls and a good deal of subterfuge besides, the Indian Board of Control let him have the rights for the 1996 World Cup for six and a half million dollars. TWI and Sinrich were his closest rivals. There was any amount of intrigue about, and even the next morning after the deal had been done, Jagmohan Dalmiya, the chairman of the Indian Board, was saying privately that the rights could still be renegotiated. He and Mascarenhas were two of a kind. Who knows what passed between them before Mascarenhas and WorldTel were sure of victory.

Mark later took me via New York to Barbados to try and persuade the West Indies Board to turn their backs on TWI and sell their rights for international cricket to WorldTel. Not surprisingly, for TWI had served West Indies cricket well, they remained loyal to TWI and Sinrich. There was a lovely moment when Mascarenhas and Sinrich met and hissed at each other on the stairs behind the boardroom at the

Kensington Oval. Mascarenhas was mortified and was upset that I had not managed to twist the arm of my old friend Stephen Camacho, who was secretary to the Board. Soon after we had got back to England I was summoned by Mascarenhas and told that as I could not deliver, my services were no longer required. When I had joined him, he had refused to sign a contract and so my bank manager and I were left high and dry. A few years later in India during an England tour, he and I resumed what had started as a most amusing and thirsty friendship. He drove me back to my hotel after a day/night game in Madras and we shook hands. The next day, when he was in pursuit of tigers near Nagpur, a lorry drove into his car and he was killed.

7

SUBCONTINENTAL
SHENANIGANS

THERE is still a huge public misconception about India. It is the country in which I most enjoy watching and commentating on cricket. When I say this, many people look at me in horror, as if I have just passed the port the wrong way or committed some other ghastly social solecism. India is the most wonderful country. My first overseas tour was to India, in 1963–64, working as a freelance journalist for various British newspapers. I fell in love with the country the moment I landed in Bombay. I can understand how the ninety-minute drive in those days from Santa Cruz airport to Apollo Bunder where our hotels were situated might have put some first-time visitors off for life. You passed through scenes of poverty so awful that, not surprisingly, some Western eyes were unable to cope. Another long, initial drive, from Dum Dum airport into Calcutta was probably even worse, as you drove through the poverty which produced the extraordinary Mother Teresa. Although the poverty is still dreadful, visitors arriving today do not have it thrust under their noses in quite the same way. As far as I was concerned, the magnetism of India was as strong then as it is now, even though prohibition was the order of the day – another hurdle to be jumped. To be able to buy a drink in the Permit Room in your hotel, you had to have it stamped in your passport before you left England that you were a confirmed alcoholic. Fortunately, neither my doctor nor the Indian High Commissioner in London had any problem with that.

On that 1963–64 tour I acquired my taste for both India and its cricket, though the series itself was as dull as any I have watched. Two strong batting sides against weak bowling produced five drawn matches. England were captained by M.J.K. Smith, and India by Tiger, the Nawab of Pataudi. He and I had played cricket against each other at school when Eton played Winchester in 1956. He was just fifteen and even at that tender age his undeveloped genius was unmistakable. In Bombay on that first tour, I took a young Bollywood actress out to dinner – and her mother came too. I quickly learned that in India two and two did not always make four.

I also came within half an hour of playing in a Test match in Bombay when Delhi belly had ravaged the England party. It was the nearest of misses and one that I still have 'if only' thoughts about. Unfortunately for me, Micky Stewart, the vice-captain, got out of his hospital bed to play, though he was back in it again well before lunch on the first day. I continue to think that one less Test match would have done him little harm, whereas one for me would have made all the difference. Sadly, all of this was eight years before my radio career began, but it was a tour which, as you can see, gave me plenty to talk about when rain stopped play in the years ahead.

I did not visit India again until late in 1976, when Tony Greig captained the England side. For that tour, Johnny Woodcock, the famous cricket correspondent of *The Times*, and I drove with three others from London to Bombay. It was a long tour which was to end with the Centenary Test match in Melbourne in March 1977. The idea of going to India by car had started in Perth in December 1975 when Australia were playing the West Indies at the WACA. At dinner one evening, I said to Woodcock that in a year's time we would both be in India. He told me that the last time he had gone there, he, Brian Johnston and Michael Melford of the *Daily Telegraph* decided they would go by car. For some reason it had not worked out. Now, well before dinner had ended that night at the Weld Club in Perth, he and I had decided that this was the time to do it. When we were later in Sydney we signed up our first passenger, the irrepressible and lovely Judy Casey.

On Tuesday, 6 October 1976, five of us drove out of a lock-up garage by the Albert Hall in a magnificent 1921 claret-coloured Rolls-Royce and a new yellow three-litre Rover. We were bound, that morning, for Margate, and ultimately for Bombay. Forty-six days later, we parked in the forecourt of the Taj Mahal Hotel in Bombay. Along the way, we had many unforgettable experiences. We met lots of interesting and extraordinary people, ate some improbable food, stayed in one or two even more improbable hotels, drove on terrifying mountainous roads. In Mashhad, the most holy city of Iran, we discovered, if you can believe it, a cache of champagne in an hotel which was almost within touching distance of the famous Holy Shrine of Imam Reza. We saw Lord Curzon's embassy in Kabul and, in the Khyber Pass, were told the scores in the current Test match between Pakistan and New Zealand which was being played in Karachi. In those days it was a relatively straightforward journey. It was to become an extremely hazardous one, especially by the route we selected. As it was, no one actually shot at us, which, in a way, was a trifle disappointing, for it would have quickened the pulse no end.

The best story from the drive came within an hour of setting out from the Albert Hall. It was a wet Tuesday morning and a bit chilly too. I was perched on the assistant chauffeur's seat in the Rolls, which was draughty and a little damp. Adrian Liddell, who owned the Silver Ghost, was driving, and continued to do so for the entire journey. Johnny Woodcock was in the back reading the paper, surrounded by much luggage. The window separating the two chauffeurs from the family in the back was wound up. The windscreen-wipers looked thin and fragile and I wondered if they were up to all that lay ahead. I need not have worried. It was slow progress in the early rush hour and eventually we came to a longish halt in a sizeable traffic jam in New Cross. There was a loud tapping on the window behind me. Seeing Woodcock was anxious to speak, I wound the window down.

'Good heavens,' he began while pointing towards New Cross station. 'When I saw all those Indians at that bus stop, I thought for a moment that we had got there.' It made us all laugh.

I had somehow persuaded the BBC to take a few updates on our progress to Bombay on *Sport on Two*, the four-hour sports programme on Saturday afternoons. In order to make this possible the BBC had given me some special equipment. To be able to broadcast on the telephone from wherever I was, I had first to unscrew the mouthpiece on the receiver. Then I had to screw on a gadget which presumably improved the quality of my voice. Organising a transfer-charge call was an interminable business. In those days, it was not always that simple even in England. When I eventually got through, I invariably had to compete with plenty of background noise. It was reasonably straightforward in Salzburg, while Salonica was not too complicated either, but when we got east of Istanbul it became somewhere between bloody difficult and impossible. Telephones were not thought to be essential in most of the hotel bedrooms we came across. This meant I had to enlist the help of the hotel receptionist, which was not always willingly given, especially as it involved dismantling her receiver. This usually caused chaos. Harsh words were sometimes spoken. Tehran was an exception as we were staying with friends who helped me jump the language barrier. Even so, the call always took ages to come through. It was quite a business in remoter places like Sivas in

Turkey, where in the end I had to give up, or even Ankara, where we stayed with the Turkish Judge Advocate – we had come across one of his sons in a petrol station just outside the city where he was also filling up his car and offered to try and find us somewhere to stay the night and ended up putting us up himself.

A good deal of shouting went on before we actually got through to London. Then, if all went well, I found myself being put through to the right studio. I remember having one splendid conversation with no less a man than Desmond Lynam. I am not sure either of us could hear what the other said, which made it even more intriguing. In a poky little hotel in Herat in Afghanistan just over the border with Iran, I was shouted down and had to give up. Every time I started the process of trying to connect with London, a lady inter- rupted and screeched at me in a voice which seemed either to be starting World War III or imitating a highly strung peacock. It was only later I discovered she was in the room across the passage and our wires must have been inextricably crossed. I learned this later that evening when she began to screech at the waiter in the dining room in that unmistakable voice. She had a deceptive head of long, dark blonde hair, which she flicked from her face as though she was teaching it a lesson. She was small, with a thin face, the tightest of mouths and an impressive array of militant front teeth, though she was not easily given to smiling. When I asked the receptionist about her, she shook her head and then tapped her finger meaningfully against her forehead. So this time Radio 2 listeners simply had to miss out on the racy stuff about that champagne in Mashhad.

The 1976–77 tour of India was the first occasion on which *Test Match Special* mounted its own operation from abroad, and even then it was only by chance. After our stately arrival by Rolls, Woodcock and I watched Tony Greig's England side make the most remarkable start to that five-match series. They won the first Test in Delhi thanks to John Lever finding plenty of swing and taking ten wickets in his first Test match. For the second match in Calcutta, the groundsmen had prepared a typical Eden Gardens pitch on which the ball turned almost square. It was ready made for India's own spinners. To their amazement, the Indians now found themselves out-batted by Tony Greig, who made a remarkable hundred in just under seven hours. They were then out-bowled not by England's spinners, but their seamers, who took sixteen of the twenty Indian wickets. England were therefore two matches up with a good chance of winning the series in the third, in Madras, which began on 14 January. Back in Broadcasting House in London, inspired by Peter Baxter, it was decided that *TMS* should broadcast commentary from Madras. CMJ was in India covering the tour for the BBC and I was writing about it for the *Guardian* and the *Observer*. The third commentator was India's Pearson Surita, a splendid Anglo-Indian character with an unforgettable voice which was both fruity and correct in what now seems a curiously old-fashioned way. It was a voice which gave off more than just a hint of the British Raj. Pearson lived amid all-pervading Dickensian gloom and splendour on Chowringhee in Calcutta, where I often visited him. He kept an unrelenting supply of Black Label Scotch whisky which his eighty-year-old bearer (male servant) dispensed with alarming freedom. The redoubtable, delightful and combative Robin Marlar, who was writing for the *Sunday Times*, agreed to be one of our summarisers, which guaranteed excitement and controversy. Tony Lewis, writing for the *Sunday Telegraph*, was another, so we were in plentiful supply. It was an exciting adventure, not least from the technical angle. In spite of their enormous enthusiasm, our local engineers sometimes found that their way of doing things differed considerably from ours. Connections and one or two other essential things like that did not always go according to plan. There were frequent breaks in transmission, which caused much shaking of heads and a few frayed tempers – in London as well as Madras.

The commentary went well and told the heart-warming story of England's third successive victory, which will have cheered up some cold January mornings at home. It was fun too, to be breaking new ground. The match was given an added flavour by what became known as the Vaseline Affair. John Lever had another five-wicket haul in India's first innings in Madras and, in all, had taken 19 in the first three Tests. During this match, the Indians complained that Lever was using grease from his face to shine the ball, suggesting this had been helping him to swing it as much as he was.

This accusation put England in a tricky situation. During the tour, Lever had been finding that sweat had been running down his forehead into his eyes, which were always stinging as a result. Bernard Thomas, England's long-standing physio-therapist, was an inventive chap. He had with him some sheets of gauze impregnated with Vaseline. He cut a sheet into strips and stuck one just above each of Lever's eyebrows to divert the flow of sweat. When bowling, Lever would often rub his forehead in order to disperse the sweat. Of course his fingers touched the Vaseline and, in turn, the ball became greasy. This helped the process of keeping the shine on the ball, making it more liable to swing – or so the argument went. The Indians were certain this was being done deliber-ately, while Lever was saying it was entirely unintentional. The upshot was that Thomas stopped putting the Vaseline strips on Lever's forehead, but he had already taken a hatful of wickets and India were poised to lose their first three Tests in a series at home for the first time.

Feelings ran high and on the Sunday, the rest day of the Test match, there was a packed press conference in Ken Barrington, the England manager's suite. Some of the Indian press were accusing England of deliberately cheating. I remember Rajan Bala, who worked for a paper in Madras and, as his size suggested, was a good trencherman, rising to unusual heights of elegance on the subject. Poor old Barrington found it a hard one to handle and was floundering. Seeing this, Tony Greig stood up and took over. He made an impassioned speech imploring the Indian journalists not to allow themselves to waste their time over such an unimportant issue, but to turn their thoughts instead to how India could pick up their cricket, which was at such a low ebb. He exhorted them to encourage the young and to look for ways of discovering and developing the enormous amount of natural talent there was in this vast country. He spoke for several minutes with vibrant messianic enthusiasm, without once pausing, in front of an audience that soon became spellbound. The next day this was the story which was all over the Indian papers and there was hardly a mention of the Vaseline. It was the ever-plausible Greig we came to know so well when he was later extolling the virtues of his new employer, Kerry Packer. CMJ was covering the press conference for the BBC. He tried to record the goings-on, but was defeated by the technical requirements. I tried to help him, although my knowledge of these things is, if anything, worse, and when CMJ attempted to play the tape back later, there was nothing there except that frustrating hiss. In public CMJ had his own homespun swearwords. The Madras air was now full of a succession of 'Fotheringay Phippses', although I don't think he ever told us who Fotheringay Phipps was – he was probably a Wodehouse invention, I would think. Greig's immortal words were not, therefore, handed down to posterity.

This Indian tour was Greig's finest hour in his short

tenure as England's captain. In the middle of the tour, Gubby Allen, the man who effectively ran England's cricket for a great many years after the war, came out to India. One evening there was a big dinner when the administrators of both countries got together and the captains were also there. At some stage, Greig and Allen must have had a conversation. Afterwards, Allen said to a friend that it was almost impossible to believe that Greig was as good as he was. He even went so far as to say that butter wouldn't melt in his mouth. Little did Allen or anyone else know that England's captain was already in cahoots with Kerry Packer.

For the time being, all was well – both with England's cricket and *TMS*. England won that Third Test by 200 runs and the series with it. It could hardly have been a more auspicious start for *TMS* on its first adventure overseas. Our efforts at the microphone must have hit all the right chords back at Broadcasting House. It was a triumph for Peter Baxter, whose original idea it had been. India then won the next Test in Bangalore, where I remember the umpiring was interesting, to say the least. The fifth, in Bombay, was drawn and it was the first time England played at the newly built Wankhede Stadium. This ground does not have the charm or the character of the old Brabourne Stadium, the home of the Cricket Club of India, which it had replaced. These two grounds are at most a quarter of a mile apart. It seems ridiculous that the Wankhede should ever have been built in the first place. It came about because of an epic and typically Indian row between the Cricket Club of India and the Bombay Cricket Association over the allocation of tickets for the big matches. It was a fight to the death.

My next visit to India was in March 1980. Mike Brearley's side stopped off on the way back from Australia to play the Golden Jubilee Test match at the Wankhede Stadium. It was played to celebrate the golden jubilee of the foundation of the Board of Control for Cricket in India. England won by ten wickets and Ian Botham made the match his own. Having picked up six wickets in India's first innings, he made 114 before taking seven more wickets in their second, finishing with thirteen wickets for 106 runs. England were 58–5 in reply to India's first-innings 242 when Bob Taylor joined Ian Botham. When they had put on 85, Taylor was given out caught behind the wicket off Kapil Dev. Taylor was not happy with the decision and India's new captain, Gundappa Viswanath, fielding at first slip, did not think he had hit the ball. He persuaded the umpire to change his mind. Viswanath's chivalry probably cost India the match, as Botham and Taylor added another 86 runs and assured England of a more than useful lead. There have been other incidents of such chivalry and I especially remember seeing Rod Marsh recall Derek Randall in the Centenary Test in Melbourne in 1977 after he had been given out caught behind by Marsh himself. Marsh realised the ball had bounced before going into his gloves and said so.

There was an amusing broadcasting moment from that Jubilee Test in Bombay. On the second day there was a total eclipse of the sun. At that time there were still rest days during Test matches. As a result of the eclipse, the rest day which always came after the third day was pushed forward to the second day so that any ensuing bad light would not interfere with the progress of the match. I was covering this game for the BBC with intermittent reports. It began on Friday, 15 February and on the rest day, the Saturday, I had to go to the Overseas Communication Services studio in Bombay to record a piece for *Sport on Two* which was to be about the first day's play and also the eclipse. Tony Lewis came to the studio with me, for he had to record a piece for *Sport on Four*, a programme he presented.

I did mine first and started off by saying, 'The streets will grow eerily dark as the eclipse takes over, the cars will have their lights on, the birds will have stopped singing and of course cricket would have been impossible.'

As soon as I had finished a voice spoke to me from the studio in London: 'Thanks for that, Henry. The only problem is that we will be playing it *after* the eclipse. You've done this piece looking ahead to the eclipse. Can we have a post-eclipse piece?'

'Right ho,' I replied. 'Keep the tape rolling and I'll go in five [seconds] . . . Here in Bombay, the streets are still eerily dark, we can hardly see anything out of the windows, the cars have got their lights on, the birds have stopped singing. They couldn't possibly have played cricket in this appalling light. The sun's completely blotted out.' There was still about two hours to go before the eclipse was going to happen.

'Great stuff. Just what we wanted,' the voice came back in my headphones.

Tony Lewis, sitting on the other side of the studio, was laughing his head off.

As it happened, I thought the eclipse was a frightful disappointment. The umpires would probably have brought the players off for bad light and side lights were perhaps necessary, but that was about it. The birds maintained a stiff upper lip throughout and continued to sing. It was easy, too, to see across the street, while the sun itself never quite gave up the fight. If it was ever completely eclipsed, it was only for about five minutes. Never let facts ruin a good story.

I was back in the Subcontinent a couple of years later. Keith Fletcher had taken an England side to India in 1981–82 and lost the series 1–0. I had been working for commercial radio in Australia and so had missed the series. I joined the party when the side flew down to Colombo for Sri Lanka's first ever Test match, at the Saravanamuttu Stadium. In the end, England won the match comfortably by seven wickets, but for a time it had looked as if they might lose the game. Then David Gower batted like an angel and John Emburey, the off-spinner, took 6–33.

I joined Don Mosey, Tony Lewis and Peter Baxter in the commentary box, which suddenly had to be changed on the morning of the match. The day before, Peter Baxter had successfully set up the commentary point at the side of the press box with all the equipment. When we arrived the next morning we found that typical Subcontinental initiative had caused a temporary stand to be erected directly in front of our original position. We couldn't see a thing. A new position then had to be found for us, somewhat begrudgingly, in the front row of the press box. Once, on another tour, much further north in Chandigarh, in India, we had found that the press box itself had been put up directly behind the sight-screen. When the groundsman was questioned about his choice of position, he replied, 'They asked for it to be wicket-to-wicket, and what could be more wicket-to-wicket than behind the sightscreen?' His logic was impeccable.

It was during this Test match in Colombo that my credit cards disappeared. I am deliberately not saying 'stolen', because my absentmindedness knows no limits. There was a dreadful hue and cry and I had an in-depth interview with the head of security at the ground. The wallet was eventually found amongst all the electronic equipment under the press box. I found that one card was missing, but it was never used and the surviving one was in mid-season form, when I came to pay my hotel bill. This was not the first time I had lost something in Sri Lanka either. After England's series in Pakistan in 1977–78, we flew via Colombo to Singapore. The England players then caught another flight to New Zealand and I went on to Perth to have another look at the Packer matches. I was writing a book, eventually published as

The Packer Affair. On the flight from Karachi to Colombo, I was trying to keep up to date and was writing about my Packer-related adventures in the last few weeks. I was in good form and words flowed off my pen. By the time we landed in Colombo, I had written more than two thousand words on the flight alone. When we went to the in-transit lounge to stretch our legs, I left all my papers in my seat. When we reboarded the aircraft I found they had disappeared.

Immediate panic. The stewards were not much help and I burst through the door onto the flight deck – this was 1978 when that could still happen – and pleaded with the captain. I told him there was no way he could take off until my papers had been found. I had lost two and a half chapters and if it meant searching the cleaners' rubbish baskets, then they would have to be searched. The captain was so surprised by my appearance and my persuasive powers that he found himself helplessly nodding his head. Ken Barrington, the England manager, was not happy with this extra delay, as the England party had a tight connection with their flight from Singapore to New Zealand. It was all rather fraught, but not long afterwards a figure came running across the tarmac waving a sheaf of papers. My outpourings had been found in the big rubbish dump where the cleaners' baskets had been emptied. We could proceed – and England, under the firm leadership of Geoffrey Boycott, just managed to catch their flight in Singapore.

Pakistan can be a more difficult nut to crack than India. I find it different, but still the greatest of fun. As it was a Muslim country, I went there wondering where my next drink was coming from. I need not have worried. There was a healthy black market. On my first visit to Pakistan in the seventies I took with me a forty-ounce bottle of Scotch I had bought in duty free at Heathrow. Stupidly, I declared it at Karachi airport and it was confiscated by customs. About three days later I met a chap at a party who was head of customs at Karachi airport. I told him that he owed me a forty-ounce bottle of Scotch. He asked me what I meant, and I told him my Scotch had been confiscated at the airport. 'Don't worry,' he said, 'you'll never see that again, it would have been drunk within half an hour of being taken off your hands'. He said that what I should do when I next visited Pakistan, was to let him know I was coming. A year later, I bought four forty-ounce bottles in duty free at Heathrow and I let him know I was heading to Pakistan. When the aeroplane landed I was summoned to the front before anyone got off. There, I was met by his deputy who took my cases and led me by a circuitous route to his office where the head of customs was thrilled to see me, shook me warmly by the hand, gave me a large glass of Scotch and lent me his car and driver to take me to my hotel. So far so good – four bottles of Scotch. At six-fifteen that evening the telephone rang and a lovely lady told me, 'There is a Commander Jilani here to see you.' 'Splendid chap, send him up!' He came up and it took us forty-one minutes to get through the first bottle. Oh well, I thought, one down, three still to play. The next evening at ten minutes to seven the telephone went again and it was another lady saying, 'Mr Blofeld, there is a Commander Jilani in the hall to see you'. 'Send him up, lovely chap!' He came up and we got rid of the second bottle. He did it again, but I had managed by then to have hidden one of the bottles, so at least I had one to myself. When I went to a party a few days later, I met a businessman who came frequently backwards and forwards to Karachi, I told him this story, but didn't mention the Commander by name. He laughed and said, 'Oh, you've met him too. He's done that to me three times!'

I shall never forget a day's wild-boar hunting in 1984 with Imran Khan's cousins on wild scrubland about forty miles out of Lahore. Imran's family live in a special, almost feudal, area in Lahore called Zamaan Park. There were a number of impressive houses built round this small park and they all belonged to his relations. I was one of the *TMS* commentators and we had just arrived back in Lahore from the delights of the second Test in Faisalabad, where *TMS* had had a good match with the bat. Vic Marks had made 83 in the first innings and helped David Gower in a record seventh-wicket stand of 167 in a drawn game. Pakistan had beaten England in Pakistan for the first time in the first Test in Karachi although, needing only 65 to win, they had lost seven wickets getting there – left-arm spinner Nick Cook took 11 in the match and 5–18 in that second innings.

On the rest day of the third Test, in Lahore, we met at Hermyun Zamaan's house soon after six o'clock in the morning. There were several cars and quite a number of people who were going to shoot. The most noticeable was a small, friendly and very determined middle-aged man who had made a great deal of money selling carpets. He was dressed to kill in a weird – to Western eyes, at least – and colourful selection of garments. He was good value, with a disarming smile but a way with a gun which made you worry whether your insurance policies were in the rudest of good health. While there was presumably little you could tell him about carpets, we were soon to find out that shooting wild boar was not his strong point, although he had definite views on the subject. We did not see many wild boar, but I despatched one most unlucky Pakistani partridge. While all this was going on, the carpet wallah, with great single-mindedness, stood facing the wrong way as masses of beaters drove a huge area of land towards us. No amount of shouting would make him turn round and face the same way as the rest of us. We never got to the bottom of this. In the middle of the day there was a splendid packed lunch, yet for some reason our carpet champion had brought along his own picnic. The others pulled his leg all the time and he laughed, but it was only a tolerant laugh and I am not sure he would have been an early choice to make up the numbers on my desert island.

I commentated on two World Cups in India and Pakistan, in 1987 and 1996. What fun they were too, with all the usual friendly chaos of airports, hotels, commentary boxes, taxi journeys to the wrong places, all those lovely curries and people, people, people. Before I had arrived on the Subcontinent from

Australia in early 1987, *TMS* had been suffering from a short-age of commentators. To the rescue came no less a man than Tim Rice, one of cricket's greatest ever supporters, who, after playing for more than thirty years, is now in grave danger of reaching two thousand runs for his own club, the Heartaches. Peter Baxter signed him up for his first match, in Jaipur. Even with Tim's outrageous talents, however, he found that commentary presented problems he had never really considered, particularly the pronunciation of some of the names. He had a relatively gentle warm-up in Jaipur, where the West Indies played England, he found that 'Kallicharran' tripped easily off his tongue, but life became more complicated when he moved on to Pune. England's next opponents were Sri Lanka, who at that time were recent additions to cricket's upper echelons, and their players were far from being household names. For the untutored, 'Ratnayeke' could be tricky and 'Anurasiri' was harder still, but he had a bit of luck that Kuruppuarachchi was kept on the bench. The one name Tim was at home with was Vinodhan John, one of the opening bowlers who he subsequently had fielding at third man and fine leg and all places in between, as well as bowling at both ends.

The last game before the semi-finals was played between India and New Zealand in Nagpur. Trevor Bailey and I were sent to cover it for *TMS*. We had first to fly from Delhi to Nagpur on a midday flight. I put my bags on the scales in Delhi and, after a good look, the official behind the desk asked me to pay an extra US$125. I started by saying there must be some mistake because

I had been in India for two weeks and had made several journeys with the same luggage without being asked to pay a cent. Nodding his head, the official smiled but remained utterly implacable in, I thought, an increasingly hostile manner. I grew angry, raised my voice and flung out a few pertinent epithets before, of course, paying up, bristling with annoyance. Trevor and I went through to the boarding lounge and when we were sitting down, Trevor told me I had behaved disgracefully and that it really would not do. Oh dear. Kipling wrote something about the fool 'who tried to hustle the East'. I knew what he meant and felt suitably ashamed of myself.

Trevor and I sat together on the aeroplane and during the journey he showed me a new, all-powerful credit card he had just signed up for with, I think, American Express. He was immensely pleased, not to say proud of it. I dutifully admired it and I rather think I was allowed to hold it. We arrived in Nagpur and the next day watched an extraordinary game between India and New Zealand. New Zealand had made 221 and to make sure they qualified for the semi-finals, India had not only to win but also to score the runs in fewer than 34 overs. Thanks to a remarkable display of controlled strokeplay by Sunny Gavaskar who made 103 not out in 88 balls, they got there in 32.1 overs. Gavaskar of course is much better known for his adhesive qualities than his agression. I shall never forget him despatching the first ball of the second over, bowled by Ewen Chatfield, into the president's box over the sightscreen at the pavilion end. In the front two rows, several ladies dressed in beautifully coloured sarees had been looking resplendent, but Sunny's six forced them to flutter furiously like a collection of indignant peacocks as they took avoiding action.

The day after the match, Trevor and I also moved on to Bombay for the semi-final. Our flight was in the morning and we met in the foyer of our hotel. I had already paid my bill and stood watching while Trevor pulled his magnificent new credit card from his wallet. He gave it to the cashier rather as though he was performing a particularly subtle conjuring trick. The cashier looked at it for a moment or two before shaking his head and handing it back to Trevor.

'I am afraid we don't take that here,' was the unpromising reply.

Trevor could not believe it and soon was involved in an exchange of invective which made my efforts at Delhi Airport look as if I was an inadequate beginner. Trevor was off his long run and in the end, of course, had to suffer the humiliation of taking his champion back. He then suffered the additional ignominy of having to produce a much less august card, which was accepted with alacrity and did the business. With the help of porters, a silent Trevor and I piled everything into the waiting taxi.

When Trevor had settled into his seat, he turned to me and said quietly and with less certainty in his voice than usual, 'I don't think I did very well then.'

'On the contrary,' I replied. 'I thought you were at the top of your form. You made the ball move both ways all right. That chap couldn't lay a bat on you.' He did not reply and I am afraid I felt horribly smug.

Telephones were a great problem when I first went to the Subcontinent. No one was more aware of this than Don Mosey when he was covering the 1977–78 tour England made to Pakistan. A few days before the third Test in Karachi, we had one of those rather pointless games which host countries love pushing into touring schedules. England had to play a one-day game against a Sind provincial side on the old Gymkhana Club ground in the middle of Karachi, where India had played Test cricket before the war. The Gymkhana side included Sikander Bakht, a quickish bowler who had played several matches for Pakistan. Brian Johnston once said of him that Sikander's Bakht was worse than his bite. Typical Johnners He now bowled a short ball to Mike Brearley, the England captain, who tried to hook and the ball broke his right arm. The result of this was that Geoffrey Boycott, the vice-captain, took over the captaincy for the third Test as well as taking England on to New Zealand for three more.

This was a big story and there were no press facilities at the ground. Mosey was watching the game to keep a precautionary eye on things. When the extent of Brearley's injury was known, he realised he had to get the news back to Broadcasting House in London as quickly as he could. There were no telephones on the ground and so he got a taxi back to our hotel, the Midway House, which was one of the airport hotels. As soon as he arrived he asked the receptionist to put through a transfer-charge call to London, then he went back to his room for the inevitable long wait.

The call took about four hours to come through. It was getting on for ten o'clock when there was a knock on his door and the woman outside shouted, 'Telephone, Mr Mosey, telephone.'

Mosey opened the door, notes in hand, ran past her to the reception desk, snatched up the receiver and shouted into it, 'Don Mosey.'

The woman on the BBC switchboard replied, 'I'm afraid he's in Pakistan,' and put the receiver down.

8

MEMORABLE
MATCHES

IT was at Headingley in 1981 that I commentated on one of the most remarkable Test matches I have ever watched. Ian Botham's short adventure as England's captain had come to a gloomy end in the previous Test at Lord's. He failed to score in either innings and resigned the captaincy a moment or two before it was going to be taken away from him. Everything came naturally to Botham who never had to think about and work out the mechanical intricacies of the game. He had no need to. As a result, he found it difficult to understand the plight more normal mortals sometimes go through. This made it difficult for him to help them come to grips with their own game when things were not going according to plan. This is such an important aspect of captaincy and his predecessor, Mike Brearley, was the past master here.

Brearley had handed the job over to Botham two years earlier. He was now happy to come out of retirement for the third Test nine days later at Headingley. In the build-up Brearley gave his well-known impersonation of a swan: calm, smiling, peaceful and relaxed on the surface, with furious activity under the water. Botham was, of course, still in the squad for Headingley. In the nets the day before the game, Brearley sauntered over and asked Botham if he wanted to play. He did, with a vengeance.

England's other hero in that Test, Bob Willis, might not have played at Headingley either. He had had a touch of flu in the Lord's Test and had missed Warwickshire's next home game. This illustrates one of the big differences between Test players then and now. In those days they played for their counties when not playing for England. Willis was told on the telephone by Alec Bedser, the chairman of the selectors, that he had not been selected for Headingley. Mike Brearley did not want any bowlers who had not had any cricket since the Lord's Test. Willis managed to persuade Bedser that he should play and Bedser then got Brearley to change his mind.

Australia were ahead in the series, having won the first Test at Trent Bridge and the second was drawn at Lord's. At Headingley they won the toss and batted. They had reached 55 when Botham came on to bowl. He took a wicket with his third ball, a beauty which nipped back and had Graeme Wood lbw. Botham went on to take 6–95, but Australia still crept past 400, a devastating score on a pitch which was giving plenty of help to the bowlers. Dennis Lillee, Terry Alderman and 'Henry' Lawson then made short work of England, even though Botham hit a typically robust fifty. Although he refused to admit it, being freed from the responsibilities of the captaincy must have been the reason for his emphatic return to form. He later described this innings as 'the turning point'. Nonetheless, England were bowled out for 174 and were asked – a delightful touch that the game's terminology should suggest this is an invitation, with the implied possibility of a refusal – to follow on 227 runs behind. The mood in the *TMS* box was one of shoulder-shrugging gloom.

The old commentary box at the back of the Football Stand at Headingley was always uncomfortable. It was a box in which commentators needed to combine the sprightly agility of a ballet dancer with the resigned humour of a saint and the imagination to determine what had happened when the ball disappeared to the outskirts of the ground that were invisible from where they sat. The box was narrow and on two levels. There was a deep step the commentators had to jump down before they could take up their position at the microphone. When two commentators were trying to change places, it was rather like watching Laurel and Hardy attempt a tricky *pas de deux*. There was a good deal of noise and often the new commentator was still in mid-air, if not in a heap on the floor, when he had to describe the next ball.

Alan McGilvray, the Australian commentator, was not normally given to displays of emotion, yet he voiced his agitation when descending into the commentators' pit. As a rule, his emotions never seemed to change when he was on air. You could never tell from his voice how Australia were doing, and he spoke in an unemotional whisper. Johnners took the rough with the smooth in his usual jaunty way. Don Mosey was darkly profound and even-handed in his descriptions, apart from an endearing north-country bias. In the summariser's chair, Fred Trueman was both busy and gruff as he failed to understand 'what's going off out there'. Trevor Bailey was brief and to the point in a disapproving and clipped 'It never happened in my day' sort of way.

Dennis Lillee's first ball on the fourth morning had Graham Gooch caught at third slip. England's progress was now even worse than it had been in the first innings. There was a glimmer of hope when Boycott and Willey put on 64 for the fifth wicket but it was only brief. Their stand ended when Kim Hughes placed Dyson with great care at fly slip for Willey, two-thirds of the way back to the boundary. Lillee's next ball was short and, as if giving fielding practice, Willey dutifully chipped it so that Dyson did not have to move. That stroke summed it all up.

Trevor Bailey was not exactly a bundle of joy. 'That really means the end of it as far as England are concerned,' he said with an irritated finality. When the seventh wicket fell at 135, he followed up with a despairing if hardly original, 'And then I think one can say the writing's on the wall.'

With three hours left, England were still 92 runs behind. I came on soon after that and, like everyone else, was resigned to England's defeat. I started by saying, 'We're in the dying moments of the match.' If ever a game was over and done with, this was it. Botham was now joined by Graham Dilley, the tall, fair-haired fast bowler from Kent. He looked more of a skittish character than he probably was, although he was over-placed at number nine. Botham greeted him in the middle with a cheerful, 'Right then, let's have a bit of fun.'

I fear the outpourings from the commentary box faithfully reflected England's plight. But even then, with Australia winning the match in a hurry, McGilvray still never let his hair down. As usual, his mouth was only a millimetre or two from the microphone. He spoke so quietly that if you were standing immediately behind him it was impossible to hear what he was saying. His tone hardly changed and I never felt he was luring his listeners in Australia to the edge of their seats as he might have been. In the far corner, Fred Trueman's pipe moved into overdrive. It underlined the appalling fog of despair that had settled over the rest of us. Johnners did his best to jolly us along with a good-looking chocolate cake, but he was the only taker. In fact, even his jollity was sounding a trifle hollow – the situation was that grim.

Botham was true to his word and he and Dilley were soon having terrific fun. Botham led the way, lofting Terry Alderman over mid off and pulling Lillee with great power over midwicket for four more. When an immaculate drive by Dilley brought him four through the covers, even the most optimistic of us would only have felt that England might just save the follow-on. They were magnificent blows, but it was hard to take them seriously. It seemed they were just putting off the inevitable, but on it went. I was commentating with Fred when Lillee came in again to Botham.

'Lillee bowls a short one and Botham hammers it square

through the covers. It goes racing into the boundary and Australia are going to have to bat again, 227–7. It's too little too late, I am afraid.' I gave a hollow chuckle.

'I dunno,' said Fred thoughtfully. 'Funny things can happen in this game of ours.'

'Not that funny, I don't think,' I answered, with a verbal shrug of the shoulders.

Yet Botham and Dilley went miraculously on, with some of Dilley's strokes matching Botham's. Gradually our optimism had a more permanent ring to it. This was underlined when Botham thundered Alderman through midwicket for a four that brought up the hundred stand in only seventy minutes.

Now it was Fred again: 'Australia have been in command for so long. Suddenly they don't know where to bowl. They're bowling too wide and giving Dilley the room to swing that bat and he's liking it. When he hits the ball it doesn't half go.'

Fred was cheering up. The pipe had gone and he was leaning forward in his seat, nose towards the window, stroking his chin with his right hand. Moments later I was describing the drive through the covers that took Dilley to fifty. By now, he was looking grossly under-placed at number nine. In the last hour in the box, despair had moved through gloom to distant hope. Those sitting in the chairs behind the commentators were chattering away, smiling and even occasionally laughing. We all looked at each other and shook our heads in disbelief. Botham and Dilley had put on 117 in just eighty minutes when Dilley was bowled by Alderman. His 56 was the highest score he made for England in 41 Test matches. He had chosen his moment. There was still no solid evidence to support this new-found optimism for England. They were only 25 runs ahead with two just wickets standing.

Chris Old, not always the most reliable of batsmen, now played an heroic innings of 29 while helping Botham add 67. McGilvray was commentating when Botham swung Lawson away on the leg side for the four which took him to his hundred. He reported the facts precisely, but without any exotic added extras. Old and Botham had taken the score to 319 and a lead of 92 before Lawson hit Old's stumps. Bob Willis, tall, angular, submerged in a helmet, and, as always, slightly discombobulated, walked purposefully out. He had once come out to bat in a Test at Edgbaston without his bat, and had had to go back and fetch it. Now, he manfully blocked his way through to the close, when England were 351–9, 124 runs ahead, with Botham on 145.

In the last hour's play that day we had been all over the place in the box. McGilvray was generously saying England had a real chance, I fear the rest of us were almost as gung-ho as Botham. Trevor's feet were still planted firmly on the ground, although the general English euphoria did catch up with him at one point. Rubbing his hands together, as if the thought had suddenly come to him, he said, 'A couple of wickets in the first ten minutes of their innings and then what a game we've got on our hands.' Fred was puffing away and there was a lot of 'I dunnoing' going on. Realistic hopes or whistling to keep up our courage? I should think when the Australians went to bed that night, one or two of them would surely have been nervous. One thing was indisputable. What a day it had been for Ian Botham. He had lost the captaincy after the previous Test, having averaged 13.80 with the bat in twelve Tests while he was in charge. Now he had taken six wickets in Australia's first innings, had made 50 in England's first and had reached a hundred in 87 balls in the second. He had given England an outside chance.

The next day, one of the most important principles of *Test Match Special* was to be severely tested. *TMS* has always prided itself on its impartiality. I well remember something else Henry Riddell said when he had listened to those two trial tapes of mine back in 1968: 'It is extremely important to remain impartial. The first time you refer to England as "we" in a broadcast will be your last broadcast.' Now, on 21 July 1981, it was going to be difficult to keep the balance. Impartiality could hardly fail to go out of the window and, in all honesty, what the hell, as long as it did not become a too blatant 'them and us' rant.

Fred's pipe made an early start on the last day. There was a huge amount of nervous energy floating around Headingley. I started things off in the box. Five more runs had been scored before, 'Alderman in, bowls to Willis. He's gone. Willis is caught at second slip by Border low to his left.' Botham was 149 not out at the end of an innings which had brought Gilbert Jessop back to life. (In 1902 at The Oval, England had needed 263 to beat Australia. They were 48–5 before Jessop hit a hundred in 75 minutes, and at the end George Hirst and Wilfred Rhodes had famously 'got 'em in singles' and England won by one wicket.) Trevor Bailey put his finger on it in his prosaic way before Botham was off the field: 'One of the great innings of Test cricket.' No one would have disagreed with him. Botham had faced 148 balls and hit 27 fours and one six. Australia now had plenty of time to score the 130 they needed to win.

What we did not know until later was the reaction of one dyed-in-the-wool Aussie, Dennis Lillee, before play began on the last morning. When bad light interfered late on the fourth day, the scoreboard flashed up that Ladbrokes were offering 500/1 against an England victory. Godfrey Evans, who kept wicket for England after the war wearing gloves covered extravagantly and unforgettably in red table-tennis bat rubber, was the bookmaker's special adviser. Ever a showman, he presumably suggested what had to be ridiculous odds for a two-horse race. Lillee tried to persuade Rod Marsh to join him in the bet. Marsh refused and Lillee asked the driver of the team coach, Peter 'Geezer' Tribe, to go round to the betting tent and put a tenner on for him. When the Australians took the field, Marsh saw Geezer walking round to the betting tent. He caught his attention and splayed out his right hand to indicate he also wanted to put on a fiver. Such an act would have caused an outrage today, with deafening accusations of match-fixing and general skulduggery and who knows, perhaps a prison sentence thrown in. Lillee and Marsh's reputations as whole-hearted Aussies were such that no one for a single moment doubted their honesty or intent – and nor need they have done. There would have been more chance of Winston Churchill sending Adolf Hitler a wedding present than of Lillee and Marsh helping England to victory in a Test match. Lillee realised those odds were just too good to miss. When Marsh had done a certain amount of swallowing, he too saw the picture and was happy to join in. Johnners let us know later that he had run into a great friend of all of us on *TMS* on the way back from the betting tent. He had reluctantly owned up to having had a slice of the 500/1 himself.

There was a good crowd at the start and it built up rapidly on this extraordinary last day. As it developed, the whole country was captivated. In the first innings Willis had been bowling up the hill from the Football Stand End and had not found it easy. At the start of the second, he again found himself lumbering up the same hill and into the wind too, to no great effect. He told Brearley he was too old to be doing this. 'Give me a go downhill,' was his request. His captain agreed and when Australia were 56–1 allowed him to mark out his run at the Kirkstall Lane End. It was from that end that Botham had taken the first wicket. Australia were 13 when Graeme Wood's bat was drawn to a ball outside the off stump and he was caught behind. This seemed to tee things up nicely. But John Dyson and Trevor Chappell showed some composure and took the score past 50, with the England bowlers trying almost too hard. The pitch had been giving the bowlers plenty of help, but now it seemed obstinately flat.

Even Brearley must have begun to scratch his head. Australia were surely over the worst. It was life-threateningly tense and it was typical Johnners that he should break the spell and make us all laugh. He had arrived at the microphone with a listener's letter in his hand and a mischievous look on his face.

'I've had a letter from a Mrs Williams asking me if we know the names of the two ice-cream makers in the Bible. Boil, do you know the names of the two ice-cream makers in the Bible?' he asked Trevor Bailey, his summariser. (Trevor was known as the Boil because years before, in a football match in Switzerland, his name had been spelt as 'Boiley' in the programme – and his England and Essex colleague, Doug Insole, made sure it stuck.)

'No, I'm afraid I don't,' came the predictable reply.

'Mrs Williams knows them all right. We've got Wall's of Jericho and Lyons of Judah.' Much laughter and the odd groan too.

McGilvray, who had not seen the joke and may not have liked ice cream either, took up the commentary. He told us in those discreet and mildly conspiratorial tones that Trevor Chappell, in trying to take his bat away from an awkward lifter from Willis, had been caught behind. There were twenty minutes to go before lunch and he handed over to me while Kim Hughes was approaching the middle. Willis, down the hill, was bowling like a man possessed. He ran in with a rhythm I don't think I ever saw from him again. It was rhythm and inspiration combined with animal brute force. Australia were 58–2 when he began what happened to be the last over of the morning. What an over it turned out to be.

The target of 130 was only 72 runs away – too close for any sort of comfort for England. But what if England could take one more wicket in those last few minutes before lunch? The crowd was in great voice as Willis raced in to bowl. Hughes safely negotiated the first two balls. This is how I took up the story, somewhat breathlessly as Willis came in for the third:

'Willis again, in to bowl to Hughes. He's out, he's out, he's caught by Botham at third slip low to his left. Hughes nought and Australia 58–3. 72 more needed and Willis bowling for his life. That's the wicket England badly wanted before lunch. This game's by no means over … Willis in again, now to Yallop. He's out, he's out. Yallop's caught by Gatting at short leg. The ball lifted on him and he couldn't keep it down. Gatting moved forward and took the catch. Australia go into lunch at 58–4 needing 72 more. What an over that was, Fred.'

Fred's pulse was racing too: 'What an over. What a transformation.'

Three more wickets fell soon after lunch. Dyson fiddled at Willis outside the off stump and got an edge. Chris Old then made a crucially important contribution when he found a way through Allan Border's defences. Rod Marsh, looking more like a bristling pocket battleship than ever, took his place. Willis bowled him a short one. He swivelled and hooked. The ball steepled down to fine leg, where Dilley, less than a foot from the boundary rope, remained calm and judged the catch perfectly. Australia 74–7. One run later, Willis bounded in again and Geoff Lawson, nibbling outside his off stump, gave Bob Taylor his fourth catch of the innings. It looked all over. But was it? No, of course not. Out strode Lillee in that purposeful what's-all-this-about way of his. If ever a man was determined to make sure his cheeky bet was a loser, this was him. In four overs, without the slightest problem, he and Ray Bright added 35 runs. It seemed heart-breakingly easy for them. I was back on the air as Lillee faced Willis at 106–8. Australia needed 24 more to win.

'Willis is accelerating up to the wicket, bowls. Lillee, stepping away, square-cuts and that's into the boundary for four. Australia 110–8 needing 20 more. What a fine stroke. These two have put on 35. Lillee has 17, Bright 19 … Here comes Willis again to Lillee. It's short, he's chipped it in the air. He's going to be caught at mid on – no – yes – I think he is. Gatting ran in and took it low in front of him as he fell forward. The players surround Willis – Taylor goes jumping in. Lillee's out, caught Gatting, bowled Willis for 17 and Australia are 110–9 … Willis to Bright. Bright's bowled, Bright's bowled, the middle stump's out of the ground. England have won by 18 runs. Willis has taken 8–43. What a phenomenal performance by Willis. He runs round punching the air. The players sprint helter-skelter to the pavilion as the boys come racing onto the ground. And one of our friends will be collecting a princely sum from the betting tent.' Perhaps I should have said 'reluctantly collecting'. Anyway, I needed a cold shower after those last two wickets.

We just looked at each other. Alan McGilvray shook us all by the hand. You would never have known from his voice or his manner that his own side had suffered what must have been the most agonising of defeats. A final irony was that the iced champagne ready to celebrate Australia's victory was now drunk in their team bath by the England side. In the island of Alderney, John Arlott must have been feeling that he had retired a year too soon. He would have loved every moment and his inimitable voice would have made the game even more memorable.

I was not selected by *Test Match Special* for the fourth Test at Edgbaston, where Ian Botham continued his magic. On the fourth day Australia needed 142 to win, with nine wickets standing. At 105–4, they wanted another 46. It was now that Brearley had a significant change of mind. He was about to bring on Peter Willey to bowl his off-breaks, but suddenly decided to throw the ball to a surprisingly reluctant Botham. Nonetheless, from the City End, bowling faster than usual, he proceeded to take five wickets for one run in 28 balls. The commentators had a job to find the right words to describe it.

Ten days later we were once again staying at the Swan Hotel at Bucklow Hill – old habits die hard – for the fifth Test at Old Trafford. By now new roads were making the approach to Old Trafford easier, although on that first day I still drove through Altrincham. I did this in honour of the journey I had made with John Arlott the year before, 1980. Then, it was the first day of the third Test against the West Indies, his final Test match at Old Trafford. Arlott asked me the night before if I would come with him the next morning. On the way we visited a favourite wine shop in Altrincham for a different sort of farewell. He was greeted on arrival by a cheerful guard of honour standing outside the entrance with raised corkscrews. An early glass or two of Puligny-Montrachet helped him clear his throat and set him up for the day.

England always had the better of this fifth Test in 1981, gaining a useful first-innings lead of 101. In the second innings we had to suffer Chris Tavaré making the slowest ever fifty in English first-class cricket. It took him 306 minutes. He made Mudassar and Boycott look like a couple of dashers three years before, in Lahore. Things were not going well for England when, at 104–5, Botham strode out enthusiastically to join Tavaré. His mood could hardly have been in sharper contrast. His strokeplay was sensational and in 102 minutes he made 118, hitting six sixes, the record number for a Test innings in England, and thirteen fours. It was an extraordinary innings on which to commentate and the best Botham ever played for England. I can only compare it to Viv Richards's innings of 189 not out against England three years later at Old Trafford in a one-day Texaco Trophy match. Richards then took the West Indies from 102–7 to 272–9. I was commentating when he came down the wicket and drove Willis far over extra cover for six. I have never seen such a stroke, before or since. That was another innings that stretched my vocabulary to breaking point.

I have one other commentary box memory from that Test at Old Trafford. In those days it was just about the smallest and most uncomfortable box in which I have ever commentated. It might well have been designed by a person who had once seen the Black Hole of Calcutta and rather admired it. The journey over the roof after climbing through the scoreboard, to our second position, where various reports for other programmes were broadcast, would have had dear old 'Elf 'n' Safety' in a flat spin.

During the closing stages of England's second innings on the third day, John Emburey was facing Terry Alderman. He snicked him for four in the air past first slip, who should have caught him. After describing the incident, I added, 'Well, that's the final nail in the Australian coffin.'

At which point I heard Alan McGilvray, who was sitting just behind me, say in a gruff voice, 'We're not dead yet.'

'That doesn't quite fit in with Alan McGilvray's way of seeing things,' I went on, 'but I must say I can't see much life left in the Australian corpse.'

I finished describing Alderman's over and then it was, 'Now, after a word from Fred Trueman, it will be Brian Johnston to take you through to the close of play.'

I got out of my chair to let Johnners in. It was a tight squeeze but not as tight as when I tried to leave the box a moment later. Alan McGilvray was standing in the narrow doorway as I tried to shuffle past him. We were more or less tummy button to tummy button when he spoke to me in the same gruff voice.

'You'll be all right, young Henry, when you learn to grow up.'

I thought he was being funny. I should have known better.

I cheerfully answered him back, 'I only wish I had the same high hopes for you.'

He did not speak to me again on the tour, or for a long time afterwards. On a previous occasion he had chosen not to speak to me for quite a while after I had had the temerity to vote for Derek Randall when it came to deciding on the Man of the Match award at the Brisbane Test in 1978–79. Randall had scored seventy in each innings of a match England had won by seven wickets. McGilvray's choice would have been Rodney Hogg, who in his first Test had taken six wickets in England's first innings. McGilvray was not a man who found it easy to give way.

He was by no means *always* angry with me, though. I remember on one tour of Australia, meeting him for a drink in Sydney in the Lord Dudley, a well-known watering hole in Paddington in the Eastern Suburbs. He was with another friend and it became an extremely thirsty evening. I don't think the intake of solids was allowed to interrupt things at any point. It was late when the three of us went back to his house in Double Bay. He immediately disappeared into his kitchen, coming back with an unopened forty-ounce bottle of Black Label. He pulled the cork and proceeded to lob it out of the window with the immortal words 'We won't be needing that again.' The only problem was that no one was allowed to leave on these occasions until the bottle was empty. McGilvray and Arlott's differences extended to the bottle too. McGilvray seldom deviated from beer and whisky, while Arlott's loyalty was exclusively to the wine industry. Both were stout defenders of these strongly held personal beliefs.

Australia has always been a joy and two of my fondest commentary moments, twenty-four years apart, have come from the huge and irresistible Melbourne Cricket Ground (MCG). It became the home of the Olympic Games in 1956 and this was the point at which it was turned from a cricket ground into a huge sporting stadium. Cricket was the ground's original purpose, although it was later to become the centre-piece of Australian Rules Football. For all that, it was Vladimir Kuts's famous 5,000 metres in the Olympics that did the most to bring the ground worldwide fame.

Bob Willis's England side came to the MCG in 1982–83 for the Boxing Day Test, two matches down with two to play. Our 'box' was effectively half a dozen seats on the top deck of the pavilion, and from this remote perch we watched as close and fascinating a Test match as you could wish to see. All forty wickets fell for the first time in a Test match – and this was the 943rd Test – and all four innings ended within 11 runs of each other. England made 284 and 294, Australia 287 and 288. Australia's target in the last innings was 292. First England seemed to be winning, then Australia were on top. On the last day, England's bowlers came back strongly, reducing their opponents to 218–9 when an England victory seemed certain. Jeff Thomson now joined Allan Border and slowly but surely they inched their way towards victory. Willis decided the best tactics were to set a deep field to Border to allow him a single whenever he wanted, to try to get Thomson on strike. This backfired spectacularly. The MCG is a huge ground and Border was able to place the ball craftily for a number of twos and also hit a few boundaries, for they are not easy to protect on such a big ground. It had been an extraordinary last day in our commentary box. However even-handed you may want to be, it is sometimes impossible to stifle your innermost feelings. As Border and Thomson got closer and closer to their target, English eyes became more and more frustrated by Willis's tactics, which seemed to have handed the match and the Ashes to Australia.

I was on the air for the final session of the match. Border, who had been so skilful in keeping the strike, was now unable to score the necessary single off the last ball of the over and it was up to Thomson. Australia needed only four runs to win and in desperation Willis threw the ball to Botham, for whom nothing was ever impossible. He was bowling to Thomson with three slips in place. As he started his run, the crowd were making a terrific noise. The close fielders went down and the atmosphere was brilliant. Thomson looked imperturbable in his stance and Border got busily ready to back up. Botham's first ball was short and just outside the off stump. Without the help of any footwork, Thomson's bat was drawn irresistibly towards it. The ball flicked the outside edge and flew at just above waist height – an awkward height for the fielder – to Chris Tavaré's right at second slip. He jerked both hands towards it. The ball probably smacked into the heel of his right hand, for it bounced agonisingly up in the air to his right. Tavaré had dropped the catch, but ... Geoff Miller, at first slip, almost literally a greyhound in the slips, moved quickly round behind Tavaré, and with some difficulty held the rebound.

England had won by three runs. I did not hold back on air. Some of the Australians sitting around us at the top of the pavilion raised their eyebrows more than a fraction. It takes a lot to shock the Australians. But if they had won ... It was unforgettable, only slightly undermined by Bill Frindall's determination not to let this frenzied moment pass without interrupting to tell the world that this wicket completed Botham's double of 1,000 runs and 100 wickets against Australia. After that, England needed to win the last Test, in Sydney, if they were to hang on to the Ashes. In the end, they were lucky to draw at the SCG and so the Ashes were anyway restored to Australian hands.

*   *   *

Twenty-four years later, 'Freddie' Flintoff was England's captain and he was not even in Willis's class as a tactician. His side arrived in Melbourne in December 2006 having been trounced in each of the first three Tests. Shane Warne was on the point of retiring and the faithful had flocked to the MCG to say goodbye. Those who were playing for England must by that stage have felt sympathy for those poor old Christians all that time ago in the Colosseum. It was going to be tough going and extremely noisy; as it happened, it was worse than that when Warne bowled Andrew Strauss, and took his 700th wicket in Test cricket. We were sitting on the same seats we had used twenty-four years before. Our feeling of general despair lifted briefly when, after bowling England out for a pretty spineless 159, Australia found themselves languishing at 84–5.

It was then that the highly talented but controversial Andrew Symonds joined the flamboyant Matthew Hayden at the crease. I was on the air, with Geoffrey Boycott sitting alongside me. I don't think he had seen Symonds before. Steve Harmison was bowling from the far end. Symonds groped at his first ball, which was outside the off stump, and missed.

'Doesn't look a Test batsman to me,' was Geoffrey's reaction to that stroke.

Moments later Harmison produced another which raced through Symonds's hastily arranged defensive push.

'He's not a Test batsman,' Geoffrey insisted. 'My mother in her pinny could've played that one better than that.'

Harmison sprinted in again and Symonds was beaten for a third time.

Boycott was adamant. 'If this man's a Test match batsman, I'll eat my hat.'

When, the next day, Symonds passed 150, we turned to Geoffrey, wondering whether it was to be his own curious brand of sunhat or something more substantial. He was typically unabashed and, of course, resisted the temptation to eat his or anyone else's headgear. He even seemed to be mildly offended we had had the temerity to suggest that he should.

England v Australia

(3rd Test)

Played at Headingley, Leeds on 16, 17, 18, 19, 20, 21 July 1981

Umpires: David Evans, Barrie Meyer

Toss: Australia

AUSTRALIA

J Dyson	b Dilley	102	c Taylor b Willis		34
GM Wood	lbw b Botham	33	c Taylor b Botham		9
TM Chappell	c Taylor b Willey	27	c Taylor b Willis		8
KJ Hughes*	c&b Botham	89	c Botham b Willis		0
RJ Bright	b Dilley	7	b Willis		19
GN Yallop	c Taylor b Botham	58	c Gatting b Willis		0
AR Border	lbw b Botham	8	b Old		0
RW Marsh†	b Botham	28	c Dilley b Willis		1
GF Lawson	c Taylor b Botham	13	c Taylor b Willis		1
DK Lillee	not out	3	c Gatting b Willis		17
TM Alderman	not out	0	not out		0
Extras	(b 4, lb 13, nb 12, w 3)	32	(lb 3, nb 14, w 1)		18
Total	(155.2 overs)	401/9d	(36.1 overs)		111

ENGLAND

GA Gooch	lbw b Alderman	2	c Alderman b Lillee		0
G Boycott	b Lawson	12	lbw b Alderman		46
JM Brearley*	c Marsh b Alderman	10	c Alderman b Lillee		14
DI Gower		9	c Border b Alderman		9
MW Gatting	lbw b Lillee	15	lbw b Alderman		1
P Willey	b Lawson	8	c Dyson b Lillee		33
IT Botham	c Marsh b Lillee	50	not out		149
RW Taylor†	c Marsh b Lillee	5	c Bright b Alderman		1
GR Dilley	c&b Lillee	13	b Alderman		56
CM Old	c Border b Alderman	0	b Lawson		29
RGD Willis	not out	1	c Border b Alderman		2
Extras	(b 6, lb 11, nb 11, w 6)	34	(b 5, lb 3, nb 2, w 1)		16
Total	(50.5 overs)	174	(81.2 overs)		356 (f/o)

ENGLAND	O	M	R	W	O	M	R	W		Fall of wickets:			
RGD Willis	30.0	8	72	0	15.1	3	43	8		Aus	Eng	Eng	Aus
CM Old	43.0	14	91	0	9.0	1	21	1	1st	55	12	0	13
GR Dilley	27.0	4	78	2	2.0	0	11	0	2nd	149	40	18	56
IT Botham	39.2	11	95	6	7.0	3	14	1	3rd	196	42	37	58
P Willey	13.0	2	31	1	3.0	1	4	0	4th	220	84	41	58
G Boycott	3.0	2	2	0					5th	332	87	105	65
									6th	354	112	133	68
AUSTRALIA	O	M	R	W	O	M	R	W	7th	357	148	135	74
DK Lillee	18.5	7	49	4	25.0	6	94	3	8th	396	166	252	75
TM Alderman	19.0	4	59	3	35.3	6	135	6	9th	401	167	319	110
GF Lawson	13.0	3	32	3	23.0	4	96	1	10th	–	174	356	111
RJ Bright					4.0	0	15	0					

Result: England won by 18 runs

9

THE OLD
AND THE NEW

B Y the time I returned to the *Test Match Special* commentary box in 1994, society was relentlessly on the move and so was cricket. T20 might not yet have been with us, but Adam Gilchrist's one-day international debut for Australia was only just over two years away. No player did more to change the character of all forms of international cricket than the amazing Gilchrist. He succeeded Ian Healy as Australia's wicketkeeper, but before his first Test match, he had played in a remarkable 76 ODIs. He was an amazing striker of the ball and it was with his batting that he changed the course of cricket. While he opened the innings in the ODIs, he batted at number seven in Test matches and scored runs there at an extraordinary pace. Not only was he largely responsible for Australia making the big scores they did, but he was also the reason they scored their runs so quickly. Gilchrist's example was seized upon all round the Test-playing world. The side batting second would often find themselves chasing a total of around 500 reasonably early on the second day and as a consequence matches were finishing much sooner. Test cricket was becoming a more compelling product and, therefore, much better value for spectators. Although this was Gilchrist's natural way of playing, it was honed in the one-day game and he burst on the Test scene like a firework display. He made sure the one-day message was not lost on the game's more stately format.

On my return to arms in 1994, I suddenly realised I was now rather higher up the *TMS* batting order, if, understandably, still on approval for a while. CMJ was the senior commentator, but I was close behind, for we had both started out in that one-day series against Australia in 1972. The Alderman had begun just after the two of us, although he was sometimes reluctant to admit it.

One of the reasons I was brought back by Peter Baxter was to lighten things up a bit. There may have been a thought that *TMS* was becoming a trifle solemn. The gentle process of change and innovation continued in South Africa in 1995–96, when Geoffrey Boycott joined us for the first time in the summariser's chair. No other individual has made a greater impact on *TMS* in recent years or caused more discussion and argument than Geoffrey. He is a man who does not like keeping his views to himself. He is always happy to repeat them too, just in case his audience did not pick them up the first time round. Those who switch on even later need not worry either, for they are sure to be given a reprise. Geoffrey's forceful comments put cricket's frequent periods of inactivity to good use in the commentary box. He gives our coverage a sharper sound when compared to the mellifluous outpourings of the old days, and gives us too a more meaningful cutting edge, which is no bad thing.

Boycott was not immediately selected for home Test matches because Trevor Bailey and Fred Trueman were still there. They came together in 1974 and were worthy successors to Norman Yardley and Freddie Brown. Bailey and Trueman remained in office until they unexpectedly found they were not going to be offered contracts in 1999. Those in power at the BBC have not always shown the greatest tact when wanting household names to move on. This was not a happy parting of the ways for two *TMS* stalwarts who should have left with a fanfare ringing in their ears.

An interesting and most welcome newcomer in our ranks at around this time was the first female commentator, Donna Symmonds. A highly successful lawyer from Barbados, Donna had already made her mark inside the commentary box in the West Indies. Her family had been close friends with Frank Worrell, one of the three famous Ws, Everton Weekes, Clyde Walcott and Worrell, who carried all before them for the West Indies after the Second World War. Donna knew the game well and had a great feel for it, as was reflected in her measured commentary, which just occasionally burst into moments of emotion and excitement. She joined *TMS* for England's series in the Caribbean in

1997–98, fitting in beautifully and becoming a great addition to the team. She was so well received that the BBC invited her to England to commentate on the World Cup in 1999. Her career in the box continued for a few years, but she was so successful in her lawyer's robes that before long she could not find the time for commentary.

Donna was sadly missed, although, of course, the number-one West Indies commentator was Tony Cozier, one of the greatest of them all. Like Symmonds, he was a Bajan, and he had first joined the *TMS* team for the Headingley Test against the West Indies in 1966, when their Jamaican commentator, Roy Lawrence, had to return home for a short while. Cozier died in 2016 and was commentating almost until the end. The other West Indian commentator who came on the scene later was Reds Perreira, who hailed from Guyana. He found it difficult to get his tongue round certain English words. When a batsman ran a third run, Reds had a habit of saying, 'And he turns for a turd.' At which point, if Johnners was in the box, he would invariably say, and loudly, 'There's a dog on the pitch.'

Of course, by the 1990s one-day cricket was second nature to us. Every home series included its share of one-day matches and *TMS* covered them all. I can remember some thrilling one-day finishes in both county and international games. A one-day game I will never forget was a semi-final played in 1981 between Northamptonshire and Lancashire at Wantage

Road, Northampton. This was the year that the NatWest Bank took over the sponsorship of the first one-day competition from Gillette, who were beginning to feel they were becoming better known for cricket than for razor blades. Lancashire were bowled out on a typically slow Northampton pitch for 186, which today seems an incredibly low score, especially as in those days they were 60-over matches. How times have changed.

Wantage Road in Northampton was not the most glamorous of grounds. For this game the press box from where we normally commentated had been taken over by BBC Television. Radio were allowed to perch uncomfortably in one corner. I was the only commentator; Trevor Bailey was our summariser and Peter Baxter the producer. The other semi-final, between Derbyshire and Essex, was being played at Derby and through the day we went back and forth for commentary and reports. Events at Derby were exciting enough, too. At the finish, the scores were level at 149 and Derbyshire won having lost fewer wickets. A total of 298 runs from 120 overs is unthinkable today. That game ended earlier than ours at Northampton, so in the closing stages we had the commentary to ourselves. Northamptonshire found it as much of a struggle as Lancashire and lost their ninth wicket at 174. Thirteen runs were needed from the last pair of Tim Lamb and Jim Griffiths, who was widely considered to be as bad a batsman as any who had ever played county cricket. The overs were running out, but somehow these two inched their way to victory. When the winning run was scored with one ball remaining, I had been banging on non-stop for more than an hour, with Trevor, as forthright and succinct as ever, beside me. It was a good rehearsal for what we would get up to fifteen years later in Bulawayo. Incidentally, this excitement carried over to the final at Lord's, where Northamptonshire were bowled out for 235 and after their 60 overs, Derbyshire were 235–6 and, as in the semi-final, won because they had lost fewer wickets.

I will always remember, too, the only T20 I was ever unleashed upon. In 2005, when the Australians toured England, their third game was the first T20 international to be played in England. The game took place at the Rose Bowl in Southampton. It was a packed crowd and an extraordinary game of cricket. England won the toss and made 179–8 in their twenty overs. In the third over of their innings Australia were 23–0. Three overs later they were 31–7, seven wickets having fallen in the space of twenty balls. In those now far-off days, T20 was a recent invention and it was perhaps hard to take it too seriously. When I was on the air I took a fair number of these wickets and found myself saying, when their seventh wicket fell, 'If Australia are 31–7 it can only be the greatest of news for an Englishman, even if it is a game of beach cricket.' Which implies that I felt it was a situation to which there was no need to attach much importance, even though I hugely enjoyed every moment of it. I was sad that I never again caught the selectors' eye when it came to choosing the commentators for another T20. Even so, I feel I can rest on my laurels after such an impressive debut. At the time it may have seemed a frivolous occasion, but the lie to this was to be found in the money that game raised, which came to just over £400,000. For the inventors of T20, this postscript was the most important part of this particular equation – as it has continued to be all round the cricketing world ever since.

For a long time, the two domestic one-day competitions, the Gillette Cup and the Benson & Hedges Cup, provided us with a lot of enjoyment. *TMS* always covered the quarter- and semi-finals as well as the final. It was such fun going down to wherever it was and staying the night before. Just occasionally we had a bit of luck when rain meant we had to stay a second night. They were great bonding adventures. Shilpa Patel, Baxter's number two, would arrange the hotel – and we had our favourites for just about every part of the country. What was also fun was that with commentary in the quarter-finals, say, coming from four different grounds, there was a certain amount of lively on-air banter between the commentators. I remember Neil Durden-Smith being late on parade once when the baton was passed to him at Leicester. He explained his absence by saying he had been having tea with the Bishop of Leicester. Neil eventually handed over to Alan Gibson in Bristol, who started off with 'No such episcopal visitations here . . .' and then probably told us about his loquacious friend, the red-headed lady behind the bar in the pavilion. On this occasion the next commentator on *Sport on Two* that afternoon was Max Robertson at Wimbledon. He was not a natural for this sort of badinage and made a rather laboured attempt at continuing the sequence with a little thing about the Bishop of Wimbledon and strawberries and cream – which did not entirely work. But it was all good fun.

With the packed programme of international cricket these days, domestic competitions of this type have lost some of their glamour and relevance. They are no longer the occasions they were, both in and out of the commentary box. Of course, there are now plans for a city-based T20 franchise competition to start in 2020. This, like its older brothers in India, Australia and elsewhere, will produce its own, more frenetic fun, in which contemplative or anecdotal commentary is unlikely to play a major part. It will obviously be a great money spinner, which is its *raison d'être*. At the end of it, the cricket will bear as little resemblance to a Lord's Test match against Australia as the commentary will to an evocative description of the Pennines by John Arlott on a rainy day at Old Trafford. But in their different ways, one will be as good as the other. Just as Arlott complemented the Pennines, so the commentary will now complement the cricket on show, and that has always been the true essence of

Test Match Special. So much has changed and yet so much remains the same.

One change that was thrust upon us came along in 1999 with the opening of the space-age capsule that is the Media Centre at the Nursery End of Lord's. *TMS* was forced to leave its position in the top turret of the Pavilion over the visitor's dressing room. The Pavilion was in so many ways a better position for us. It is not that we are against the space age, but our old home complemented the nature of *TMS* better than its ultra-modern replacement, which is rather impersonal and too high to be ideal. It is not especially comfortable either, although the recent refit has improved things. In the Pavilion, *TMS* seemed to be more a part of the fabric of Lord's. One enormous advantage for us was that the great and the good who watched the game from the committee room in the Pavilion were only a passage and a couple of flights of stairs away. As a result, more people used to pop into the box and stay on to say a few words. That was something we all enjoyed and, of course, no one more so than Brian Johnston, who incidentally did not live to see or use our new home. I am not sure he would have welcomed it with open arms.

The change came about because the authorities had felt, logically enough, that as we approached the twenty-first century, the media should all be together under the same roof, even if it made *TMS* more inaccessible for some. We still managed, thanks to Peter Baxter who was in charge at the time, to make our mark on the new building. When it was in the later stages of planning, it was he who insisted that we should have a window that could be opened. Only then would we be able to absorb the atmosphere of the ground and the occasion, which is so important for our commentary. The new box was first used by us in July 1999 for the second Test match against New Zealand. This was the first Test match New Zealand had ever won at Lord's. I will never forget Iain Gallaway, the president of the New Zealand Cricket Association, coming up to the box in the closing stages of the match with a look of complete disbelief on his face. Gallaway, the most delightful man, was the best cricket commentator New Zealand has ever produced. He had just retired and the presidency of the NZCA was his deserved reward.

Peter Baxter retired in 2007, and during the last few years of his reign, it seemed that *Test Match Special* was being pulled inexorably towards Radio 5 Live. In 1991, Radio 5, as it was called for a few years, had become the new home for sport, having taken over the frequencies of Radio 2 MW. *TMS* had hitherto been something of a wanderer. Radio 3 LW owned us for a time and later Radio 4 LW became our paymasters. To the outsider – and to this insider – it always seemed strange that no one particularly wanted to provide a permanent long-term home for one of BBC Radio's most successful programmes. There may have been the feeling that since much of the commentary was provided by freelance commentators like myself, we succeeded in spite of the BBC Sports Room and not because of it. As demonstrated by that acrimonious meeting at the Swan at Bucklow Hill when Slim Wilkinson was Head of Sport, our position was far from secure. Now Radio 5 Live existed as a sports network, it was not surprising that they felt they should take us on board. From their point of view, there would have been one problem: *Test Match Special* did not sound like the rest of Radio 5 Live, so we had better change our ways.

Baxter was under increasing pressure to go down the Radio 5 Live passage. This is a style of broadcasting which has probably been designed more to suit the needs of a football rather than a cricket audience. Understandably, Baxter wanted to protect his heritage and the *TMS* way of doing things. His retirement was looming and in the build-up to it, two 5 Live regulars joined us for a short time. Arlo White spent a year or two with us and, I daresay, found himself in a difficult position, with a 5 Live briefing in his head and Baxter as his boss. He is now doing brilliantly in the United States as a commentator on American football. In the end, he may not have been too enthusiastic about the combination of cricket and BBC politics. Mark Pougatch was another from 5 Live who dipped his toe briefly into the vibrant tributary of *TMS*. Mark is a charming man and a wonderful commentator on so many sports, especially football. I am sure he would have gone on to do cricket as well as he did everything else, but he may have found *TMS* a little too ring-fenced compared to the things he was used to.

In the end, Peter Baxter decided to retire midway through the 2007 English summer. It had been in 2003 that his successor, Adam Mountford, first caught up with us as Peter's deputy. At first, his principal occupation was to look after the box that supplied Radio 5 Live with live reports throughout the day. He took over the producer's chair from Baxter in July 2007 after England's series against the West Indies in the first part of that summer. I have often wondered if Adam came to us on a mission from 5 Live to turn us from the *Test Match Special* of Arlott and Johnston – *Old Test Match Special*, if you will – into a programme that fitted more into the pattern of 5 Live – *New Test Match Special*. There was undoubtedly a gradual change in the way things were done – as you would expect with any new boss. Over the next few years, the personnel began to change. It sometimes seemed that unashamed individuality became less important than general conformity. As one who had thrived in the era when this individuality was encouraged, the contrast was sharp. For most of my life with *TMS* the commentators had instantly recognisable voices; now there was rather more of a sameness to them. You only had to listen to one syllable from Arlott, Johnston and CMJ and you knew exactly who they were. Aggers, who has his own splendidly distinctive tones, continues this tradition. This is not a criticism, because things are always changing and who is to say that one way is better than the other; it is just an observation. And it may well be that this was not deliberate, but simply how it naturally happened. In recent years, we still had a good laugh in the box and the jokes were often underlined by our new producer's loud and infectious laugh from behind. In the old days it was Bill Frindall's imperious adenoidal snorts that acknowledged the moments of high humour.

While all this was going on, I carried on in my *Old TMS* way. I continued trying to paint the picture and enliven the scene as I had always done. Buses were becoming a problem, however, because of the way that Lord's and other Test grounds were being developed. The tendency was for the media to be massed together, as had happened at Lord's, and *TMS* was shifted from some of its old commentary boxes into newly painted glistening white corridors with media to the right and media to the left of us. We had become massively corporate, and the change in topography had also robbed us of some familiar views. In our new home at Lord's the red double-decker buses in the Wellington Road were behind us, or they passed unseen down the St John's Wood Road behind the New Mound and Tavern Stands. The same applied to the Kirkstall Lane at Headingley, the Radcliffe Road at Trent Bridge, and the Harleyford Road at The Oval. By stretching my neck in giraffe-like fashion, I could still just catch a bus or two in the Loughborough Road at Trent Bridge, but I could no longer see the old Chester Flyer in the Warwick

Road Station at Old Trafford. The Riverside at Durham, a newcomer, does still buses on view, but rather disappointingly they are coaches rather than good old red-blooded double-deckers. Edgbaston, sadly, was always a busless ground.

In the last few years I made up for the lack of buses by turning my gaze and voice on the seeming idleness of neighbouring cranes. Then, of course, there was all the aerial activity, both feathered and otherwise, such as a helicopter buzzing noisily across a ground or the constant stream of aircraft in the distance behind the Lord's Pavilion on the way into Heathrow. Like the pigeons, it all added to the picture I had tried to paint ever since Baxter had that word in my ear. Some of my more recent colleagues seem to shy away from these added extras, but I feel they are all a part of at any rate the mount and frame of the picture in front of me and deserve a mention. They are particularly useful, of course, when the cricket is dull and maiden overs are proliferating. It is then, I think, that commentators should be acutely aware of the fact that part of their role is to be an entertainer. Anyway, in my case, it was too late to try and teach an old dog new tricks.

One of Adam Mountford's great achievements has been to persuade Phil Tufnell to come and sit in the summariser's chair. He is a wonderful character, and although he seemed to spend his entire career trying to prove there was not a grey cell in his head, he shows now just how shrewd he is. You've got to be pretty canny to win *I'm a Celebrity, Get Me Out of Here*. And he was a real dasher on *Strictly Come Dancing* too. Nowadays you seem to hear him every time you switch on the wireless or television. He knows so much about so many things. None of our newcomers understood what *TMS* is about better or quicker than Tuffers. His humour, his choice of words and, above all, his sense of timing make him a fine broadcaster. That chuckle is irresistible too, and in the box he plays the team game so well.

The funniest moment I had on air with Tuffers was during the first Test against Australia at Trent Bridge in 2013. There is a two-man pop group from Ireland called the Duckworth Lewis Method. Both members of the group are passionate about cricket. They named themselves after the system which two clever statisticians, Frank Duckworth and Tony Lewis (not the cricketer), successfully invented in order to balance a one-day game after rain had unfairly tilted it sharply one way. The two Irish pop artists, Neil Hannon and Thomas Walsh, felt that the name rolled nicely off the tongue and also bore testimony to their love of cricket. They had just put together a new album called *Sticky Wickets*, and were recording it in London during the winter of 2012–13. To make the most of the lead song called 'It's Just Not Cricket', they required the services of a well-known and trustworthy rapper. I believe Snoop Dogg tried to strike too hard a bargain, while Jay-Z couldn't make up his mind. In the end they decided to look elsewhere and, as you will have presumed by now, gave me a ring. Luckily I was free on the date they suggested. A lovely lady explained on the telephone what I had to get up to, and I didn't understand a word of it. On the agreed date I drove to the studio in the East End of London and when Neil and Thomas had gone through what I had to do, it all seemed just about possible to do.

The two of them strummed away on a double bass and a keyboard. Every so often they would stop and I had to come in with some derogatory comment like 'How perfectly ghastly', or 'You simply can't believe it' and, once or twice, 'My dear old thing' in as disagreeable a voice as I could manage. Standing in the middle of the technical equipment, it felt more than slightly unreal. Everyone seemed totally relaxed and after a couple of rehearsals off we went. At the end they made me feel as if I had just won or was about to win an Oscar. A week or two later I was told that we had even climbed to number 29 in the charts.

Fast-forward now to the first Test of the following summer, at Trent Bridge. At lunchtime on the Saturday of every Test there is the 'A View from the Boundary' slot on *TMS*, when well-known figures from the outside world who enjoy cricket – actors, pop stars, businessmen, authors, politicians and many others – submit themselves to Jonathan Agnew for half an hour's interrogation. Because of all the fuss about my rapping, the Duckworth Lewis pair had got the nod at Trent Bridge. It was the full ensemble too, for they not only brought the double bass and the keyboard with them; they also found they

could not manage without me. At the start of the slot, we did
our stuff. They strummed away and sang and I burst in with
the occasional despairing 'My dear old thing' or 'It's just not
cricket'. My efforts sounded pretty tinny to me, but again
they seemed pleased and there was much laughter at the end.

Nick and Tom were then cross-examined by Aggers. They
were followed by a hurried lunchtime county scorecard and
the afternoon session began with Tuffers and me at the microphone. The lunchtime session had been so full of chaotic
laughter I thought we should quickly go back over it once
again to make sure our listeners had some idea of what had
been going on. The first over of the afternoon was bowled by
Mitchell Starc who, walking back to the start of his long run,
gave Tuffers and me the time we needed to recap. We somehow got through it and after the fifth ball I said in my most
Churchillian of voices, 'Yes, the Duckworth Lewis Method
and Blowers', effectively drawing a double line under it.

Instantly, I heard a half-stifled giggling on my right.
Looking round, I saw Tuffers, puce in the face, shoulders
shaking, with his head in between his arms on the green baize
desk in front of us. Realising he would be no help, I turned to
Malcolm Ashton, our scorer, on my left. He had thrown his
pencil down and was resting his head on his scoresheet while
making spluttering noises. I then heard Adam Mountford
laughing as only he can. I had no idea what was going on and
I think I said, 'What on earth has happened? Did I say something dreadful?' Nothing but squawks and guffaws came back.

I doggedly kept on commentating until the end of the over. Then I paused, hoping Tuffers would come in with some lively comment about the events of the over. There was nothing but a long silence, and another quick look showed me he was in no fit state to say anything. So I kept on talking and then commentated through the next over. When that was finished, I said, 'Now, Tuffers, if you can think of anything coherent to tell us, I shall make way for Jim Maxwell.' There were a few gurgles, but Tuffers managed to get through it.

As I took my headphones off and stood up, Henry Moeran, our ever-attentive assistant producer, was at my side.

'Blowers, do you know what you said then?' he asked.

'Yes,' I said, taking a moment to think about it, 'I said, "Yes, the Duckworth Lewis Method and Blowers."'

'Are you sure?'

'Yes, absolutely.'

'It didn't come out quite like that. I think you ought to listen to it.'

'Surely there's no need for that. I know exactly what I said.'

He handed me some headphones and, shaking my head and smiling at him, I put them on. He then pressed the button and this is what I heard myself say:

'Yes, the Duckworth Lewis Method and Blowjob.'

For a moment I couldn't believe it, but there it was in aspic, as it were. Goodness knows where it had come from. The only thought I had was that at one of the two schools I attended, that had been my nickname for a time. Maybe all these years later my subconscious mind had suddenly dug it up. I didn't know whether to laugh or cry, but luckily everyone seemed to think it hysterical and, realising I had not done it on purpose, no one at the BBC or anywhere else called for my head.

By the time it was all over, I had begun to get rather a taste for the music business, but subsequently Nick and Tom have disappeared over the horizon, or are still getting over the shock. I suppose I shall therefore go down in history as a one-rap wonder.

10

DOING A
BULAWAYO

O NE of the common denominators of *Old Test Match Special* and *New Test Match Special*, up until the end of 2012, sadly his last year in the box, was Christopher Martin-Jenkins's dependable voice. Without fail, his commentary was as charming and as accurate as his unpunctuality was supreme and unrivalled. It earned him the well-deserved soubriquet of 'the late CMJ' many years before he died. One of the great unsolved mysteries was why he bothered to wear a watch. There are some people who cannot help being late and CMJ was unquestionably one of them. His life was, I think, mildly disorganised, to say the least. He always hoped he was going to be on time, but it never worked out and he never seemed to learn from experience. He would turn up in the box hot and bothered, as if life had somehow dealt him an unfair hand. Those who knew him only as a splendidly organised and professional commentator may be surprised by this. Yet the commentary box was the only place in which his life was tidily arranged. Even then, no one was more aware than our two producers, Peter Baxter and his successor Adam

Mountford, of the inherent dangers in asking CMJ to come to the ground to do the early-morning slot for the *Today* programme. Then, after Baxter had retired, Mountford knew what he would have to suffer if he asked CMJ to open the next day's programme. This meant going out onto the middle of the ground well prepared for a quarter of an hour's chat before the start which was later extended to half an hour, but that was post CMJ.

I particularly remember in 2012, during what turned out to be his last Test match at Trent Bridge, CMJ was chosen to do this first piece on the third day of the match. No one loved playing golf more than CMJ and if a course was handy, he would be determined to fit in nine holes in the early morning before coming to the ground. He would by then have discovered the shortest time it had ever taken anyone to get from whichever clubhouse it was to the commentary box. This was the time he would aim to leave himself, but at least another five to ten minutes would always have been lost before he let in the clutch, at which point his lateness was guaranteed. Of course, these timings took no account of traffic jams or roadworks or of losing his way, another likely occurence. On this occasion he was staying in the Vale of Belvoir and had located a golf course in precisely the right spot. When he arrived, in a hurry, he was already late for his appointment on the first tee. Self-indulgence now played its part, for if he had stuck to his original intention and been content with nine holes, it might not have been too bad, but as was invariably the case, he found the tenth hole an irresistible attraction. After a wayward tee shot had called for a bit of a search, his timings were even more all over the place.

At 10.33, Mountford bit the bullet and asked me to do the start for the second day running. This caused another slight rush, for there were various bits of information I had to collect. Just in time, I headed out to the middle with the intrepid Henry Moeran, who was always there to hold our hands if need be. A few minutes later, hurried, breathless and red in the face, CMJ arrived with stories of major roadworks and traffic jams that the other 14,000 people in the ground had all cleverly avoided. He was then out of sorts for the first part of the day – he had that pained, innocent look – mystified that no one else in the box had believed a word he had said. We knew him too well – that tenth hole.

When he was safely in the box, CMJ was the most reliable commentator I worked with. His description told listeners the precise story of what had happened. He was also good at identification, an area in which if there were four commentators, I always came a distant fourth. CMJ's career in our box became even more frenetic when he took on the job, first of the *Times* cricket correspondent before moving to a similar role with the *Daily Telegraph*. It was remarkable how he succeeded for many years to write long accounts for these papers as well as doing a full day's commentary. As newspaper deadlines require promptness and punctuality, I shall never know how he managed to do both jobs so amazingly well.

CMJ was a wonderful mimic and had a good sense of humour, which probably came through more in his broadcasting than in his writing. He was at his funniest making after-dinner speeches, when he was able to give full vent to his mimicry. He was also an outstanding storyteller. Sadly, we did not see a great deal of one another away from the cricket. After finishing his work, with the hands of the clock still pointing at him like two accusing fingers, CMJ would scurry off to his home in Sussex or to a speaking engagement. I suppose, in a way, we never saw each other as natural companions because he took a less extravagant line when it came to the wine industry and he liked to start his lie-down before breakfast earlier than me. The only thing I had over him was that from time to time I looked at my watch.

He had a delightful habit of getting into difficult situations on the air and contriving to make them worse. I shall never forget one such moment on a tour of New Zealand when we were playing a Test match in Christchurch. Their left-arm spinner, Daniel Vettori, was batting. He played no stroke to a ball outside the off stump from one of the faster bowlers. CMJ said, '. . . bowls to Vettori, who does not fish for that one outside the off stump. He kept his rod down, as it were.' This prompted much laughter in the box, at which point CMJ did not follow the golden rule and stop digging. He went on: 'I don't know if Vettori is a fisherman. Jeremy [Coney], perhaps you could tell me if he is a fisherman, many cricketers are.' The laughter now got out of hand.

CMJ was nearly always late in handing over to his next commentator. We do twenty-minute spells, and he almost invariably went on for anything up to half an hour, but there was one occasion, in the World Cup final at Eden Gardens in Calcutta in 1987, when he presented us with a rather different problem. Tall, thin, angular and fair-haired, CMJ tended to pick up any illness that was going around in India – and there was usually something. England were playing Australia in the final and on that day CMJ was looking even paler than usual. He was about ten minutes into a spell in the middle of the day when he suddenly got up, handed over to whoever was follow-ing him and stage-whispered to anyone within earshot, and principally Peter Baxter, 'I'm just going back to the hotel for a comfortable one.' The hotel where we were staying, the Oberoi Grand on Chowringhee, was twenty minutes' walk across the Maidan. From the back of the stand, we spotted him striding out across the grass, accelerating with every step, but only from the knees downwards. Rumour had it that he made it, just.

Simon Mann is another commentator without frills or blem-ishes who has helped steer us surely into the twenty-first century. 'Grumpy' is a most unfair nickname for Simon, who is the good fun that his slightly naughty smile suggests. He was given this nickname early in his life with the BBC, appar-ently because back then there were times when he might not have been mistaken for a bundle of joy. By the end of my time with *TMS*, I think I was the only one in the box who still called him Grumpy. When I did, he gave me a smile which managed to be both tolerant and disapproving.

Simon began his Test commentary career in Zimbabwe in December 1996, where he had just about the most irritating start imaginable – and I am ashamed to say I was entirely to blame. England were making their first tour to Zimbabwe and with Robert Mugabe flexing his muscles all over the place, it could hardly fail to be an interesting experience. The first ever Test match between the two countries was played in Bulawayo. For most of the match on a charming ground, England had the upper hand. In the final innings, on the last day, England needed to make 205 to win at just over five and a half runs an over. Mike Atherton was soon out and when I took over the commentary from Simon Mann, Nick Knight and Alec Stewart were beginning what looked like a match-winning partnership of 137. When Stewart was out, England needed another 51 from eight overs. Three more wickets then fell quickly and when it came to the final ball of the match, England still needed three runs. Knight was facing Heath Streak and drove to deep cover. He and Darren Gough scampered two and Knight was run out going for an impossible third run. It was the first time a Test match had ever finished as a draw with the scores level. After the game, David Lloyd, the frustrated England coach, produced his immortal epitaph to this history-making affair: 'We flippin' murdered them.' Which did not endear him to everyone in Zimbabwe.

Before I took over commentary from Grumpy, I had seen that my name was the last one on Peter Baxter's commentary rota. This was not because he wanted me to go on until the end of the match; it was merely an indication that he had no idea what time the game would end. Anyway, the long and short of it was that I stayed at the microphone, with huge enjoyment, I have to say, for something like an hour and a half until, amid scenes of great excitement, the match finally ended. Peter, who was acting as both producer and third commentator, had obviously been expecting me to hand over to him after the usual twenty minutes. Looking back from this distance, I have no idea how I had the nerve to go on for as long as I did. I also find it difficult to understand why Simon and Peter did not strong-arm me out of the way. Of course, I was completely caught up with the drama unfolding in front of us, but that is a commentator's job and cannot be used as an excuse.

Vic Marks was also with us as a summariser in Zimbabwe and what an important member of the *TMS* team he was to become. This book is coming out in the year we have all been celebrating *TMS*'s sixtieth birthday, which speaks for itself. Of course, the heavyweights are crucial to the programme: the Arlotts, the Johnstons and the CMJs, and the big summarisers too: Fred and Trevor, Geoffrey and Tuffers, Vaughny and Swanny and also Victor Marks, heavy perhaps only on the scales. The former captains of England as well as those who piled on the runs or took buckets full of wickets, all of whom will have been getting on for perhaps a hundred Test Matches, are essential to our programme. These players have become the pillars around which *Wisden* and the history of the game are built. They give us *gravitas*. But, so too, in a different way, do the Vic Markses and Mike Selveys of this world, who bring another sort of cricket knowledge to the box. It is a knowledge based on hard work, uncertainty and a constant struggle to stay at the top level as a player once they had got there, which, sadly, they were unable to do. These are experiences the giants of the game have not been through in the same way. These lesser players give a different, more human perspective on what they are watching and talking about – and, just as important, a greater humility. They have a better understanding of human fallibility and realise the game is more than just moving chessmen around the board. They have found the game more difficult than their more illustrious colleagues who, because of their continued success, are able to talk with an uncompromising certainty. They have not themselves, had to face failure in the same way. *TMS* needs the input of those who gained a brief toehold at the top level of the game just as much as the confident assurance and criticism of the great players who never had to cope with failure. They are all part of the blend of voices, styles, experience and know-how that makes *TMS* what it is, a programme celebrating its sixtieth birthday.

I happen to think that Victor is one of the most valuable and understated of our commentary team. For me, he stands out as the best of all the summarisers I have worked with. He was an efficient off-spinner who could bat a great deal more than just a bit. He played six Test matches for England, has a wonderful intrinsic knowledge of the game and a real feel for it. No one in my experience reads a game much better or has been quicker to spot a moment when it is changing course. He never has a personal position to defend; his comments are always shrewd and well thought out. The listener knows that a delightful sense of humour is lurking only just around the corner. It is backed up by a chuckle which says, yes, this may be serious, but it is still only a game. Victor never patronises or shouts at the microphone; he does not bully or hector and he always shows a respect for the players themselves. He has been there, knows what it is like, but is never superior. He is a joy to have sitting next to you – in the commentary box or, indeed, anywhere else.

Victor joined *TMS* for the first time in Delhi in somewhat curious circumstances. He went to India as a player with Keith Fletcher's side in 1984–85. Mike Selvey, who was finding his way as a *TMS* summariser on that tour, went down with a severe attack of Delhi belly, in Delhi itself, appropriately enough. This made him unsafe for duty. Another summariser, the former Indian batsman Abbas Ali Baig, had had to go off in the middle of the second Test in Delhi for a business meeting in Bombay. This stretched resources beyond breaking point and so Peter Baxter, who was running the show, went down to the England dressing room to ask the manager, Tony Brown, the former Gloucestershire player, if a member of the squad not playing in the match could come up to the box and lend a hand. This is something that would never happen today; the question would never be asked, let alone answered as it was then.

'You might as well have Vic,' was Tony Brown's immediate reply to Baxter. 'He's the only one not playing who's here.'

Within minutes that well-known chuckle was making its *TMS* debut. Since then, Victor has always been used more on tour than in England, for a pragmatic but perhaps unsatisfactory reason: as a journalist, he would have been on the tour anyway for his newspaper, which meant that the BBC would not have to pay his full expenses. I am sure during his career some within the BBC may have wondered if Victor is a big enough name at a time when celebrity seems to be everything. Thank goodness they realised he is even more than that.

The other lovely thing about Victor is his impeccable dress sense. When the dress code is 'smart casual', he modestly takes up the reins on behalf of 'casual'. There is always a well-lived-in look about his clothes. The old faithful shirts keep turning up year after year. Some of the creases, too, have become hardy annuals and old friends. Somehow his clothes set off his underlying cheerfulness to perfection. If we had a commentary box full of Victor Markses, we would not have to worry about the ratings even if it made it unlikely that a modelling agency would be on the line any time soon.

Now, back to my less than virtuoso performance in Bulawayo. I have to admit that at the end of each over, while Trevor Bailey was giving his views, I did sense that Peter was moving around in a predatory and rather agitated manner over my right shoulder in the forlorn hope that I was going to hand over to him. Simon, in his first Test, must have felt that if Peter could not dislodge me, there was not much he could do about it. Victor simply slotted in at my side when the rota told him to. At the end, after Trevor and I had summed it all up, I returned us to the studio in London and jumped up. It was, I am afraid, with a feeling of elation rather than embarrassment that I turned to face my colleagues. I remember some amused tut-tutting from Trevor Bailey, but that was about it. Simon has never had a better reason to live up to his nickname, but, as I remember it, he looked more bemused than grumpy. He swallowed, smiled and let the moment go past the off stump. The upshot was that the phrase 'doing a Bulawayo' entered the *TMS* lexicon to describe the behaviour of any commentator who goes seriously over his time. Of course, it was not the way to play a team game. I was as guilty as hell, but I enjoyed every moment of it.

The fun in Zimbabwe did not stop there. I was lucky and enjoyed a wonderful Christmas on a friend's farm near Harare. Sadly, it was the last Christmas the family spent on their farm, for during the next year it was snatched by Robert Mugabe's thugs. On Boxing Day 1996, the *TMS* team gathered once more, at the Harare Sports Club for the second Test. The match itself was ruined by the weather, but it was an occasion I shall never forget. On the second day President Mugabe himself came to lunch and met the players. He had also agreed to be interviewed at the ground by the assembled press.

The press conference was going to be held in the big upstairs room in the pavilion. I am not sure whether it was to pay me back for my sins in Bulawayo or to show that he had forgiven me, but Peter Baxter selected me to interview Mugabe. He said later that I had asked him if I could do it, which, if I did, showed him to be even more forgiving than I thought. The process was going to be heavily policed, although obviously with the international press there we were likely to be in for a display of bravado. First, a cavalcade of at least twelve of the vulgarest-looking cars I have ever seen streamed into the ground. The first – the vulgarest of all – was one of those American jobs that seemed to go on for ever. Predictably, it decanted Mugabe in the shiniest of dark suits. From the other cars there erupted platoons of thugs in ill-fitting two-piece pale-grey suits with sinister bulges up by the shoulder. With a collective scowl, they distributed themselves around the place and you would not have wanted to pick an argument with any of them. As the members of the media attempted to mount the stairs, a few of these less-than-svelte gentlemen watched us closely and there was a bit of jostling. The heavies seemed to regard Peter Baxter, who was strung about with outside-broadcast equipment, with particular suspicion. Finally, with ill-humoured reluctance, they let us through.

By then Mugabe and his closest chums had shaken hands with the officers of the club and headed up some back stairs. There was an inner door in the committee room through which Mugabe would emerge. Peter and I took up our stance at the front of the throng of journalists and waited. In order that the BBC should appear to have been given an exclusive interview, I was to ask the first half-dozen questions before the press joined in. The thugs were now strutting around again and some of them began to flex their muscles. One or two people who were not journalists were rudely and firmly dispatched downstairs. Then one of the thugs, wearing an ungovernably hostile pair of dark glasses to complement his scowl, advanced on me, gesturing at the microphone in my hand.

'What's that?' he asked, without a great deal of charm.

I told him it was the microphone through which I was about to interview his president.

'You come with me,' was his blunt response.

It was an invitation it was going to be difficult to refuse. I looked quickly at Peter, who pointed sharply over my left shoulder. I followed his gaze and, lo and behold, there was Mugabe, who had just come through the inner door and was shuffling towards me. Was I the only person in the room who had actually been saved by Robert Mugabe? I stood my ground facing the president. I later wondered how my thug had taken his leader's arrival, for it had forced him to watch his catch wriggle off the hook at the very last moment.

Mugabe had been warned that I was his starting point and he had come straight across the room to me. Baxter had told me that it had been agreed that no political questions should be asked. In one way that let me off; in another it made it more difficult. I was not certain how I should address him, so I played it safe.

'When did you last come to a cricket match, sir?' I asked.

'I can't remember,' was the helpful reply.

I cleverly countered with, 'Do you enjoy cricket, sir?'

'No,' was the uncompromising answer. It was going awfully well.

I soon discovered that if ever at the Olympic Games there were a competition for spitting, Mugabe would be guaranteed a place at the top of the rostrum. I was having to use my microphone to ward off the gobs that were not flying over my shoulder.

'Have you ever played the game, sir?' I tried next. I felt there simply couldn't be too many 'sirs'.

'No,' he said, taking half a step towards me and enveloping me in a truly memorable cloud of halitosis.

I took a deep breath and changed course: 'What games, sir, did you enjoy playing when you were young?'

'Tennis,' was the reply. Thank heavens, we were up and running.

He talked about playing tennis against and beating his predecessor as president, the splendidly named Mr Canaan Sodindo Banana. I suggested that the next time they played, the Centre Court at Wimbledon should be the venue. A reluctant rictus grin now appeared and with it another surge of halitosis. Trying not to breathe in, I asked if Sir was happy to meet the press. My journalistic friends took over, the rictus grin reassembled itself into a scowl and I moved sideways out of halitosis range. Thus ended one of the more inspiring exclusive interviews ever undertaken by the BBC.

At the bitter end of the twentieth century, *Test Match Special* bravely withstood another shock. In April 1999, I was walking down the King's Road in Chelsea when I felt a tightness across my chest, which I later discovered was angina. I sat down thankfully on a passing bench – whose presence I still acknowledge gratefully on a daily basis – and the next morning found myself in the Harley Street Clinic. The day after that, I had an angiogram, a curious business that involves delicately and disconcertingly sticking a camera up your groin and wiggling it all the way up to your heart. Amazingly, I could not feel a thing and yet I was able to watch its progress on a screen on the far wall. It was an eerie experience. There were three blocked arteries and the next day I was in the operating theatre for a bypass operation. To make it even more exciting, I had apparently gone into heart-attack mode as I was being wheeled into the theatre.

I don't think it went quite as well as they had hoped, because when I was pushed back to intensive care, all sorts of exciting things happened. I believe they had to do another operation on the spot without moving me back to the theatre. Actually, I have been told so many versions of what happened that I am really not quite sure how it all went. I know I took an unconscionable time to come round and there was profound relief when I did. I know also that my brother-in-law, Anthony Salmon, who happens to be a vicar, had to give me the last rites. This turned into a moment or two of high humour. At any rate, I hope the Almighty had a chuckle. Anthony had been well briefed because he had brought along some holy oil, just in case. He found when he got there that there was not a moment to lose. He had to roll up his sleeves and get down to it, but, as I suppose happens from time to time, he lost control of the oil at the crucial moment and, by all accounts, damned nearly drowned me. A lucky escape, but his efforts were successful, although I suppose it may have been that the Almighty had decided, as he had done once or twice before in my life, that he simply wasn't ready to face me quite yet.

The Harley Street Clinic has quite small rooms and it was stifling hot. I longed to go home, but my splendid surgeon, Christopher Lincoln, was keen to hang on to me. He had won his spurs all right when I met him for the first time on the day I clocked in. A couple of weeks earlier I had been given a dozen bottles of Gruaud-Larose from a very good year. There were eight bottles of this delicious claret left when I packed, so I took the precaution of slipping them into my bag. When my bag was unpacked a nurse rather ostentatiously, put all eight bottles on a table at the foot of my bed. When I met Christopher that first evening, he pointed to the bottles. Then he turned to the sister who was with him, with something that looked like the Leaning Tower of Pisa on her head.

'You see those bottles, sister? Mr Blofeld can have them

whenever he wants.' And then turning to me, he went on, 'The benefits of red wine with heart illness are only just beginning to be understood.'

It seemed an entirely sensible attitude. I took him at his word and without a doubt it did me nothing but good.

With Broadcasting House just round the corner, Peter Baxter and Shilpa Patel, his gorgeous deputy, came to see me several times. At first they looked at me as if I was the ghost I so nearly had been. Before long the conversation turned to *TMS*. The World Cup consumed the first part of the 1999 summer. Then New Zealand were due to stay on and play four Test matches. I told Peter I was determined to be back in the *TMS* box on 1 July for the first day of the first Test at Edgbaston. I was always certain I would be there, but the doctors kept scratching their heads. In the end they agreed that although it might be a little too soon, it would probably do me more good than harm.

I shall never forget driving myself from Hoveton, the family home in Norfolk, to Brockencote Hall in Chaddesley Corbett, where we were all staying for the Edgbaston Test. In some ways it was almost unreal, even though I do not think I realised how close to death I had been. Soon after I arrived at the hotel I had a wonderful moment which helped me realise how incredibly lucky I had been. It was a glorious day and after I had signed in I wandered through the bar and took a glass out with me onto the terrace. I had hardly sat down when a figure burst through the glass door and embraced me tightly, exclaiming, 'I never thought I was going to see you again.' It was Graeme 'Foxy' Fowler, one of our summarisers. In saying that, he said it all. It was an extraordinary, and deeply touching moment. After that, the Test match itself was almost an anticlimax, with England winning in under two and a half days, but I think I just about got away with it in the commentary box. What a joy and relief it was to be back. I cannot tell you how wonderful it felt.

The great success of *Test Match Special*'s first overseas venture in India in 1976–77 was confirmed when England went to Pakistan the following winter. Don Mosey, who was the official BBC man on that 1977–78 tour, and I mounted another *TMS* adventure from Lahore, Hyderabad and Karachi. It was an intriguing series, and for me it was part of a remarkable few months, which started with a visit to Australia. In late November 1977 I flew to Melbourne to watch the first official Kerry Packer-inspired World Series Cricket (WSC) game, played between his Australian and the West Indian teams out at VFL Park in the Melbourne suburb of Waverley, one of the more important homes of Australian Rules Football. To begin with, cricket's traditional authorities had managed to prevent Packer from playing on the Test grounds in Australia. WSC, therefore, had to improvise. In the early stages of all this, Packer had employed a groundsman, John Maley, whose first job was to prepare pitches in vast trays which could be dropped into the middle of whichever ground it was they found themselves playing on. One of these was now being used at VFL Park.

It was an extraordinary, almost militant 'them and us' atmosphere to fly into. No one was indifferent. The Establishment was sure their birthright was being threatened. The supporters of Packer were convinced it was they who had the moral high ground: top-class cricketers had, until now, been paid a pittance and thanks to the foresight and wealth of Mr Packer, this was going to end. The Packer camp was energetically evangelical and it almost became a religious battlefield. One of my briefs was to commentate for the BBC on the first ever Packer ball. Armed with every sort of press ticket and identification card, as well as the inevitable Uher, I embarked with Johnny Woodcock upon the considerable taxi drive from the middle of Melbourne out to VFL Park.

It was a strange but exciting journey and for an Establishment supporter it felt like a foray into enemy territory. Neither of us had any idea of what we were going to find. The huge, chain-smoking figure of Packer was very much in evidence on that first day. Like me, many of the journalists present at VFL Park were strong supporters of the Establishment. Packer did not mince his words with any of us. His Australian side batted first and it turned out to be a fairly bloodless cricket match. I could not help but feel that no one cared much about the result. What mattered was that Packer's Australian team were playing the West Indies and World Series Cricket was under way.

Sitting in the press box with my Uher, I commentated on the first over. It was bowled by Andy Roberts to Rick McCosker, who was caught at third slip off the second ball. There were not 500 people in the ground and McCosker's dismissal did not even produce a ripple of applause. At the same time as WSC were going through birth pangs, the official Australian side captained by Bobby Simpson, who had been persuaded by the Australian Cricket Board to come out of retirement to their rescue, beat India in front of good crowds in the first official Test at the Gabba in Brisbane.

Packer received one highly encouraging and crucially important piece of news during that first WSC match. The previous summer in London a fierce battle had been fought in the High Court between Packer and the MCC. Packer's argument was that in banning their own players from taking part in his cricket, the MCC and, by inference, similarly inclined cricket authorities around the world, were seriously breaching the laws governing restraint of trade. Mr Justice Christopher Slade, the brother of Julian Slade who had written the post-war musical *Salad Days*, had heard the case. He had reserved his judgement, which he finally handed down while we were at Waverley. He found comprehensively for Packer who, with a facial expression which somehow combined a licking of the lips with a militantly triumphant smirk – he was no smiler – relished his victory. He had every justification for doing so.

He had started the whole business simply to make money. His internal think-tank at Channel Nine, his television network in Australia, had persuaded him he would be onto a big winner if he could get hold of the exclusive rights to televise international cricket in Australia, at the time held by the Australian Broadcasting Commission. The refusal of the Australian Cricket Board even to talk to him ultimately made him stamp his foot and decide to lay on his own SuperTests. The gloves were off. This decision turned it into an all-out battle between Packer on the one hand and Establishment cricket on the other. Being the man he was, victory was the only possible outcome for Packer, no matter how much money he had to throw at it. It is worth going into all this again to explain what we all felt on that first day at Waverley and why emotions ran so high. It was a day unlike any other I have experienced in nearly fifty years of broadcasting cricket, and yet the actual cricket at Waverley was essentially irrelevant. I can still feel that same tension I felt on the drive to VFL Park as I write these words now.

I left Melbourne at the end of the first week in December 1977, but the dramas of that ongoing battle were to follow me round the world until the end of the following April. My next port of call was Lahore, for England's first Test against Pakistan, where I joined Don Mosey. The ground was called the Gaddafi Stadium in honour of Colonel Gaddafi, who had presumably given Pakistan a hefty tranche of Libyan money. The *TMS* 'box' was perched on the bare, slate-grey stone roof of the pavilion. It provided the Alderman and me with a splendid if rather exposed and isolated spot from which to commentate. It did little to protect us from either sun or rain. There was plenty of fun to be had trying to make contact with the appropriate studio in Broadcasting House in London. The local radio engineers were men with firm views and their own way of doing things. The Alderman was no shrinking violet, mind you, and there were some lively exchanges on our rooftop – and the odd ultimatum too.

The first Test, which started on 14 December 1977, was one of the dullest games of cricket I have ever seen. While commentating, I really had to hitch up my trousers to try and prevent listeners from switching off. Things were livened up, if that is the right expression, by two innings that must be high on the list of the worst served up to entertain the human race. First, Mudassar Nazar made the slowest first-class hundred known to mankind. It took Mudassar the small matter of 557 minutes to reach three figures. England's ever dependable Geoffrey Boycott clearly thought the record should be his. He made an impressive attempt upon it too. When he reached fifty he was more than just a short head in front, as he had taken twenty minutes longer than Mudassar to reach that landmark. When he had made another thirteen, Homer mercifully nodded and he missed a straight ball.

Mudassar's hundred did not leave us empty-handed. As far as the crowd was concerned, a century was a century. In the later stages, as he dawdled towards three figures, the spectators were cheering in excited anticipation as every ball was bowled. Mudassar, unmoved by any of this, eventually got to 98, which meant that at some point in the next hour the chances were that he might just possibly reach a hundred. The cheering grew louder and louder. Bob Willis was bowling from the end opposite to the pavilion. Mudassar half steered, half snicked a short one to third man, where Graham Roope was fielding. It was only ever going to be a single, but the crowd thought the moment had arrived, and they boiled over.

A great many had been standing up and pressing against the high boundary fences designed to prevent the spectators from running onto the field. As Mudassar completed the leisurely single, many spectators were already climbing over the wire with inspiring athleticism. Once over the wire, they ran in a torrent towards Mudassar, who tried to shoo them away. He then realised, as King Canute had once done, that the tide of these things cannot be stopped. He moved quickly towards extra cover so that the stampede would not damage the actual pitch. Mudassar was soon surrounded and then submerged under the mass of hysterical supporters, while the scoreboard showed with a discouraging finger-wagging firmness that his tally was still only 99.

Not before time, the police realised they had better try to restore order. The gates were opened to allow them onto the field, dressed in khaki shirts and shorts and carrying long wooden lathi sticks. Although hopelessly outnumbered, they came out barking commands which were completely ignored. They then began to use their lathi sticks to whack any of the invaders who came within range. Seeing the treatment being meted out to their fellow spectators, those still in the stands felt it was their time to join in. There was another even bigger invasion. The police swung their lathi sticks even more meaningfully. It was soon clear they were fighting a losing battle. Mudassar, meanwhile, was still submerged by spectators desperate to get close enough to touch their hero, all convinced he had reached a hundred.

When the senior policemen who had sensibly remained behind the scenes saw the plight of their colleagues on the field they whistled up the riot police. It was not long before they made a rather more impressive entrance than their lathi-sticked colleagues. Wearing long trousers and huge, clumsy gas masks straight out of a World War I movie, they strutted onto the ground like prehistoric monsters carrying masses of tear-gas canisters. When they pulled the pins out of the canisters and lobbed them into the crowd, dense clouds of tear gas stopped the rioters in their tracks. Realising the party was over, they headed back to the stands, holding their noses and rubbing their eyes.

All this had taken quite a while. Don Mosey and I were busily describing the scene to our listeners, and I am ashamed to say I found it all rather fun. I think I talked about it with perhaps a little more relish than the Alderman. Of course, when the tear gas began to fly about, we adopted a stern 'it serves them right' attitude especially when some of the gas wafted its way up to our lofty perch. Now, I was an experienced tear-gas hand, having learned the relevant tricks at Sabina Park in Kingston, Jamaica, during Colin Cowdrey's tour in 1967–68. I had been working for Jim Swanton who, when the tear gas was first thrown, kindly ordered me out onto the ground to find out exactly what was happening. The police then made the silly mistake of throwing the stuff into the strong wind rather than downwind. The result was that I found myself submerged by a thick cloud of the stuff. Most painful and unpleasant it was too, something I was never sure that my employer sitting in the air-conditioned press box fully appreciated. Back at the Gaddafi Stadium experience took over, I had my handkerchief out in a flash, with my head as close to the ground as I could get. The Alderman, who was not so well trained, sat where he was and breathed it all in. Soon he choked and, in time, expostulated vigorously and at length.

The field was eventually cleared and play restarted. It would be stretching the truth to say that Mudassar now raced to his hundred: after carefully playing himself in again, he squirted that last, elusive single somewhere behind square on the off side. There were one or two brave spirits who had not learned their lesson and tried to come over the fence again. This time the police were on red alert. They were none too gentle either. At that moment, I was able to tell listeners that Mudassar had 'at last reached a truly riotous hundred'. It produced a good old Yorkshire groan from the Alderman. If he had had a moustache, it would have bristled.

After all three Tests in Pakistan had been drawn and we had, among other things, survived the delights of our rather dreadful hotel in Hyderabad, England departed for New Zealand. I, however, flew from Karachi to Perth via Colombo where of course my manuscript had been deposited ruthlessly into the refuse bin, for another quick dose of Packer cricket. In Perth, World Series Cricket had made their home at the Gloucester Park trotting track, just across the road from the Test ground, the WACA. In another WSC SuperTest, at the end of January 1978, Australia were playing the Rest of the World on one of Maley's drop-in pitches, with the trotting track encircling the playing area. In the SuperTest that I had watched at the beginning of December at VFL Park, the players had seemed to be going through the motions. What I saw in Perth could hardly have been more different. Every one of them was going to the limit and beyond. It was as tough and competitive a game of cricket as one could have wished to see. It also produced the most remarkable display of batting I think I have ever seen. The Rest of the World reached a massive first-innings total of 625. The three principal individual run-scorers – Barry Richards 207, Viv Richards 177 and Gordon Greenidge 140 – made my point better than I would be able to myself. It is very seldom I have seen two great batsmen play at their best in partnership, but now it was first Barry Richards and Greenidge and then the two Richardses. They also showed that John Maley knew a thing or two about drop-in pitches.

After two days at Gloucester Park, I flew to Adelaide to watch the end of the 'official' fifth Test between Bobby Simpson's non-Packer Australia and India. Amid great excitement in front of good crowds, India failed by 48 runs to make the 493 they needed to win in the fourth innings. Australia won the series 3–2. Then I dashed across the Tasman Sea to New Zealand, where Geoffrey Boycott became the first England captain to fail to win a series in New Zealand. He also had to suffer the indignity in the second Test in Christchurch of being run out by Ian Botham, who had been promoted in the order to number four and sent in with specific instructions to do so – because his captain was batting much too slowly for England's needs. In mid-pitch, when he realised he had no hope of getting back, Boycott shouted to Botham, 'What have you done?' Botham's reply was short, entertaining and conclusive. During this series World Series Cricket tried to obtain the services of Richard Hadlee, but this time Packer was thwarted, much to the delight of the whole of New Zealand.

After England's series in New Zealand, which was drawn 1–1, I flew to the Caribbean to watch Bobby Simpson's official Australian side play a series against the West Indies. For the first two Tests, in Trinidad and Barbados, they were up against the full West Indian contingent of Packer players and lost heavily. Even so, in Bridgetown, Jeff Thomson bowled one of the great spells of genuine fast bowling I have been lucky enough to see. If there had been neutral umpires, he might have had as many as four wickets with the new ball late on the first day. As it was, he had to be content with Gordon Greenidge's. It was a spell to rival Michael Holding's against England on the same ground three years later, which I also saw. The series then moved to Guyana, where after endless bad-tempered discussions concerning the presence of the Packer lot in the West Indies side, Clive Lloyd pulled all the Packer players out for the remainder of the series. Before the match there was furious diplomatic activity, and rumour had it that Packer himself was making the journey. In the end, we had to settle for a visit by Austin Robertson, who was one of the WSC's main warriors.

It made for plenty to talk about on Radio Demerara, for whom I commentated under the auspices of the unique and idiosyncratic B.L. Crombie, a broadcasting legend in Guyana. His lack of knowledge about the more intricate details of cricket made him, if anything, even more delightful, inconse-quential and entertaining. He shouted unmercifully at the microphone with a gravelly voice. Commentating with the one-eyed B.L. was as interesting an experience as working in the Radio Trinidad commentary box with the absurdly patri-otic Ralph 'Raffie' Knowles. Raffie spoke in an almost contin-uous high-pitched scream in unintelligible Trinidadian English, whereas B.L.'s commentary was one long, vociferous rant in deep bass Guyanese English. Raffie was a tall, thin man with a terrific sense of humour and an insatiable love of the ladies. He had played hockey for Trinidad. B.L. was a large and essentially genial man who had to be shoehorned into his prehistoric Morris Minor, which he drove with the disconcerting fierceness of his commentary. Both were hugely loved figures in their own domains. They greatly enhanced the joy I found in watching and commentating in the Caribbean at this time. Both were dear men, if outrageous cricket commentators.

11

BROADLY
TRENT BRIDGE

THERE was one recent spell of *Test Match Special* commentary I shall never forget. Under the new order that rules Test cricket, England play Australia more frequently than in the days of the old four-year cycle. The Aussies were here in 2013, then England went Down Under in 2013–14 and Australia were back again in 2015. The greed that seems to be encroaching on all big sports these days is the principal reason. One unfortunate by-product of this is that the baggy green cap has lost some of its mystique. If we had seen Don Bradman every other year, he would soon have seemed a mere mortal rather than a deity from Mount Olympus. But, of course, Ashes series against Australia fill the coffers quickest of all.

When Australia came to Trent Bridge for the fourth Test in 2015 they were 2–1 down in the series. They lost the first and third Tests at Cardiff and Edgbaston and in between won with great ease at Lord's. England's victory in three days at Edgbaston had given them back the psychological advantage. There is something special about Test matches at Trent Bridge. I cannot think of a friendlier Test venue. It is presided over by a committee which has always cared equally for the game, the players and the spectators, whose interests some grounds almost seem to forget.

Another reason I love going to Trent Bridge is that it allows me to stay at Langar Hall in the Vale of Belvoir. This has long been my favourite hotel anywhere in the world, cricketing or otherwise. It is an hotel which, with its lovely ochre colour, looks and feels as if it might have been transplanted from Tuscany. Langar is as gloriously eccentric as its unique owner, Imogen Skirving, who was tragically run over and killed by a car while walking back from the beach in Menorca in July 2016. Imogen was then seventy-nine and still ran everything in her hotel, down to the smallest detail. I once described her, in the foreword of her book, as a benevolent despot with a stern-ish finger on every pulse. She was delighted. Nothing escaped her ever-searching eye. The hotel was nothing more than a wonderful extension of her own personality. It was supremely comfortable, the food and wine were delicious, the service was good, the menu was original, and the cooking a joy.

Brian Johnston was the first member of the *TMS* team to stay at Langar – CMJ had told him that the sister of a friend of his owned a good hotel near Trent Bridge – and ironically dear old Brian was the only one who was not entirely happy there. The reason for this was that he was the most fastidious of eaters. He preferred food that was English through and through. All he really wanted was bangers and mash, fish and chips or something along those lines, with a spoonful or two of soggy cabbage and lumpy mashed potato thrown in. The only words that were more of an anathema to him than 'al dente' were 'nouvelle cuisine', and when he first went to Langar the food was, he felt, outrageously nouvelle cuisine. After that first visit, he decamped to another billet. John Arlott never stayed there either, but then he always had his own hideaways. He liked somewhere that took a relaxed view of a guest who brought his own wine to stay with him. For the rest of us, Langar Hall was as near to heaven as it gets – and still is.

At the end of July 2015, we all arrived at Trent Bridge in good heart. We went up to the commentary box at the Radcliffe Road End in one of those outrageously slow and temperamental lifts which seem to be compulsory in the new media centres of every Test ground in England. Aggers, who by then was an experienced pilot and latter-day Biggles, was, as usual, full of stories of looping the loop. His recent adventures with Mrs Aggers, the beautiful blonde, chic Emma, quickened all our pulses and, I daresay, those of the listeners too, as they were recounted later on. The lovely Agnews live in the Vale of Belvoir, which they bestride in style, giving the Duke and Duchess of Rutland a good run for their money. Adam Mountford soon put up the day's rota. While Aggers was going to start things off out in the middle, I was down to do the first twenty minutes of commentary. I always love kicking off the commentary, and there is a special excitement on the first morning of any Test but especially, for me, at Trent Bridge.

Aggers gave us a great start out in the middle, after Alastair

Cook had won the toss. There was a tinge of green on the pitch and he invited Australia to bat – that terminology again. Michael Vaughan, Phil Tufnell and Jim Maxwell were in splendid form, out in the middle with Aggers with a dash of Vic Marks thrown in to spice it all up. Overhead, it was grey and threatening. At about five to eleven it began to drizzle gently and the pitch covers were rushed on, but within a minute or two it had stopped and by the time Aggers handed over to me in the box, the covers were coming off again. Although the ground staff were putting the stumps back in and generally tidying up and the umpires were coming out, play was bound to start a few minutes late.

The only problem for England was that Jimmy Anderson, who swings the ball round corners at Trent Bridge, had been injured in the previous Test and could not play. Nonetheless, Stuart Broad was looking taller, sharper and more menacing than ever. He was visibly champing at the bit at the end of his run at the Pavilion End. Would this be his day and could he do it on his own? Would this be the day for one of his purple patches, when he threatens to take a wicket with every ball? The Australian openers, Chris Rogers and David Warner, had a pugnacious look to them as they walked out – Australian openers usually do. Both were four-square and stocky. The left-handed Rogers took guard and looked round the field with exaggerated care. Cook, from first slip, made sure his fielders were in the right place; the clock showed it was five minutes past eleven. Rogers was ready and Broad started in.

Tuffers was sitting on my right-hand side, with Andrew Samson, pencil poised, on my left. Broad was fast that morning. Australia got underway with four leg byes. Then Rogers pushed half forward to the third ball, bat away from body, and Cook held the edge at first slip. The crowd could hardly believe it and I was almost blowing a gasket in the commentary box. But this was only the start. A flashing square drive for four showed us that the next man in, Steve Smith, was going to take the battle to Broad. He was then squared up as he pushed defensively at his third ball and Joe Root took a comfortable catch at third slip. Tuffers and I were screaming our heads off. 'He's gone, he's gone' was becoming my theme song.

Two out in the first over and now it was Mark Wood's turn. The other Australian opener, David Warner, also left-handed and looking as if the boxing ring would be more his natural habitat, had a nasty one that nipped back on him and flicked the inside edge. Jos Buttler did the rest behind the stumps. Warner's departure is always a moment of immense joy for his opponents. There was bedlam in the commentary box. I even saw a policeman on the steps of the Fox Road Stand to our left cup his hands round his mouth. He appeared to give the sort of yell he would have normally reserved for burglars he caught red-handed. Meanwhile Tuffers was making a cat on hot bricks look like John Arlott with a hangover. Australia's captain, Michael Clarke, anxiously played out Wood's over while trying to look reassuring and not really succeeding. The crowd were expecting a wicket with every ball. I have seldom seen spectators in such a ferment of disbelieving excitement as they were now. And then it was Broad again. Shaun Marsh, another left-hander, never looked as if he would make much difference – and he didn't. He pushed forward and instinctively followed his fourth ball. Ian Bell came up with the catch at second slip. Marsh, mystified and out of his depth, slowly trudged off.

Australia were already 15–4 and we were only in the third over. Tuffers and I were still shouting our heads off and jumping up and down. The sublime and the ridiculous, Tuffers and Blowers, were on song. Andrew Samson was frantically trying to find a moment to give us all the relevant statistical details, but he had no chance. He accepted his fate with a resigned grin. Then I heard in my ear the first voice of sobriety I had heard for fifteen minutes. Producer Adam Mountford's gentle, measured tones told me it was time for me to hand over to Ed Smith. Which I think I did in tones which suggested yet another wicket had fallen. As I got out of my chair, those in the box gave me a round of applause. It was the only time this ever happened, to me or anyone else when I was in the box.

I recounted this moment on stage a year later when Graeme Swann and I were doing our hilarious theatre tour together. 'Don't be stupid, Blowers,' he said. 'They were clapping Broad.' Thank you, Swanny.

I fear he may have been right. But what a spell of commentary it had been. I cannot remember another in which quite so much happened or where the excitement was so unrelenting. I suppose Tuffers and I are the product of our times. I hardly think, for example, that John Arlott and Norman Yardley would have cut loose like we did when Peter Loader took a hat-trick against the West Indies at Headingley in 1957.

During that match at Trent Bridge in 2015, I couldn't help thinking back to another crucial game that England had won there, in August 2005. This was the series when England won back the Ashes for the first time since 1986–87, when Mike Gatting's side had won in Australia. After making Australia follow on, Michael Vaughan's England had to score 129 to win and they lost seven wickets getting there. It was nerve-wracking. In the end, England's left-arm spinner, Ashley Giles, batting at number eight, played Shane Warne off the front foot, with a bit of bottom hand thrown in, to the midwicket boundary for the winning runs. There was a lovely story after the game. When he had finished everything he had to do in the commentary box, Jonathan Agnew went round to one of the hospitality suites in our stand. He was talking to some friends when he spotted an elderly lady sitting on her own at the back of the box with a handkerchief up to her eyes, crying. He went over to her and asked what the problem was and if he could help. She looked up with tears in her eyes and said in a tearful voice, 'My son has just scored the winning runs.' It was Giles's mother.

There were two moments in the match itself which still live on. In the first innings the fifth Australian wicket fell at 99. This brought in Adam Gilchrist, always a dangerous batsman. He started well, but when he had reached 27 he faced Flintoff.

The ball was just outside the off stump. From the angle of Gilchrist's bat you could see he began by wanting to cut. Then he decided to defend but could not quite straighten up his bat. He edged the ball and Andrew Strauss at second slip dived far to his left and held the ball when he was horizontal, with his entire body off the ground. Mercifully, one camera at least preserved the catch for ever.

The other moment, unforgettable for a different reason, came in Australia's second innings. Simon Jones had sadly limped off with a knee injury and the substitute was twenty-two-year-old Gary Pratt of Durham, who had not played a single Championship match that season. He was fielding at cover when Damien Martyn pushed a ball slowly to his right and called the Australian captain, Ricky Ponting, for a single. Pratt swooped on the ball right-handed and threw the stumps down at the wicketkeeper's end all in the same movement. Ponting was run out, and he was none too pleased about it.

Before this match, the Australians had been protesting that England had been using substitutes too often in both the one-day series and the Test matches. On this occasion Ponting had words with the square-leg umpire Aleem Dar, who gave him no sympathy. Then, as he left the field, he spotted the England manager Duncan Fletcher on the England balcony, took off his helmet and gave him a verbal blast. His behaviour cost him 75 per cent of his match fee. This was another incident that was discussed over and over again in the *Test Match Special* box, and we all came to the same conclusion. He should never have done it. It was sad that Ponting reacted as he did, but under pressure disappointment can lead so easily to resentment. When he cooled down Ponting would have been only too well aware that he had behaved stupidly. I felt rather sorry for Gary Pratt, whose magnificent piece of fielding received far less attention than it deserved. The story was Ponting when it should have been Pratt.

There was almost a replay of Broad's brilliant spell at Trent Bridge in 2015 when he took 8–15 a few months later in Johannesburg in January 2016, during the third Test between South Africa and England at the Wanderers. England had won the first in Durban and come north after a high-scoring draw in Cape Town, when Ben Stokes had played his extraordinary innings of 258. On the last day of that match England batted badly in their second innings, at one point giving South Africa an outside chance of victory. As a result, South Africa had the psychological advantage coming to Johannesburg. They won the toss at the Wanderers and were bowled out for 313. The innings was curious in that it was only the thirteenth time every batsman had reached double figures in a Test innings. A brilliant innings of 110 by Joe Root was principally responsible for giving England a slender first-innings lead of ten runs.

Now, *Test Match Special* has been blessed with a striking array of scorers over the years. Roy Webber was the first, who was succeeded by Arthur Wrigley. Then in 1966 Bill Frindall's long reign began. He was in the scorer's chair for forty-two years before he contracted legionnaires' disease while playing cricket in Dubai and sadly died early in 2009. Malcolm Ashton, who had for a long time been Frindall's understudy, succeeded the Bearded Wonder. When England went to Australia in 2010–11, however, Ashton was asked to score, but only if he paid his own expenses, and not surprisingly he decided to stay at home. As a result, our present Test match scorer, Andrew Samson, a South African who lives in Johannesburg, was asked to step in. He was quick to show that he is the best of the lot. He is extremely quick, with a wonderful statistical memory of his own. Not only that, he also has the most extraordinarily complex database which enables him to produce unlikely facts in a matter of seconds.

We had a wonderful example of this at the Wanderers. South Africa had selected for this third Test a rather unlikely seam bowler called Hardus Viljoen. He was a big strong man, but on this evidence not obviously a Test cricketer. He came in to bat on the second morning and hit his first ball, from Stuart Broad, for four. Later the same day, he came on to bowl and with his first ball he had Alastair Cook caught behind the wicket, trying to glance a short one. Before the next batsman had faced his first ball, our irrepressible scorer revealed to the world that only one other player in the history of Test cricket had hit his first ball for four and also taken a wicket with his first ball. His name was Matthew Henderson and he had taken New Zealand's first ever wicket in Test cricket. England, under Harold Gilligan, were taking on New Zealand at Christchurch in January 1930. Henderson had Eddie Dawson, the captain of Leicestershire, caught by the New Zealand captain, Tom Lowry. Henderson and Viljoen are likely to have one other thing in common. That was Henderson's only Test match, and it will be a surprise if Viljoen should play another. Although I would put nothing past Samson, I cannot believe that he had this fact tucked away at the back of his mind, but what a remarkable database he must have if such an old and remote statistic can be found with not much more than a flick of the fingers. Samson's only blemish is his handwriting, which not even a drunken spider would be proud of. He, too, is bearded, perhaps a necessity for a successful *TMS* scorer. Samson oozes wisdom and, without doubt, bears a striking resemblance to Erasmus – the theologian, not the umpire.

At the Wanderers in 2016, our commentary box was high up at the top of the stand at the Corlett Drive End. In the summariser's chair, South Africa's recently retired captain, Graeme Smith, was splendidly and amusingly philosophical as Broad proceeded to destroy South Africa's second innings. They had been 16 for no wicket at lunch on the third day and the game seemed delicately poised. Then, three overs into the afternoon, Dean Elgar's bat was drawn to a short ball he could have left alone and he was caught behind. After that, it all happened in a rush and it was crescendo level in the *TMS* box – for me at any rate. Vic Marks was with me, and he could never be described as a screamer. In fact, there have been times when I have playfully had to chide him for being too solemn – as if he is reading the second lesson in a church service. Controlled happiness was now the order of the day. Five more runs were scored and then Stiaan van Zyl pushed wide of his stumps at a ball of full length from Broad. He was comfortably caught in the gully by Stokes. Broad in this mood is thrilling to describe. There was an urgency about him as he strode back to his mark. When the ball was returned to him by a fielder, he grabbed it one-handed in an almost impatient gesture which told of his eagerness to get on with the next ball. His run-up was springy and irresistible. The force was with him. He pounded in to A.B. de Villiers who, along with his partner, Hashim Amla, were now the key to the match. If one settled in, it was bad for England; if they both settled, England's batsmen were going to have an uncomfortable time of it in the fourth innings.

Broad, bowling to the left handed de Villiers, produced an extraordinary ball. It was that perfect length which has a batsman in two minds as to whether he should play back or forward. In the end, de Villiers shuffled across his crease. I should think it may have pitched just to the off side of middle stump and cut back in to de Villiers, who was in no position to play it. The ball found the inside edge of a bat for there was a small gap between bat and body. It then thudded into Jonny Bairstow's gloves. De Villiers walked away quickly, almost scurrying to the pavilion, which was at square leg. This was a decisive moment and the all-round body language told the story. South Africa were 30–3.

One run later, in his next over, Broad bowled to Amla. He

played him firmly away off his legs just in front of square. James Taylor, all of 5 feet 4 inches tall, was at square short leg, standing a little deeper than usual. This was to give himself time to react when the ball came off the middle of the bat. He was right down on his haunches when Amla played the stroke. The key was that Taylor stayed down and was able to take the ball very close to the ground in both hands. It was a wonderful catch and from that moment there was no doubt that South Africa were beaten. Broad was fizzing and he was bowling every ball as if he knew he was going to take a wicket. All the parts of his fast-bowling mechanism combined to produce a rhythm which was as exquisite as it was unstoppable. Four runs later Temba Bavuma, scorer of a hundred in Cape Town, played a hurried defensive stroke at Broad and edged the ball into his stumps. In thirty-six balls Broad had taken five wickets for one run, which had come from a dropped catch at second slip. It was all over and England won by seven wickets on the third day.

That performance in Johannesburg was my own personal hat-trick of amazing spells of bowling by Broad. The sequence had begun in 2011 against India at Trent Bridge. In India's first innings Broad, 6–46, had made sure that their first-innings lead was kept within bounds. India had lost the first Test at Lord's. They were now 258–4 in reply to England's 221 when the second new ball was taken. In Broad's third over, Yuvraj Singh was caught behind. He pushed defensively at one that, on his walk back to the pavilion, he will have

The rogues' gallery: the *TMS* team for the Test against the West Indies at Trent Bridge in 1995.

The Queen, in sparkling form talking to Peter Baxter, Blowers and CMJ, gives *TMS* a fruit cake in the Lord's Committee Room in 2001.

CMJ is either recommending me a restaurant or checking a batting average. I can't remember which.

Frank Keating enjoying the West Indian sun in 1980–81. A great friend and guiding light – a supremely wise and much-missed old owl.

A typically jaunty Jonty Rhodes in the covers – where else? – South Africa v Australia at Newlands, Cape Town, in 1994.

TMS at the ready. England's first Test against Zimbabwe, at Bulawayo in 1996: Chris Cowdrey, Trevor Bailey, me (standing), Simon Mann and scorer Jo King.

The power, elegance and composure of Michael Vaughan as he pulls Jason Gillespie at Old Trafford in 2005.

Andrew Strauss's magical airborne catch at second slip puts paid to the dangerous Adam Gilchrist in the Ashes Test at Trent Bridge in 2005.

England's unforgettable last pair of Jimmy Anderson and Monty Panesar. They held on for 11.3 overs in Cardiff for a draw against Australia in 2009.

Stuart Broad, 8–15 in Australia's first innings, leaves the field after England's three-day win at Trent Bridge in 2015.

James 'Titch' Taylor, brilliant at short leg, holds Kyle Abbott of South Africa off Moeen Ali at Durban in December 2015.

A great addition to *TMS*. Former South African captain Graeme Smith and I sort things out at Lord's in 2017.

Shilpa Patel, Peter Baxter's glamorous number two, sees if she can upset scorer Andrew Samson's unbreakable concentration at a *TMS* party.

Jim Maxwell and I seem to have spotted something on the pitch before the third day's play at Lord's in 2015.

Aggers and Vic Marks at our *TMS* party in London in 2017, with Henry Moeran, who could be hoping for a part in *The Godfather*.

The cake of the century, sent to the Old Trafford Test against South Africa to mark my retirement.

The Nottingham City Council have named a bus after me! Here we are at a neighbouring bus stop during the first lunch interval of the 2017 Test at Trent Bridge.

My Jägerbomb debut. During the Edgbaston Test in 2016 I was put in to bat by Vaughany, Tuffers and Warney – I had five straight off.

The amazing, beautiful and incomparable Valeria. She has not only withstood me for nearly ten years, but it is she who has made it all happen.

wished devoutly he had left alone. By then, Rahul Dravid had passed his hundred. In his next over Broad was bowling to M.S. Dhoni, the Indian captain. He flashed at a short one without any footwork and Jimmy Anderson held an awkward catch easily at second slip. Harbhajan Singh was caught on the crease by the next ball and was given out lbw. For some time after its introduction, India had obstinately refused to use the referral system whereby players can appeal if they think the umpires have treated them unfairly. If they had been using it on this occasion, Harbhajan would have been recalled, for he clearly got a thick inside edge into his pad.

Aggers was commentating when Dhoni and Harbhajan were out, but now, with Broad on a hat-trick, his time was up. He generously handed over to me. I had never commentated on a hat-trick and I was into the build-up even before I was sitting down. Broad, like an old-fashioned knight with his lance, roared in again, this time to Praveen Kumar. It was the perfect ball: it cut back into the batsman, tore through a shuffling defensive push and crashed into the middle and off stumps. In my usual high state of excitement, I shrieked, 'That was a humdinger of a ball, a real beauty.' I remember Shilpa Patel who stayed on as Adam Mountford's number two for a while, kept smiling and saying 'humdinger' to me every time I saw her for the rest of the summer. Broad had now taken five wickets for no runs in 16 balls. I know I only nipped in right at the end of this magnificent spell, after Aggers had done all the hard work, but these heady moments are wonderful. When the time came to hand over the microphone after such dramatic spells I was always on a high. The thrill and satisfaction of having to communicate great events of this sort to the outside world was marvellous. It gave me a real buzz. Now I am retiring from the microphone, Broad must be beginning to wonder where his next Test wickets are going to come from.

India were back again in 2014 and played the first Test at Trent Bridge. This time, Broad didn't get it right, wasting the new ball by continually bowling wide of the stumps. The batsmen were therefore not being made to play a stroke. I was commentating with Geoffrey Boycott alongside me. The great man criticised Broad for not putting the batsmen under enough pressure. This started a conversation about the excessive amount of appealing we had been getting from Broad.

With a slight smile, which of course cannot be seen on the wireless, Boycott said, 'His mum didn't smack him enough when he was little, I reckon.'

I said, 'You're a hard man, Geoffrey. Anyway, Broad—'

Geoffrey cut in: 'See, I grew up when that happened. No political correctness then. You got a little clip from your mum. That sorted you out.'

'Yes,' I said, 'I had a bit of that too . . .' (I certainly did, and I'm sure it did me nothing but good.) 'Here comes Broad again . . .'

After the day's play, a listener complained about the broadcast, saying Geoffrey had 'condoned the physical abuse of children'. He described the comments as 'insensitive and inappropriate'. This complaint was rejected by the BBC's editorial complaints unit, who said that light-hearted conversations were the hallmark of *TMS* and that Boycott and I had both laughed during the exchange. It was later taken to the BBC Trust, but the trustees ruled out an appeal. It shows how careful one has to be with this sort of thing in the modern age. What Geoffrey and I were saying was surely light years away from condoning the physical abuse of children. Political correctness does not always take common sense into account. On the other hand, there have certainly been occasions when I have found myself saying things I wish I hadn't.

In recent years, three new grounds, Chester-le-Street, Southampton and Cardiff, have been added to the Test list. Riverside at Chester-le-Street is a lovely ground in the shadow of Lumley Castle, but sadly, Test matches have not proved as popular up there as they need to be in these cash-conscious times. In one of the early matches I covered there, I'm afraid I made an extremely crass remark on air.

I can't remember why, but we were talking about putting on weight. I had recently seen my doctor in London and he had pointed a finger at my steadily increasing girth. I told him I had really been trying to lose weight and nothing much had happened. He had replied, in the sanctity of his surgery, that it was a good idea to eat rather less and underlined his point by saying that there were not many fat people in Belsen. I can hardly believe it, but I came up with this story while England were playing a one-day match at Riverside. Mike Gatting, who was sitting beside me in the summariser's chair, instantly looked round at those behind him and clearly did not know what he should say, before vigorously shaking his head in mystified horror. The last thing I had meant to do was upset anyone, and seeing Mike's reaction, I realised what a thoughtless idiot I had been.

I remember Mark Saggers, who had been commentating for us on several ODIs, wagging a formidable finger in my direction too. Oh dear – the more I thought about it, the worse it sounded. Saggers, who had been a vibrant and successful sporting host over the years on many sporting shows on both radio and television, was relatively new to *TMS*. He joined us for one Test match too, in 2002, against India at Trent Bridge, and he did a splendid job. I always think that if he had made up his mind that this was what he wanted to do he would have become a regular. After my unfortunate reference to the last war, he certainly showed that his moral compass was in the right place.

My remark had resulted in some agitated telephone calls. For a while I got the feeling that I was now definitely part of the castle not normally shown to visitors. I often wondered later what my old adjudicator, Henry Riddell, would have made of it. Maybe, in those distant days, he would have simply shrugged his shoulders, but I rather suspect he would have prepared himself for our final interview. As it was, I was mercifully not cast into the outer darkness I probably deserved.

While I am on the subject of career-threatening bloomers, I

had better get the other stinker out of my system. England were playing the West Indies at Headingley, a match they lost by nine wickets. The Cardigan Road runs behind the ground in the north-east corner. There is a row of formidable red-brick Victorian houses on the Headingley side of the road, some way back from the cricket. For that match, two of the houses had turned their adjoining balconies into a stand for their friends, and there was quite a gathering. I took listeners on my usual journey round the ground and mentioned this impromptu stand. I speculated that the ticket price was small. Then I likened it to a similarly makeshift stand at Eden Park in Auckland where, in one corner of the ground I remembered a balcony being used in the same way. I knew that the stand in Auckland had been given a jokey name which suggested cut-price tickets. I thought it would be a suitable name for this stand at Headingley. Suddenly I found myself calling it 'the Jewish Stand'.

This time there was an immediate shocked, eerie silence in the box. Bill Frindall was never quiet for long on these occasions and he made a few short and meaningful comments. Otherwise my fellow commentators just looked at me, and there was some awkward fidgeting. I knew I had got it wrong, but as my mind raced I could not work out why they had used that name in Auckland and got away with it. Then it came to me. At Eden Park it was actually known as 'the Scottish Stand'. I realised the magnitude of my folly. Peter Baxter was not at all happy, while CMJ just shook his head silently and sorrowfully.

After I had handed over to the next commentator and

stood up, I could see that my colleagues were looking the other way. After much discussion I was told by Baxter that I must apologise on air, which I did in my next spell. Telephone calls poured in from the bosses back in Broadcasting House in London and, of course, complaints followed from listeners. I have never been good at handling things like this. I soon realised that my excuse over Eden Park in Auckland did not have much to commend it either. If I had called it 'the Scottish Stand', how would those on the other side of Hadrian's Wall have taken the news? A flurry of tossed cabers perhaps. I have never been remotely anti-Semitic, but as with my effort at Riverside, I had plunged in without giving it enough thought. It was not until the words were out of my mouth that I began to realise what I had really said and what the consequences might be. Obviously there was going to be a lengthy and, for me, extremely uncomfortable inquest. There was indeed, but I just managed to survive it.

It was not a laughing matter, but later on there was one amusing follow-up, though it didn't seem funny at the time. I had made my gaffe during the morning session. The unpleasant faxes began to arrive almost straight away and they continued for the rest of the day. Thank goodness emails did not exist – if they had, it doesn't bear thinking about what might have turned up. It was getting on for tea when Baxter thrust yet another long fax into my hand. This one accused me of causing racial hatred, of having a mindset like an old-fashioned colonial and a number of other unpleasant things besides. I was horrified to read the signature. It had been sent by the Chief Rabbi. I was really worried now. I asked Baxter for his advice and then settled down with some BBC paper and a pen to write a profound letter of apology. I showed it to Peter, who thought it was reasonable. With his help I sent it to the Chief Rabbi's fax number. I did not enjoy the rest of the day one little bit. I was made to feel guilty as charged, which indeed I was. I hardly slept a wink all night. Breakfast wasn't much better, as my leg was severely pulled and I feared it would continue all day.

I drove to Headingley and settled down in the box to read the newspaper. For that match David 'Bluey' Bairstow was in our number two box as the expert helping Pat Murphy with the coverage for Radio 5 Live. Bluey always made an entrance. He now appeared waving a piece of paper vaguely in my direction.

'Look what I found in my fax machine when I got home last night.'

He showed it to one or two of the others first and they began to laugh. Then he gave it to me and I found myself reading the message I had sent, shame-faced, the evening before to the Chief Rabbi. Bluey had been the 'Chief Rabbi' all along and had written the original fax. I could have hit him over the head, but I was so relieved that I burst out laughing. When, not long ago, I told this story to his son, Jonny, his reply was, 'Typical!', and he had a really good laugh.

When I returned to Headingley the following year for the

Test against Pakistan, I felt that they had forgiven me for the error of my ways. A large sheet of white cloth was hanging from one of these same two balconies. It proclaimed in bold capital letters, 'HENRY BLOFELD IS GOD'. I cannot imagine the two events were in any way connected.

One of the other new Test venues, Sophia Gardens, now the SWALEC stadium, in Cardiff, has hosted two Ashes Tests that were particularly memorable for me as a commentator, and at one of them I also received an unexpected and distinctly unfriendly response to my efforts in the *TMS* box. The ground began life as Sophia Gardens and is charming. There are trees everywhere, the River Taff glides by and the cathedral and castle are within spitting distance, but, and it is a big but, the ground only holds about 15,000 people. On the evidence so far, the Welsh are keen enough to see an Ashes Test match, but they find other opponents less compelling than the Australians. Their diet in the future may be confined to one-day internationals.

Having said all that, I love going to Cardiff and Sophia Gardens, and I was lucky enough to commentate on the Ashes Test there in 2009 and then again in 2015, by which time the ground had metamorphosed into the SWALEC Stadium. I hope I am not alone in loathing the way well-known cricket grounds take on commercial names. Thank goodness Lord's is still Lord's, and I pray it will be Lord's for ever. I can see administrators all over the place throwing up their hands in horror at this. 'We need the money!' will be the cry from those who run the grounds that are afflicted in this way: an eternal modern dichotomy.

The first of those two matches, in 2009, produced an extraordinary draw. England's last pair of Jimmy Anderson and Monty Panesar came together with eleven and a half overs remaining. England were facing an innings defeat. In what was an agonising last hour, those two held firm. It made for the most dramatic commentary. I love getting my teeth around moments of high drama like these. It makes it all doubly worthwhile. Nobody expected those two tailenders to save England, but they played forward as if they had spent all the previous evening reading the MCC coaching book. There were one or two splendid strokes as well, which saved the innings defeat. It was as exciting an hour as any I can remember. At the time, it was not inconceivable that Anderson could block his way through, but it seemed scarcely credible that Panesar might do so too. For a long time the feeling was that they were simply delaying the inevitable. Then it suddenly began to dawn on everyone in the ground that they had a real chance of saving the match. After that, each ball became a potential hand grenade. In the box we were all completely limp with exhaustion and excitement by the time the last ball had been bowled. How crucial that draw was too. Australia won the second Test at Lord's and if they had won that one as well, they would have been two matches up. It would have been difficult to imagine a way back for England then. As it was, England went on to win the 2009 series.

The other memorable Test at Cardiff was in 2015. Before the game, the superstitious among the *TMS* team approached the SWALEC Stadium cautiously. It was half an hour's walk from our hotel, and on the way we had passed a blue plaque on the wall of an old hotel which stated that it was there that Captain Scott had spent his last night on British soil before sailing for the Antarctic. We all knew about his unfortunate end and hoped that this was not an omen for England's progress over the next few days. We need not have worried. In Cardiff, England outplayed Australia, winning by 169 runs, a victory that will have given the SWALEC Stadium and its new name some well-earned kudos. More surprisingly, Alastair Cook out-captained Michael Clarke, who was not himself in that match. He got more involved than usual in the conversational 'pleasantries' around the bat that have become a hallmark of Ashes battles and, at times, he seemed distracted. The course of the game was straightforward enough. A fine hundred by Joe Root helped England to 430. They gained a first-innings lead of 122 and left Australia a final target of 412. There was only ever one side in it. Even so, I shall always remember the game – for the dastardly act of betrayal by Cardiff's fraternity of seagulls.

The gulls always play an important role on Welsh grounds. During my spell of commentary on the first morning, they swooped and glided most chirpily past the windows of the box in a most entertaining fashion. I could have sworn that one or two actually winked at me. I have always been their greatest fan and throughout the day I followed their activities closely. On the second day, which was again fine, I once more described their adventures in affectionate tones. I was confident I was on good terms with Cardiff's gull population.

On the second evening I walked back to the hotel: over the river, past the castle and down the high street. I had nearly got there when I passed a florist's shop. The owner had hosed down the pavement before shutting the shop and there was a big puddle at the side of the road. Just about every gull in Cardiff was in it and I even noticed one or two intruders from Swansea – I could tell by their accents. I was almost level with them when a car drove fast through the puddle, scattering the gulls and splashing the rest of us. The gulls squawked and took off, but quickly got into a formation the Red Arrows would have been proud of and flew over me.

Every single one of them dropped whatever liquid or solid excess they had on them. I had no fewer than twelve direct hits. I have never known a more deliberate example of sheer, naked ingratitude. Perhaps they had been sent along by listeners who had no great love for my wittering-on about gulls. I'm afraid my shirt did not re-emerge from the dry-cleaners. On *Test Match Special* the next day, my plight caused much laughter, most of it led by Aggers. From the noise they made, the gulls in the ground seemed to be enjoying my discomfort as well.

England v Australia

(4th Test)

Played at Trent Bridge, Nottingham on 6, 7, 8 August 2015

Umpires: Aleem Dar, Sundaram Ravi

Toss: England

AUSTRALIA

CJL Rogers	c Cook b Broad	0	c Root b Stokes		52
DA Warner	c Buttler b Wood	0	c Broad b Stokes		64
SPD Smith	c Root b Broad	6	c Stokes b Broad		5
SE Marsh	c Bell b Broad	0	c Root B Stokes		2
MJ Clarke*	c Cook b Broad	10	c Bell b Wood		13
AC Voges	c Stokes b Broad	1	not out		51
PM Nevill†	b Finn	2	lbw Stokes		17
MG Johnson	c Root b Broad	13	c Cook B Stokes		5
MA Starc	c Root b Broad	1	c Bell b Stokes		0
JR Hazlewood	not out	4	b Wood		0
NM Lyon	c Stokes b Broad	9	b Wood		4
Extras	(lb 11 nb 4)	14	(b 20, lb 160, nb 3, w 1)		40
Total	(18.3 overs)	60	(72.4 overs)		253

ENGLAND

A Lyth	c Nevill b Starc	14
AN Cook*	lbw b Starc	43
IR Bell	lbw b Starc	1
JE Root	c Nevill b Starc	130
JM Bairstow	c Rogers b Hazlewood	74
MA Wood	b Starc	28
BA Stokes	c Nevill b Hazlewood	5
JC Buttler†	b Starc	12
MM Ali	c Smith b Johnson	38
SCJ Broad	not out	24
ST Finn	not out	0
Extras	(b 14, lb 2, nb 4, w 2)	22
Total	(85.2 overs)	391/9d

ENGLAND	O	M	R	W	O	M	R	W		Fall of wickets:			
										Aus	Eng	Aus	Eng
SCJ Broad	9.3	5	15	8	16.0	5	36	1	1st	4	32	113	-
MA Wood	3.0	0	13	1	17.4	3	69	3	2nd	10	34	130	-
ST Finn	6.0	0	21	1	12.0	4	42	0	3rd	10	96	136	-
BA Stokes					21.0	8	36	6	4th	15	269	136	-
MM Ali					26.0	0	34	0	5th	21	297	174	
									6th*	29	306	224	
AUSTRALIA	O	M	R	W					7th	33	320	236	-
MA Starc	27.0	2	111	6					8th	46	332	242	-
JR Hazlewood	24.0	4	97	2					9th	47	390	243	-
MG Johnson	21.2	2	102	2					10th	60	-	253	-
NM Lyon	10.0	1	47	1									
DA Warner	3.0	0	18	0									

Result: England won by an innings and 78 runs

12

GUIDING HANDS AND GUESTS OF HONOUR

IN my time with *Test Match Special*, two extremely important figures behind the scenes were Shilpa Patel and her
successor, Henry Moeran. In their different ways, each brought
a huge amount to our box. They were joint firsts among equals.
For many years, Shilpa was Peter Baxter's assistant. Henry
later fulfilled a similar role for Adam Mountford. Shilpa's
special ingredients were energy and vitality, as well as a genius
for discovering famous and unusual visitors in the crowd. She
sought them out and persuaded them to come round and have
a chat with us. Her finest moment came at Lord's in 2007
when Harry Potter fame was at its height. She heard a rumour
that the actor who played the schoolboy wizard on film was
watching the match, not in a hospitality box where he would
have been easy to track down, but somewhere in the stands.
Without telling a soul, Shilpa set to work and two days later,
during the morning session, I turned round and found myself
looking into the smiling face of Daniel Radcliffe, with Shilpa
just behind him, grinning fit to bust. Aggers had a frenzied
half an hour to brush up on Harry Potter.

Shilpa was also good at looking after commentators or summarisers from overseas who was not familiar with the idiosyncratic ways of *TMS*. When she was not rushing off to collect someone or to leave tickets at the gate or run an errand for Peter Baxter, she was a sharp listener too. If she thought I had got something wrong, she would wag a firm but friendly finger when I came off the air. If I had got something right – which I just occasionally did – she was also quick to say so. She scurried busily about between our boxes, answering a telephone call in the engineers' box, then delivering messages to Baxter sitting on his pedestal behind us in the commentary box. She always looked terrific and much thought went into her dashing and succulent outfits. I hardly ever came across her when she wasn't in a hurry, but she always had a word for everyone. She was so enthusiastic about all she did, whether it was in the box during play, bouncing into the bar for a drink afterwards or, later still, tackling the menu and organising the ordering, to say nothing of the bill-paying. Shilpa was a life-enhancer. On a gloomy morning or when England's cricket-ers were getting it wrong, her cheerful face gave us all a lift.

Shilpa always stayed in the same hotel with us when we were out of London. I can remember so many dinners where she was the life and soul of the party. If I had a criticism, it was that once or twice her persuasiveness had to take the blame for that last drink, which by the next morning had become a serious mistake. Annoyingly, her powers of recovery were a great deal better than mine. I remember far too many occasions when I arrived at breakfast and it was all I could do to put one foot in front of the other, only to find that she was way ahead, even of the eggs and bacon. I would find it hard to keep up with the inquest she was conducting into the events of the previous evening. Sinners were seldom let off lightly, and the choice of girlfriends for those with the licence to have them came under close scrutiny. There was nothing indecisive or blurred about her opinions. She had, too, the dirtiest laugh in the business. She ribbed Peter a good deal and they were an excellent combination. They had the odd moment, which is bound to happen from time to time in the febrile atmosphere of a commentary box, but nothing smouldered on. Like Henry later, she did much for our team spirit.

Over the years she tried hard to keep me in line, but without too much success. When she felt I had fallen short of her own high standards, she relayed the details to the rest of the team with relish. I stayed for years at the delightful Belle Époque in Knutsford when we were at Old Trafford. Once or twice, some of the others, including Shilpa, came along too. She was there when I found a lovely companion for one of the evenings, but when we got back to the hotel, a rambling art nouveau building, I discovered I had lost my keys. On one side of the hotel was a flight of stone steps going up the wall. I assured my companion that getting up to my room would not be the slightest problem. We briskly mounted the steps, only to find a locked gate at the top. With great skill and athleticism we clambered over the top, making enough noise to wake the redoubtable Shilpa in a neighbouring room. She peeped round her curtains and not only saw the midnight marauders, but also had no trouble in identifying them. When I came down to breakfast the next morning everyone in the dining room burst into torrents of laughter, none more so than Nerys Mooney, the effervescent chatelaine of the Belle Époque. It took me a long time to live that one down and, given half a chance, Shilpa still brings it up, as does Nerys. Then there was another occasion, this time at Langar Hall, when I apparently met a pretty girl who was dining there and asked her to dine with me the following evening, only to forget all about the arrangement. When she turned up the next night at half past eight, dressed to kill, she found I was having dinner with another lady. I needed Fred Astaire's footwork to get out of that one. That was a story Shilpa dined out on for years.

When Peter Baxter retired, for a year or two Shilpa carried on working with his successor, Adam Mountford, but I think it is fair to say they were never going to fit. When part of the BBC moved to Manchester, Shilpa was asked to spend a few days a month in the north, but decided against it. Her job with us came up for grabs, therefore, and after the ensuing applications and interviews, Henry Moeran was given the job. What a brilliant choice he has proved to be. He is not quite as easy on the eye as Shilpa, he does not have her *je ne sais quoi* and his dress sense is perhaps not quite the same. In all other respects, it is hard to tell them apart. Henry is a hard worker with a huge amount of charm and plenty of dash – backed up by a lively imagination. There is something of the young David Niven about his appearance. He has much of Shilpa's talent for sussing out interesting people for Aggers to talk to. There are times when he dives purposefully away from our box, with a 'Shan't be long' over his shoulder, and comes back a few minutes later engaged in conversation with a Rolling Stone or a Pet Shop Boy. The biggest compliment I can pay him is that everyone on *TMS* knows that he is a true friend. Nothing is too much trouble and he has a grip of all the technical problems that befuddle us from time to time.

He has also developed into an excellent broadcaster himself. He has a pleasant voice and is good at doing those short, stopwatch-controlled pieces when the need arises. This gives him another important arrow in his quiver. There are times too, when his boss needs a well-deserved break. Adam is lucky to have found such a trustworthy deputy to produce *TMS*, for example, on a short tour of ODIs in the West Indies. No one is more fun off duty too. This is an important part of producerly duties. Mucking in, off hours, encourages a more intimate form of friendship and one that makes relationships easier when we are at the pit face. It is where you really learn what makes people tick, where weaknesses are revealed, if not explored, and true friendships are made. Peter Baxter and Shilpa were both good at this too. You may find someone tricky to work with, but by the time you have spent an evening or two together it has usually become a different and more workable relationship. I think this can be an important help when it comes to what we all do in the box. Being clinically efficient is all well and good. On its own, however, it doesn't necessarily lead to warmth and humour. True friendship is so important and, when there's a wobble, it can make all the difference.

While Shilpa and then Henry have been ever-presents for *Test Match Special* in recent years, there have been other characters who have flitted in and out of our lives, hitting centre stage fleetingly before going the way of the shooting star. One touched us briefly for a few glorious moments during a match at Lord's in 1979. His big moment deserves to be recorded.

In October 1976, when five of us were driving from London to Bombay in a 1921 Rolls-Royce, we felt we had done the hard bit when we arrived in Delhi. We were now at the freewheeling stage because, give or take the idiosyncratic ways of Indian drivers, it was surely downhill to Bombay. In Delhi we made friends with the staff of the British High Commission and got to know some of them fairly well as we spent a few days in the capital. One who steered us in several most agreeable directions was Michael Pakenham, who was later to become a considerable diplomat. He was one of the eight children of that redoubtable progenitor Lord Longford, whose children were as eccentric as he was himself. We were much indebted to Michael's kindness. Before we moved on, we made the sort of rather vague plan that usually ends up in the wastepaper basket – about being sure to meet up again, perhaps in London, at some point in the future.

In 1979, during the second World Cup, England played Australia at Lord's. Peter Baxter was back in the studio pulling all the threads together from the various grounds. Our producer at Lord's was Chris Rea, who had played in the centre for Scotland thirteen times and was also a British Lion. The game at Lord's had started and all was going pretty well, in the commentary box at least, when the door opened and in burst a mildly dishevelled man who was around my age. He introduced himself to me as Michael Pakenham and reminded me that we had met three years before in India. He was carrying a surprising amount of paraphernalia with him, which he put down on the floor. We chatted amiably for a few minutes before it was my turn to commentate. Shortly after I had begun, he lay down at the back of a box which was none too big, and went to sleep. I know I have that effect on many people, but it does not often happen quite so quickly.

When I came off air he was still flat out on the floor and breathing rhythmically. For a few minutes we picked our way over him. Chris Rea finally rang Baxter in the studio and asked, with some doubt in his voice, 'Is this normal?' Baxter assured him it was not. It then took us quite a while to wake him up so comfortably had he settled. He eventually and with some difficulty lifted himself up, gathered together his belongings and shuffled out of the door, never to be seen again.

Then there was my brief encounter – the phrase seems appropriate – with Trevor Howard when England were playing a Test match in Barbados in 1968. Originally, the charming old Kensington Oval was ramshackle, intimate, friendly and redolent of all that was Bajan and West Indian cricket. It has now been 'updated' – a word used to justify so many indefensible alterations to our past. It was still the old Kensington when I met Trevor in the dusty old bar behind the wall that was the sightscreen at the Pavilion End. This was adjacent to the press and broadcasting boxes. It was where thirsty broadcasters would gather when they were in need of a drink.

I burst in one day just before lunch to find this late-middle-aged man with a well-preserved and distinguished face organising himself a refill at the bar. I was standing beside him, waiting my chance, when he turned his head and with just a flicker of a smile and such friendly eyes asked, 'What would you like to drink?' And this before we had been introduced. Not everyone would do that. I was certain I knew him, but I could not place him. The voice was definitely familiar. Then a friend of his came up and said simply, 'Don't leave me out, Trevor.' The penny dropped. Only a few seconds passed before I had a rum and Coke in my hand. I was not sure of the strength of the rum in my glass, but I can guarantee it was not a single.

There was, I suppose, a roundabout family connection. My mother had once told me that before she married my father she had gone out with Peter Fleming, the brother of Ian Fleming. He, of course, had married Celia Johnson, who was Trevor Howard's co-star in *Brief Encounter*. At the bar, he started to talk most enthusiastically about the morning's cricket, which had seen Geoffrey Boycott and John Edrich go about their undemonstrative business in a stand which eventually reached 172. Trevor insisted on buying the next drink soon after the first. I then had to return to my duties, although I caught up with him on the fourth afternoon of the match, when we again talked cricket. Sadly I never saw him again except, at a distance, the night the match finished. It was after midnight and he and some friends, all laughing their heads off, were leaving Harry's Nightery, an unforgettable Bridgetown nightspot. Harry himself, in a plummy voice which would have made Winston Churchill sound like a rough end costermonger, introduced his female performers. When extolling the virtues of the naked female form, his choice of adjectives was as amazing as it was inexhaustible. The cabaret itself was basic in the extreme, but we would all have queued for hours to listen to Harry alone. It was quite a monologue. We didn't even notice that the bar had run out of ice.

On one occasion in the box we were visited by Ainsley Harriott. A brilliant chef and a man of great humour, he presented *Ready Steady Cook*, which ran on BBC daytime television for many years. When he came to our box in 2008, he asked me if I would like to do the show. It sounded tremendous fun. I was quick to accept the chance to take on Phillip Silverstone, a charming wine expert who had just moved from Essex to the east coast of the United States, where he still prospers. The programme was recorded in front of a lively audience in a studio near The Oval. We were both assigned to celebrity chefs, which meant that in our respective corners, Phillip and I scurried around like demented kitchen maids fetching this, grating that and breaking the occasional egg. We were once or twice asked to lend a hand with something it would have been almost impossible, even for me, to get wrong.

The programme began with our chefs – Phillip, I think, had Antony Worrall Thompson in his corner and I had Phil Vickery in mine – working out what they were going to cook and then getting down to it. Soon after the start, Ainsley went up to Phillip, asked how he had got into the wine business and then talked him through his career. Some fierce cooking followed before Ainsley came up to me to do much the same.

First he said, 'Henry, I want to ask you a favour. May I call you "Blowers"?'

'Yes, of course,' I replied, 'but only on one understanding, and that is that I can call you "Ainers".'

Ainsley almost choked and the studio audience had hysterics. It took me a moment to see what they were laughing at. In my mind I had spelt it as 'Ainers'. Everyone else in the studio was convinced I had meant 'Anus'. In their infinite wisdom, those in charge of the cutting room edited it out. Which was a pity.

My award for gallantry in the line of duty goes unquestionably to Marmaduke Hussey when he was Chairman of the BBC. After five days' active service in the war, he was badly wounded and a German surgeon removed his right leg in an operation carried out on the edge of the battlefield. Thereafter he limped his way courageously through life. He was a big man, standing six foot five inches tall. He weighed seventeen stone, and so lugging himself and his tin leg around on just a stick was by no means an easy or pain-free business. Before becoming Chairman of the BBC, he had been Managing Director and Chief Executive of Times Newspapers, then owned by the Thomson Organisation. Hussey was in charge when they took on the print unions in 1978–79. It was a ruinous battle for the organisation and resulted in the papers going out of business for eleven months. Hussey never lost his determination, his cheerfulness and his humour throughout it all. When publication was resumed, Thomson sold the titles to Rupert Murdoch, who kept Hussey but moved him sideways. Then, in 1986, he was made Chairman of the BBC by Margaret Thatcher and held the job for ten years, by which time he had become the longest-serving Chairman.

The MCC usually invite the BBC Chairman to one day of the Lord's Test match. Whenever Hussey was able to accept the invitation, he invariably came to see us in our turreted box at the top of the Pavilion. Not only that, he walked unflinch-ingly up three flights of unforgiving stairs with his tin leg. He knew Johnners – they had both served in the Grenadier Guards – and he would stay with us for at least half an hour, however much his aides tried to pull him away. He made sure he met and spoke to all of us and, by the time he left, we all felt he was firmly on our side. His visit was a great moment for us and he so clearly loved it himself.

His cheerfulness was a great tonic and somehow was reflected in the way he wore his comfortable, lived-in, dark grey suit. He was the friendliest and most approachable of men. No one could have been more interested in what was going on, and when he told us what a great job we were doing, he clearly meant it. He still talked about 'the wireless' too. He and Fred Trueman always had something to catch up on. There was lots of laughter when they talked. Finally, one of his entou-rage would pluck up the courage to touch him on the shoulder. By the time he left, we had begun to feel we were more impor-tant than we were really were, and just occasionally that's no bad thing. Off he would go, limping back down the three flights of stairs, smiling all the way. I believe he was usually in pain, but you would never have known. He was the only BBC Chairman who ever came near us. Director-Generals, Ian Trethowan apart, have been notable by their absence too.

It would be impossible to imagine a greater contrast from Hussey than when Alice Cooper – born Vincent Damon

Furnier – came into the box to chat with Aggers. It was the first day of the third Test at Lord's against South Africa in August 2012 when the Godfather of Shock Rock, with flowing locks to match, popped in to see us. Aggers's charm almost reduced his rasping voice to a rough-edged purr as they worked their way through his career, his songs and his bizarre stage props. These included such homely items as a guillotine and an electric chair, with a few deadly snakes thrown in.

Geoffrey Boycott was out of the box during their talk and did not come back until just after they had finished. He was told that Aggers had been talking to Alice Cooper. He then spotted a lovely lady dressed beguilingly in white at the back of the box. Geoffrey loves to make his mark with all the gorgeous ladies – as well as the famous. 'Ah, Alice Cooper herself,' you could hear him think when he saw this vision in white. With the broadest of grins and his sun hat tipped back a fraction, he moved swiftly and gave Alice Cooper's wife the handshake of the century. ''Ow do, luv. Nice to meet you.' When he discovered his mistake, he coped with his usual aplomb.

One of our greatest friends and supporters over the years was the blind pianist George Shearing, who insisted he was a pianist who happened to be blind – a subtle but real distinction if you think about it. I first met him in the commentary box at Lord's. He was seventy-one, warm and cuddly. He had come to talk to Johnners in June 1990 on the Saturday of the second Test against New Zealand, a match which was one of those interminable, old-fashioned draws. Shearing was born a cockney in the East End of London, the youngest of nine children. He turned himself into one of the great jazz pianists. He spoke with an accent that revealed a slight but charming American input – the cockney had gone years before. Sometimes when I have chatted with blind people I have felt a slight sense of guilt that I can see and they cannot. Not with George, who left you feeling that being blind was almost an asset. He was enormous fun and one of the most remarkable and memorable people I have ever met.

His father had been a coalman who delivered his coal in a horse and cart. With his usual twinkle, George said, 'I always think he should have put on his cart "COAL A LA CART" or "COAL DE SACK".' There was no musician in his family and he had a splendid explanation for his musical talents: 'I imagine, in a previous life, I was Mozart's guide dog.' He lived most of the year in New York, and listened to as much of *TMS* as he could. Whenever he and his second wife, Ellie, who was as lovely and understated as he was himself, were in London during a Lord's Test match, they did their best to come up from their beloved Cotswolds to see us.

A year or two later they visited us again, when he told a wonderful story. He was flying, with his guide dog in the days that was allowed, from London to New York. For some reason the aeroplane had been forced to land at Gander in Newfoundland. While most of the passengers went off to the in-transit lounge, George, who was in first-class, stayed put. After a short while, the captain, who knew George, came back from the flight deck to have a word with him.

He was just about to go when he said, 'Look, George, I am going outside to stretch my legs for a few minutes. Why don't I take your dog with me?'

George readily agreed and off they went. Twenty minutes later the captain returned his dog. An hour after that the passengers had still not got back on board and George was anxious he might miss an appointment in New York. He asked the steward if there was a problem. Reluctantly the steward admitted that there was.

'I am afraid, Mr Shearing, the passengers are refusing to get back on board the aircraft because they say they saw the captain being led down the steps of his aeroplane by a guide dog.'

If it isn't true, it deserves to be.

Many entertaining characters came to the *TMS* box during the lunch interval on the Saturday of a Test match for 'A View from the Boundary', the interview slot that was originally hosted by Johnners. That was how George Shearing had first come into my life. After Johnners died in 1994, the interviewing duties were shared among the team, until Aggers took over in 2007. What fun it was too. When Peter

Baxter had picked out a victim for me, Shilpa would arm me with a sheaf of background information. I devoured these and arrived in the box with a couple of pages of scrawled questions. The first two or three were useful when starting off, but usually the interview quickly turned into a conversation. Then my list of questions acted as an aide-memoire if things should get a bit sticky later on.

I had a feeling that my three favourite turns on 'A View from the Boundary' were going to be amusing, and they didn't let me down. Nigel Havers and Boris Johnson were bound to be fun, but so too, was Dennis Skinner, now the last of the truly old-fashioned Labour MPs. I first met 'the Beast of Bolsover' at Denis Compton's memorial service at Westminster Abbey. I had been placed in a pew which was pretty close to the action and effectively saving a single. Without needing binoculars, I had a reasonable view of the pulpit and the clergy. The umpires were just about to come out when I saw a short, elderly, thickset man hastening down the aisle towards where I was sitting. It was Dennis. He said later that he had spotted me. He asked my neighbour to move over so that he could sit next to me. He introduced himself and we had one of those feverish whispered conversations that happen in places where you are not meant to talk. You never quite manage to hear what the other chap says. Peter Baxter was sitting in the row behind me. He realised that the Beast and I were made for each other.

In the interview itself, Dennis started out by testing my memory about Denis Compton's figures in 1947, his *annus mirabilis* – 3,816 runs with eighteen centuries. Skinner's own credentials were good. He told me that when he was a miner he used to play in the Bassetlaw League. He said he was a touch quicker than Dominic Cork, the Derbyshire and England bowler – distance can lend enchantment. Cycling, snooker and tennis were his main sporting activities. He was not averse to running the odd marathon either, as well as relentlessly harrying politicians on the other side of the house – and his own too if need be. Then there was heel-and-toe road walking with the funny gait that goes with it. 'My dad said to me – he was a miner as well as me – "Hey, what the bloody hell are you doing? Tommy Lunn says to me tha'rt walking past his house, waggling thee arse."' He was a singer too, and, among others, took off Slim Whitman, Johnnie Ray and Frankie Laine. He once sang 'Shall We Dance' at the Albert Hall in front of six thousand people. A great man of many parts.

He told me about his early life at the Glapwell Colliery before he gave Thatcher and Tebbit a going-over. He confessed that he had once, in the House, called David Owen a 'pompous sod' and had had to take an early bath when he refused to apologise. He had also called the diminutive Colin Moynihan the 'Miniature for Sport'. His admirable motto is 'Don't moan, don't whine, don't whinge.' He had it in for Mrs Thatcher and the Tory party about something which will resonate with all cricket lovers: 'She didn't just close the pits, you know. They got rid of the cricket fields, because every mine had a cricket field and a football field. A hell of a lot of those went in the process.' Yes. They did.

It was a heart-warming half hour. When Dennis left me, I felt I would rather vote for him than a lot of wishy-washy Tories I have met.

Nigel Havers was wonderful. I met the man I had been meeting on the screen from the first time I saw *Chariots of Fire*. His charm is like Tom Graveney's cover drive, when the ball would purr its way to the boundary. His smile was such that strong girls wobbled at the knees. His manners would make Professor Higgins blush. We had the most effortless conversation I can remember. After agreeing that his success in *Chariots of Fire* was hugely important for him, he revealed that it was only his bravery that enabled him to keep going, although he did not put it quite like that. Playing the part of Lord Andrew Lindsay, he had to learn to hurdle. He was doing well when, while showing off one day to Ben Cross, who was playing Harold Abrahams, he clipped a hurdle, dislocated a shoulder and snapped his wrist. 'I thought, "If I tell them about that, I'll never make the film." So it was a very easy and economical decision to make and I just strapped it up ... and I survived.' He admitted that when he went over the hurdles with champagne glasses on them, they were taped down. He also owned up to telling porkies about his age, to preferring Burgundy to Claret, to being a Fulham supporter, to liking his steaks rare and being a good friend of Princess Diana.

I asked him who his three guests would be if the Grill Room at the Savoy offered him a table for four for dinner. His first choice was his late father, who was Lord Chancellor, followed by Judi Dench and David Niven. If they would not mind squeezing in an extra chair, he would offer it to Alec Guinness. What an evening it would have been.

Boris Johnson arrived at Old Trafford for the Test against Pakistan in 2006. He had not been there before, but he had been to the football ground, 'to give a speech for my friend, George Osborne'. I wonder if they are still friends. He expected great things later that day from Monty Panesar; he admitted to once making 25 in the fathers' match at his son's prep school. His disobedient fair hair was even more all over the place than it is today. He was delightful in a boyish, happy-go-lucky way and his massive intelligence shone fiercely through as the conversation ranged over all sorts of topics. After realising management consultancy was not for him, he had joined *The Times*. He spent a good deal of time in Brussels learning that the European Union was never going to work: 'We want to be ruled by people who speak our language. It's very difficult to persuade people otherwise.' He spoke of his visit to Liverpool to apologise for writing that people were over-sentimental when Liverpudlian Ken Bigley was kidnapped and murdered in Baghdad. Boris took it in his stride. He talked fondly of Michael Heseltine, whose Henley constituency he inherited. That friendship might not have withstood the test of Brussels either. He talked about the thought processes behind his novel, *Seventy-Two Virgins*. By then, he was the motoring correspondent for *GQ* magazine and had driven up in a fast car he was testing, but he also stuck up like nobody's business for cycling. It is partly as a result of his mayoral activities that London is now full of bicycle lanes. Boris is not flavour-of-the-month with cab drivers. He was demure when I asked if he wanted one day to become Prime Minister, but he was determined to be a success as shadow higher education spokesman. His guests for dinner at the Savoy Grill began with the Emperor Augustus, because he wanted to know how he used Latin. Mary Magdalene would be sitting on his right, because he wanted to get to the bottom of *The Da Vinci Code*. Madonna was the third choice, in case things needed livening up a bit. An extra chair would be pushed in for Ian Botham, who would be given the chance to see how the Emperor Augustus coped with a few bouncers in the nets the next morning.

There are many pitfalls commentators have to try and avoid, most are of their own making, but a few are thrust upon them and more difficult to sidestep. Alun Williams, a famous broadcaster in Wales, joined *TMS* once, when New Zealand played a one-day international in Swansea in 1973. His first major pitfall had come at the very beginning of his broadcasting career.

On his first day he reported in the morning to the head-quarters at Llandaff by the Cathedral in Cardiff. He was instructed to go down to the Arms Park where Glamorgan were playing Hampshire. He was told to sit in the press box taking notes. At the end of the day he had to catch the bus back to Llandaff, writing out his minute-long piece for the sports news as he went. Then he had to sit outside the studio and go in when he was called for. He did exactly as he was told. When he arrived back from the cricket he was under-standably nervous before his first broadcast.

One of the presenters going off for the day saw this. He went up to Williams and said, 'Boyo, there is one important thing to do. You must learn your first line by heart. Then you will find that all the rest will fall into place.'

Williams thanked him for his advice. He then walked up and down outside the studio for the next fifteen minutes repeating aloud to himself, 'I have just come back from Cardiff Arms Park, where I have been watching Glamorgan play Hampshire. I have just come back from Cardiff Arms Park . . .'

He must have gone through it about fifteen times when the studio manager put his head round the door and said it was time to go in. Williams went in and sat down. He put the headphones on, the red light above his head came on and he heard the presenter in his ear.

'And now cricket,' he began. 'We will go straight over to Alun Williams, who has just come back from Cardiff Arms

Park, where he has been watching Glamorgan play Hampshire.'

There was a pause and then Alun began rather limply, 'Yes, I have just come back from Cardiff Arms Park, where I have been watching Glamorgan play Hampshire.'

13

ENTHUSIASMS
AND INDULGENCES

C AKES and double deckers, pigeons and planes – when
I started my career in the commentary box, who could
have predicted that such things would play such an important
role for so many years? Johnners once said that my acute
busitis came about because I was run over by that bus when I
was at school, but for me they are simply a part of what I can
see in front of me. They help form the overall picture and, I
think, deserve a mention. The crowd can see them and so why
shouldn't our listeners hear about them too?

I had enormous fun over the years joining local commentary teams in other countries in between my stints for *Test
Match Special*, and I always loved joining them even if my
own idiosyncratic way of doing things may have come as a
nasty shock to their listeners. One of the most amusing
moments was in Barbados when I was working for the
Voice of Barbados. The West Indies were playing England
at Kensington Oval under Ian Botham's captaincy early in
March 1981. We had quite an array of commentators, led
by the unmistakable Les 'Shell' Harris, who had once

bowled leg-breaks and googlies for Barbados. Shell couldn't field to save his life, which may have shortened his brief career. He was the jolliest of men and had the thickest of Bajan accents. This made him incomprehensible to untrained ears. Another member of our team was former fast bowler Richard 'Prof' Edwards, who bowled fast for the West Indies in five Test matches in the late sixties. His nickname came from comedian 'Professor' Jimmy Edwards of *Whack-O!* fame. Prof Edwards was the most genial of men and a great leg-puller.

Throughout this match there were any number of small-ish brown, pigeon-like birds flying around. As you can imagine, I was soon on their case and was anxious to identify them. Prof told me they were called 'mahogany birds'. For the next five days my commentary was full of mahogany birds. In fact, I think I was calling the end from which we were talking the 'Mahogany Bird End'. Whenever I mentioned a mahogany bird, I noticed it always raised a smile among my colleagues. On the journeys back to my hotel in the evening, two of the taxi drivers had said to me, 'Man, you sure like those mahogany birds.' One of them had gone on to say, 'You be careful,' and roared with laughter. I took this as a compliment and felt as if I had just reached fifty.

On the fifth day of the match, I described at some length the antics of yet another group of mahogany birds. When I came off the air, Prof tapped me on the shoulder and finally told me, to my great mortification, that the mahogany bird is actually a scavenger that looks like a small cockroach. He went on to say that 'mahogany bird' in Barbados is also a euphemism for a lavatory seat. Thank you, Prof.

One of the strangest experiences I have had with planes occurred in India, but not when I was commentating. I was working for Mark Mascarenhas, who had bought the rights for the series between India and the West Indies in 1994–95. It was probably true to say that the huge Ilyushin transport aircraft which ferried commentators and equipment around India was not the least memorable aspect of the tour. This Russian plane, piloted by Russians, provided us with more than its share of anxious moments.

Garry Sobers, Mansoor Ali Khan, the former Nawab of Pataudi, and I were three of the commentary team. 'Tiger' (a childhood nickname) Pataudi hated flying, Garry didn't much care for it either, and this elderly, shaking heavyweight aircraft made me more nervous than usual. The heavy equipment was loaded the night before we flew. We invariably started off the next day at an hour which made one wonder if it was worth going to bed. The three of us had pleaded anxiety and had been shown by the crew into a sort of cubbyhole immediately behind the flight deck. We fitted into it without much to spare. Tiger's remedy when it came to dealing with his aeronautical demons was a large bottle of Russian vodka. He clutched it tightly as he mounted the rickety steps to our seats. We were usually well into our second glass before the engines started turning. This became an official early-morning ceremony for the three of us, ending only when the wheels were on the ground at our destination.

That first glass was usually drunk in silence. Pataudi was not a loquacious man at such moments and in the Ilyushin he communicated only in grunts. Even at that hour, Garry was cheerful enough and he and I chuntered along until it was time for full throttle, at which point a heavy thunderstorm would have had to try hard to make itself heard. I have never known an aircraft shake as this one did as it lurched down the runway, accelerating painfully slowly. It did nothing for my nerves and it always seemed long odds against it ever leaving the ground. By the time it juuuust lifted itself off the runway, the three of us were white-knuckled, clutching anything we could lay our hands on. We held our breath and prayed. Every time we took off we seemed to clear the trees at the end of the runway by about a millimetre and a half, at which point Pataudi would be in total shock while Garry and I suddenly ran out of conversation.

Tiger Pataudi was bright, patrician and determined, with the manner of an old-fashioned aristocrat which blended so well with a splendid sense of humour. One evening at our hotel in Calcutta, an American who had just been introduced to him asked him what he did. 'I am a prince,' was the measured reply; 'you had better be careful.' Then came a big grin, followed by, 'What will you have to drink?' It was his determination, together with an extraordinary talent, which enabled him to go on playing not just cricket, but Test cricket for his country with only one eye. He had lost his right eye in a car crash when he was captain of Oxford University. He took over the captaincy of India in 1962 at the age of twenty-one, not long after the accident. He was in charge for forty of his forty-six Tests and he was the captain who first taught India's players to believe they could win.

Tiger loved nothing more than to play practical jokes on his friends. Perhaps the former Australian captain Ian Chappell paid him the greatest compliment – from an Australian anyway – when he called him a 'lovable larrikin'. He tells the story too, of the Australian players, media and television officials flying from Chandigarh to Lahore for the 1996 World Cup final. The players and most of the journalists were in economy, the officials in first class. When Chappell and Shane Warne got on board, Mark Mascarenhas, who had bought the television rights for the tournament, told them to sit by him in first class. Tiger and his wife, Sharmila, a famous Bollywood actress, were sitting in the front row of economy. He saw Ayaz Memon, a journalist, about to sit up front with the nobs. Tiger asked Memon if he could see his boarding pass. Memon gave it to him and it had on it the red, first-class strip. Being in economy, Tiger had the green economy strip on his. With a good fielder's sleight of hand, Tiger swapped his own boarding pass for Memon's and handed it back upside down, so the green strip was not visible. Moments later Tiger and Sharmila were sitting in first class, Tiger with his patrician, as-of-right look on his face.

On the last day of the first Test at Lord's against South Africa in 2017, I bumped into Sunny Gavaskar, perhaps India's best ever opening batsman, in the Media Centre. He told me the story of one of the more dramatic practical jokes Tiger played on his visitors to the Pataudi estates in Bhopal. On one occasion he had a number of his Indian side staying there and had arranged a shooting expedition for them. They were out in the thick of the bush when they were suddenly surrounded and held up at gunpoint by a bunch of dacoits (bandits). The players were scared stiff and one of them, the off-spinner Erapalli Prasanna, made a run for it. One of the dacoits raised his gun and fired and Prasanna sprawled to the ground. The other cricketers were in panic, but Tiger was laughing helplessly. He had set the whole thing up. Some of his estate workers had dressed up as dacoits and Tiger had let Prasanna in on the story. He was instructed to bolt. When the gun went off – it was a blank containing gunpowder but no bullet – he had to lie still where he fell. Now, when I first went to India to cover the England tour in 1963–64, Tiger took Peter Parfitt and me partridge-shooting in Bhopal, but that day the dacoits must have missed their cue.

The story I am about to tell may be the first time, for a great many years at any rate, that Shane Warne has played a walk-on part. In early August 2016, the third Test against Pakistan was played at Edgbaston. As usual, Warne was working for Sky Television and we were all staying in the same hotel in the middle of Birmingham. When I had finished my last stint on the second day, I walked round to the car park and on the way caught up with Michael Vaughan and Phil Tufnell. We agreed to meet in the bar of the hotel and have dinner together. A splendid bottle of Italian red wine got us off to an impressive start and it was not long before this led to another. The likelihood of our actually taking on board any solids that evening sharply receded. The red wine touched the spot. It was after half past nine and another bottle when we were joined by a grinning Shane Warne, whose gleaming white teeth made him look as if he was taking part in a toothpaste advertisement. He also got stuck into the red wine.

After a while Warney must have gone to have a word with a waiter. A few minutes later the waiter leaned over the table carrying what looked like a glass bowl with some dark brown liquid swirling about in the bottom. 'Come on, Blowers, drink this,' Warney insisted. I was in no mood to refuse such an order. I took the bowl in two hands and raised it to my lips. I had had a couple of agreeable slurps and was closing in for the kill when suddenly something hit my nose. I pulled back and found there was a smaller glass standing in the middle of the brown liquid. This had caught me as I bent forward to drink. I remember being surprised to find some liquid inside. I thought, 'I'd better have that little lot too,' and down it went. It was pretty decent. My immediate thought was 'Terrific, I could do that again.' Within a couple of minutes, Warney, looking more than ever like a smiling dentist's assistant, had come up with another glass bowl. That went down even better. And on it went. The next morning at breakfast they were all laughing their heads off when I arrived. I was told I had been drinking Jägerbombs, a lethal mixture of Jägermeister and Red Bull – short pitched and fierce – and I had managed five, which was considerably over par. Although I don't remember seeing him around at the time, my stage partner Swanny (Graeme Swann) has been telling everyone he put me to bed. Sadly, I never felt a thing. I slept like a log and did not have a hangover or even feel particularly fragile the next day. When I got to the commentary box, I suggested we might try it again that evening, but there were no takers, which was disappointing. What a cowardly lot they were.

England went on to win the Test match, but not before *TMS* had learned the secret of how Geoffrey Boycott protected his wealth. On the last day he and Ed Smith were on the air together early in Pakistan's second innings. They were a couple of wickets down and Boycott said that the odds were now very much in England's favour. Smith replied that cold logic would have told us that the odds at that point were in favour of Pakistan. Boycott would have none of it and said he would have a bet with Smith that England would win the match. Smith reiterated what he had said and Boycott pretended they had made a bet. Before long it became clear that England were going to win and Boycott, tongue in cheek, said that Smith owed him money. In order to find a home for it, he got out an impressively full wallet. I am not sure I had ever seen his wallet before. Soon afterwards he told listeners of his sensible precautions in his playing days with Yorkshire and England. The last thing he did before going out to bat was always to take all the folding money out of his wallet and put it in his batting trousers. He went on to say that one of the Yorkshire physiotherapists had told him that if ever Boycott was hit and knocked out, he would make sure he was first on the scene.

Piers Morgan's connection with *Test Match Special* came about on 9 June 2007 at Old Trafford, when Simon Mann interviewed him for 'A View from the Boundary'. There is no greater cricket lover than Piers. In 1996, England cricketers Ian Botham and Allan Lamb sued the Pakistan captain Imran Khan for libel because of accusations he had made against both players in newspapers and magazines in England and India. Morgan played a small part in the story of the subsequent case in the High Court. As the editor of the *Daily Mirror*, he would have sanctioned the call made by one of his assistants asking me if I would write a daily piece about the forthcoming legal battle. They wanted it written in the idiom of *TMS*. I thought it would be fun and signed up. When I turned up, rather nervously, at the High Court, I met Peter Allen. He was actually covering the case for the *Mirror* while I was nothing more than an added extra. It was a meeting which began one of the great friendships of my life. Peter is now based in Paris, and there is scarcely a newspaper in the world he has not worked for. He is a brilliant journalist, an impressive man and an exceptional and intrepid guide when I go to Paris.

The libel case was heard in July before Mr Justice French, who was arguably past his sell-by date, in Court 13 in the Royal Courts of Justice. It lasted for thirteen extraordinary days. There was a massive cast too. George Carman, the most famous libel barrister of this time, was acting for Imran. He was five-star entertainment on his own. His opponent, Charles Gray, a considerable figure in the same trade who would only have doffed his hat to Carman, did duty in court for Botham and Lamb in a more unassuming manner. There was a remarkable array of cricketing witnesses. The first Test between England and Pakistan began at Lord's midway through the trial and interrupted with my presence in Court 13. For all his magic, one could only feel that George Carman knew he was fighting a losing battle. Nonetheless, his sharp questioning gave us some wonderful entertainment and his waspish sarcasm produced much laughter.

The two most inadvertently amusing witnesses were Geoffrey Boycott and the umpire Donald Oslear. Boycott came straight from Lord's during the Test and so I was unable to see him perform in the box. His appearance was much photographed by the papers. He had arrived looking as if he was an advertiser's sandwich board. His working clothes were clearly sponsored and most bore the sponsor's name. When the judge asked him why he was dressed as he was, he said, a trifle self-righteously, that his duties had not allowed him the time to change. Boycott, who put the judge right about any number of things, was called by Imran's side, as was David Lloyd, also in the television commentary box for the Test match – his dress was unsponsored. Oslear was tiresomely pompous when both the judge and Carman spoke about the 'rules' of cricket. He told them, rather as if he was addressing a class of recalcitrant children, that cricket had 'laws', not rules. Both Carman and Mr Justice French reacted as if they had been disturbed by an unnecessarily loud mosquito and they swatted Oslear away. The umpire did his best to leave them in no doubt that they were neither of them fit to remain in court if they did not grasp the importance and significance of the 'laws'.

While all this was going on, Imran's beautiful wife, Jemima Khan, was sitting near her husband. A long bench in the spectators' gallery was filled with her family, led by her mother, Annabel, after whom the Berkeley Square nightclub had been named. Kathy Botham was also, but more discreetly, in attendance. Mr Carman made an impassioned final speech, while Mr Gray, who must have been feeling confident of the outcome, came across as the more comfortable voice of reason when he had his turn. The judge had his say and all but directed the jury to find for Botham and Lamb.

The jury retired on the twelfth afternoon, and late on the

thirteenth morning, after more than five hours of deliberations, they came down 10–2 in a majority verdict in favour of Imran. By then I was back in court because Pakistan had won the Test match two days earlier. The jury had, therefore, brought about a stirring Pakistan double. Maybe they had sensed opportunism in Imran's opponents. Botham and Lamb were said to have refused the chance to settle out of court, an expensive mistake. When the verdict came, no one was more dumbfounded than the judge, who blinked and stuttered quite a bit as he tidied up at the end.

When it was all over and Peter Allen and I had filed our pieces for the *Mirror*, we beat it to one of the pubs on the other side of the Strand for a sharpener. After a while we were joined by no less a person than George Carman, who without letting his hair down was in understandably good form and enjoyed his red wine with a vengance. I was introduced to him and, with a brow that became suddenly furrowed underneath his dashing white hair, he proceeded to lecture me for about three minutes, telling me in no uncertain terms that Chatham House Rules applied to anything that I should now hear about the case. He went on a bit and clearly had it in for me. I later told my brother, John, a high court judge himself, that Carman had not regarded me as a friend. John told me this was probably because he had heard Carman's previous case and he had lost it.

When Peter Allen and I left the George and Dragon, we decided to continue our revelry in Chelsea. We caught a taxi and while we were going down the Mall, his telephone rang. It was Piers Morgan calling to congratulate us on what we had written. He told Peter to tell me I had the front page of the next day's *Daily Mirror* to myself. Peter, who must have been understandably put out by this, was extremely generous about it. He then told his editor we were in the taxi with George Carman. Piers told him he would like to congratulate him himself. Of course, we had left Carman drinking, a trifle unsteadily, in the Strand. Peter, bless his heart, told Piers to hold on a moment and he would put him on. He then passed his telephone to me, whispering that I was now George Carman. I thought quite hard for a moment. The chances of Piers thinking my voice was Carman's were remote. I took the receiver and in a loud whisper I first told Piers that it was me. I added that Carman had had too much to drink and was asleep in the taxi between Peter and me and could not therefore speak to him. To my surprise, he seemed to be satisfied with this. He then told me I appeared to be able to write and that if at any time I wanted a job I was to come and see him. Then, unscathed, I passed him back to Peter. I rang Piers a week or two later and said yes, I would be interested in a job. I fear that by then I had dropped back in the betting. Or maybe he had other things on his mind. Sadly, I was never to become Blowers of the *Mirror*.

When Marie Antoinette famously said, '*Qu'ils mangent de la brioche,*' or 'Let them eat cake', she was unlikely to have been having percipient thoughts about *Test Match Special*. Nonetheless cakes were to become an integral part of the programme. Maybe Brian Johnston was thinking along similar lines as the French queen when, soon after joining us in 1970, he mentioned his love of chocolate cakes. It was then, curiously enough, the British queen, Elizabeth II, who a few years later confirmed with some emphasis that fruit cakes had taken over in the post-Johnners *TMS*. I doubt Johnners himself would ever have been converted to fruit cakes. He was inflexible about his eating arrangements.

For her pains, Marie Antoinette lost her head, while the seed Johnners had originally planted went on to flourish. It all began in 1974 when a lady who had heard him talk of his passion for chocolate cake sent him a large and particularly good-looking one on the first day of the Lord's Test match. Rumour had it that on that day he ate no fewer than thirteen slices himself. It was also said that he did six twenty-minute spells of commentary and never mentioned a single ball – which may have been a slight exaggeration. But a precedent had been created. Johnners did not spare himself in extolling the virtues of this first chocolate cake. He banged on about it to such an extent that all the able-bodied ladies in the land who were listening went into their kitchens that evening and baked chocolate cakes for Queen and Country. They sent every one of them to us. We did our best, which, as it happened, was not good enough. As a result, the left-over cakes were sent to a neighbouring hospice, as still happens today.

As soon as Johnners had died our listeners mysteriously and inexplicably, I thought, began to send us an abundance of fruit cakes. There have been some who have suggested that I have been slow to spot the connection between *Test Match Special* and fruit cakes. A few years later, we received the fruit cake to end all fruit cakes. In 2001, Steve Waugh's Australians came to England and, as usual, played the second Test match at Lord's. Buckingham Palace announced that the Queen was going to come to the match. She always likes to come to Lord's to meet the players when Australia are playing. She comes to the Test matches against the other countries too, but not so frequently. We always know when she arrives because her personal standard is raised on the flagpole over the committee room. The royal visit lasts for about two and a half to three hours and is a much-loved feature of the Lord's Test. The Queen watches from the committee room and then meets the players in front of the Pavilion during an extended tea interval. I am sure she then gets a cup of tea herself before returning to the Palace.

To celebrate this visit, the PR machine at the Palace had decreed that the chefs there should make a suitably regal fruit cake, which Her Majesty would bring with her and present to us during the tea interval. I think the cake actually went on ahead of her with a motorcycle escort rather than being tucked away in the boot of the Rolls. I heard it was a bit miffed at missing out on the Rolls, but then not every fruit cake gets a motorcycle escort. At the start of the extended tea interval, five of us – Aggers, CMJ, the Bearded Wonder, Peter Baxter and me – pushed our way round through the crowd. It took a while and we arrived only just before the Queen returned to the committee room after meeting the players. We filed in and the Queen presented the cake to Peter Baxter on a salver. She looked a trifle quizzical, as if she was not sure of her brief.

She said to Peter, 'They tell me people give you cakes?'

He confirmed that this was so, while Marie Antoinette would surely have felt her fellow queen was on the right lines. Then Peter began to introduce her to the rest of us.

When I shook her hand, she said, 'You must find it awfully difficult to know what to say when nothing is happening.'

'One of the things about *Test Match Special*, Your Majesty,' I replied, 'is that when rain or bad light has stopped play and nothing is happening, we carry on talking about anything and everything, and many of our listeners write in and say how much better we are when nothing is happening.'

I hoped this might bring a smile to her face. But I got that badly wrong. She looked a trifle solemn and her head seemed to sway slightly, and she came back in a more hushed voice with, 'How dreadfully sad.'

She moved on to Aggers. They shook hands and in mid-grip Aggers said, 'Ma'am, did you bake it yourself?'

A worse case of *lèse-majesté* would be hard to imagine. If he had said that to Elizabeth I, he would have been in the Tower of London well before the close of play.

The Queen came back strongly: 'No,' she said, 'but it was made under strict personal supervision.'

I am delighted to be able to tell you that a sizeable dose of really classy royal brandy must have gone into it. When later, back in the media spaceship at the Nursery End, we cut into the cake, you only had to have half a smell. It was, of course, delicious.

The final words we had with the monarch came after we had all been introduced to her. Play had already begun again and she turned to Peter Baxter.

'With all of you here, how are you remaining on the air?' she asked.

'Well, Your Majesty,' Peter replied, 'we have an Australian.'

'Oh,' said the Queen, very cheerfully. 'They can be very useful, can't they.'

Our Australian was Tim Lane, a fine commentator, who covered that tour for the Australian Broadcasting Corporation. He most nobly held the fort for us – and was, indeed, very useful.

While cakes of all sorts still come into the *TMS* box thick and fast, nowadays they are part of a great variety of splendid delicacies. We also receive cupcakes, currant buns, mince pies, doughnuts, fudge, shortbread, cheeses, sausage rolls, nuts, raisins, pork pies – Aggers has located a regular source in Melton Mowbray, the Mecca for pork pies – and all kinds of other delicious things. At the end of a busy day, our box can look a bit like the store in *Open All Hours*. Aggers would make a good Ronnie Barker to Andrew Samson's David Jason. It is a wonder the BBC bother to give us a meal allowance when we're away from home.

The caterers at the Test match grounds sometimes join in too. Those at Lord's are especially inventive. Occasionally one of the chaps working at the entrance to the Media Centre will stagger in with an offering from the Lord's kitchens. Just lately we have enjoyed some really big cakes with a cricket motif, their surfaces iced in green, with little fielders dotted around in improbable positions. And yes, we do eat them, although 'friends' from other places such as David 'Bumble' Lloyd and Mike Atherton often pop in to pinch a slice or two. Bumble has a particularly sweet tooth – but then he did once belong to *TMS*.

I am occasionally asked if we make things up when we thank listeners for yet another chocolate cake. I can assure you we have no need to do that. I am also asked if I make up the buses or pigeons or cranes I like to describe for the listeners. I am pretty certain I have never made up a bus. I can remember, though, when nothing much was happening soon after we moved from the Pavilion to the Nursery End at Lord's, saying, 'If I were talking to you from the top of the Pavilion, I would almost certainly be able to tell you that there are two, or perhaps three, handsome red double-deckers going up and down the Wellington Road.' I suppose some might call that a form of cheating; they might also suggest that on the odd occasion I have got a little carried away with my enthusiasms.

Once, with great excitement, I told listeners that there were 'two ... no, three ... look, four double-deckers in a convention of buses in the Wellington Road!'

I then heard Peter Baxter whisper loudly from the back of the box, 'Someone tell Blowers it's a bus stop.'

14

MY ENCHANTING
GHOSTS

YOU can see from all I have written just what a wonderful time I have had working for *Test Match Special*. I
think the most important ingredient in this curious life I have
led has been luck. I was lucky to inherit from my father a
voice that for some reason worked over the air. Throughout
my career I have repeatedly been told about the distinctive-
ness of my voice. I suppose I must accept that, but at times I
find it surprising because whenever I hear a recording I think
I sound such a pompous prat. I am not sure, though, that one
ever hears one's own voice in the way listeners do. When I am
actually talking, I can of course hear myself, but I really don't
think it can be the same noise that the listeners hear. If it is, I
am surprised the BBC didn't kick me into touch years ago. I
was lucky too, to have the gift of the gab – and this was passed
on to me more by my mother than my father, who was not
such a natural chatterbox. On the other hand, the ability to
choose the right word, and maybe even to have a number of
alternatives, will have come more from my father. Then I was
extremely lucky to be given the chance to use these inherited

attributes in the way that I have. In truth, it astonishes me that I was given that chance, because I have just listened to a recording of one of my first broadcasts and I really didn't think it was very good. Maybe if there is any talent, it has been my ability over the years to knock all these natural gifts into the right shape for broadcasting.

I still get asked if I think I would have played cricket for England if I had not had that altercation with a bus. It is an unanswerable question. I have no more of a clue than I did on 7 June 1957 when I bicycled into the wretched thing. My gut feeling is that I think it would have been highly unlikely. I suppose I should feel flattered that the question is asked at all. The one thing I do know is that even if I had been that good, I would have had to retire when I was in my thirties. This means the bus did me a huge favour. I have still managed to have a life in cricket and I have been able to keep going until two weeks before my seventy-eighth birthday. That's one in the eye for the bus.

I am lucky and extremely grateful to have been left with so many happy, extraordinary and amusing memories to keep me going. Far from being sad, I am now excited about all the things that lie ahead. The one thing I am not going to do is retire altogether. Already there are nearly a hundred theatre shows lurking round the corner and and any number of speaking engagements. Maybe there will be some more broadcasting of a sort and perhaps a few voiceovers for commercials and, who knows, a cruise or two. I shall not be muted just yet.

I have been highly flattered by all the people who have asked me to think again about retirement from *TMS*. If I did, I fear their smiles might turn to frowns. Funnily enough, I have enjoyed the two Test matches I have done since deciding to retire as much as any I can remember. I am writing this chapter when I still have my final Test ahead of me, when England play the West Indies at Lord's in September 2017. As I write, there are so many thoughts and memories swirling around in my head. They mostly come from the old days when I first faced a microphone. This may have happened because, back at the start, I was less sure of myself and what the future held in store for me. That may be why I remember it more clearly. Also, when you are young you are more impressionable. For whatever reason, these moments have stayed with me. In the later part of my broadcasting life, there was no immediate threat and I just relaxed and got on with it. By then, it had become routine. Perhaps too, the eccentricities of the characters around me in the early days were more extraordinary.

I can see even now an out-of-breath John Arlott puffing his way up the last flight of stairs to the commentary box at the top of the Lord's Pavilion. He would sit down heavily and take a minute or two to get his breath back. I can also hear his final words at the end of his last spell of commentary in a Test match, the Centenary Test match between England and

Australia at Lord's in 1980: 'And after Trevor Bailey, it will be Christopher Martin-Jenkins.' Simply that. He pushed back his chair, and raised himself ponderously. Then he gathered up his papers and shuffled out of the box and away from commentary for ever. Alan Curtis, a former actor who made the ground announcements in those days, then spoke to the crowd: 'John Arlott has just finished his last spell with *Test Match Special* as a cricket commentator,' and the great man received loud, warming applause from the players and the crowd. Arlott was only sixty-six. Did he have any regrets? He said to Peter Baxter the following year in the middle of Ian Botham's extraordinary series against Australia in 1981, 'I think I went a year too soon.' I am not sure he meant it, for I think he felt the year before that his time had come.

While Arlott is in the front of my mind, Brian Johnston is there too. As he strode up the steps to that old box I can still hear, 'Morning, Backers. Morning, Boil. Morning, Blowers. Morning, Bearders,' the voice as sprightly as his stride. As sprightly too, as the neatly polished brown and white co-respondent shoes he always wore for Test matches. Sadly, there was no resounding Lord's send-off for Johnners. He was simply not there when *TMS* began again in the summer of 1994. I can also see CMJ scurrying up the stairs to meet a fretting producer who never learned from experience and had him down to start the programme. He would go feverishly into our box, brushing Peter Baxter aside. He would cram on his headphones while muttering something mildly uncouth about traffic jams. Those listening to his smooth, unruffled greeting a couple of moments later would have had no clue of how nearly he did not make it.

In those days, the unbending Alan McGilvray would have been well into his first packet of cigarettes before the umpires had even put on their coats. He would be telling someone how much 'I admire your work'. The Bearded Wonder would have beaten us all into the box that morning. He would have spread his implements and accessories around like a master chef organising a mouthwatering main course. If anyone had the temerity to suggest he had spread himself too far, he did so at his peril. Frindall felt it was his duty to establish squatter's rights in each and every commentary box. He was a difficult man to disagree with – and not only because he was usually right. If it was not already lit, Fred Trueman's pipe would be lying on the green baize which covered our desk, ready for action. He would be shaking his tousled head and saying, 'I don't know what went off out there.' There would suddenly be a mild oath, a scuffling noise, and Peter Baxter, as if going for a quick single, would be out of the door in a flash, dashing along the passage and into the engineer's box to head off the latest impending crisis. These are just some of the ghosts who have come back, not to haunt, but to enchant.

In forty-something years' time, maybe a commentator whose career is only now beginning will announce that he or she is going to retire from the commentary box. It will be wonderful if this happens, because it will mean not only that *Test Match Special* is with us still, but also that Test matches are still part of the coinage. *T20 Match Special* does not have the same ring to it. Who knows, it may even be *T10 Match Special* by then. I have no doubt this mythical future retiree will also have a wonderful story to tell. It is bound to be different to this memoir, but I am sure it will be an extremely entertaining story. I just wish that I was going to be around to read it. It only remains for me to wish everyone luck: to the commentators and producers who I know will keep up the good work and take the programme to new frontiers; to the listeners who will keep faith and spread the word so that a new and larger audience is forever switching on; and to the BBC, who, fingers crossed, will make sure *Test Match Special* is available all the time for everyone to hear.

15

AU REVOIR

AFTER describing the last ball of my Test match career, on 9 September 2017, my headphones became hopelessly entangled with my binoculars as I tried to hand over to Ed Smith. I stood with my back to the ground frantically trying to disentangle them. In the middle, led by the captain, Joe Root, the England players turned to the Media Centre and applauded, while the crowd of getting on for 30,000 stood and cheered. I saw none of it, but somehow managed to separate the headphones from the binoculars.

Ten minutes later and already becoming an experienced hand at retirement, I went down in the lift with Aggers and Vic Marks, on my way, I thought, to help with the prize-giving in front of the Pavilion which always marks the end of a series. When we reached the grass behind the sightscreen, the broadcast was thrown down to Aggers and we set off towards the Mound Stand. Aggers was next to the railings, Vic in the middle and I was on the outside. By the time we got past the huge Nursery End sightscreen I realised I had been set up.

I was now three yards ahead of the field, with Aggers and Vic shuffling along behind as they talked on air. When I emerged from behind the sightscreen there was an enormous cheer. Instinctively, I looked behind me to see who on earth had prompted this. It was then I realised that it was for me – and I was gobsmacked. It was incredible: the wonderfully kind things the crowd near the fence in the Mound Stand said to me. I am fairly sure one lovely lady asked me if I would marry her, but I kept moving and I did not receive confirmation. Everything then unfolded like some magical, surreal and unbelievable kaleidoscope.

I was wearing a pistachio-green jacket and strawberry trousers, with a pink shirt outside my trousers. While I was walking past the Mound Stand, Vic Marks apparently told the world that I looked like a cross between Winston Churchill and Dame Edna. Which I suppose was recognition of a sort. I had just reached the Pavilion when someone told me to look up at the England dressing room. All the players were on the balcony looking down at me and cheering. That was the most extraordinary moment of all. I was dumbfounded and did not know what to think. I mean, I wasn't even a cricketer. I waved rather wetly back at them, but I couldn't think of anything else to do. Matthew Fleming, the President of MCC, now came up to me and said, 'Blowers, you've done half the ground, now do the other half.'

The members in the front of the Pavilion were friendly but rather more temperate in their comments, and I'm pretty certain none of them asked me to marry them. And on it went past the Warner Stand, the Grand Stand and the Compton Stand. The noise, the enthusiasm, the kindness and the persistence was something that will ring in my head for ever. I honestly almost felt embarrassed. Part of me still cannot believe that it actually happened. I never dreamt for a single moment that people felt like this.

When I eventually walked back across the ground to the prize-giving ceremony, I found I was not wanted. That had just been a smokescreen to get me to go unquestioningly down to the ground at the end. The first half of this walk had been planned by Ralph Brünjes, my brilliant agent, and our charming *TMS* producer, Adam Mountford, and Matthew Fleming was in on it too with a number of others.

The kaleidoscope continued as I was introduced for the first time to Joe Root, by Michael Vaughan. Joe asked me to come up to the England dressing room for a glass when the formalities had finished. He persuaded Vaughany to bring me up. Through the gate, up the steps into the Pavilion, through the Long Room, up the stairs and into the dressing room. There was a wonderful atmosphere. The room was full of the players, their wives and children, but no champagne. The dregs from the six empty bottles used for shaking up and spraying on the prize-giving rostrum were drained into a plastic mug – just enough for a couple of sips. I was about to have the first when the door opened. Alastair Cook, who during the match had dropped three highly takeable catches at first slip, came in carrying his twelve-month-old daughter. I started forward just in case. He juggled with her, but happily managed to hold on.

The captain made a short speech and presented me with an England shirt inscribed and signed by the players. I replied and when I told them I had once made 104 not out from this same dressing room, the look of combined disbelief was impressive. More champagne arrived and we drank and talked until it was time to go. It was September and dusk was upon us. The floodlights were off and single bulbs burned in the stands. I shook a number of hands. Then I started the long, slow walk out of the dressing room and back the way I had come, down the stairs, through the Long Room, out of the famous door, down the steps and onto the grass.

After a few steps I turned and stood looking at the Allen Stand at the left-hand end of the Pavilion. I thought back to that first visit to the ground, on 26 June 1948. I was with my father and mother and in those days we were allowed to sit on the grass behind the boundary rope. On that unforgettable day I watched Don Bradman make 89 in his last Test innings at Lord's. I can still see Bill Edrich catching him up by his right shoulder at first slip off Alec Bedser just before the close of play.

I walked to the middle of the ground and, looking round, thought of the amazing cricketing journey I had embarked on that day almost seventy years before. More than 700 Test matches, the runs, the wickets, the catches, the players, the trips round the world, the people I had met, the places I had visited – and even the drive from London to Bombay in a 1921 Rolls-Royce. What an amazing journey it had all been. And now it was over. It was quite a moment.

But no, it was not retirement. Three days later I was into rehearsals with Graeme Swann for our two-man theatre tour of twenty shows up and down the country. Swanny is a wonderful stage and real-life companion, for he has a sense of humour which is as snappy and delicious as his off-spin bowling. We began the tour in Kettering towards the end of September and finished in front of a full house at the Lyric in the West End in mid-November. In order to gear myself up for the hectic life of retirement, I had, starting in May, written this book about my life with *Test Match Special*, in about twelve weeks, so we could grab the Christmas market. *Over and Out* was masterminded by that prince of publishers, Roddy Bloomfield, and came out on 21 October. It had meant a fair bit of work.

Then it was the cruise season. In December, Valeria and I joined the *Queen Victoria* for ten days and sailed down to the Canaries. In January the *Queen Elizabeth* took us across the Atlantic to New York by way of the Azores. On each of these cruises I did three gigs in the big theatre at the front of the ship. In New York the temperature stayed relentlessly at minus five degrees centigrade, which enlivened my hips no end. We had a sensational few days, and for me one of the highlights was going to a service in the Little Church Around the Corner on 29th and Madison, where my great literary hero, P. G. Wodehouse, was married to Ethel in 1914. Cruising has become something of a lifeline for me. These voyages usually last for ten to twelve days and mean that I do not have to get behind the wheel of a car. Also Valeria, who comes with me to everything I do, is not packing and unpacking suitcases on a daily basis and, even better, Cunard look after us extremely well.

In between all these adventures I made a good many speeches at various dinners around the country, and so it was not turning out to be the normal retirement, but what fun it was. If I had a fiver for every time someone said to me, 'You are doing far too much,' I would be drinking an even better glass of wine than I am already. I cannot do with people who take the view that if you give up everything you enjoy you will live to be even older than the hills. What a miserably boring last few years they would be. I have every intention of disappearing over the horizon with all sails flying.

As you can see, I am still pretty busy. By the end of March I had already embarked upon a one-man theatre tour of 38 shows and, believe it or not, 96 per cent of the tickets were sold. They were a terrific few weeks. I love the theatre, but I love it even more when the seats are full. The next twelve months look like being even more hectic as we are moving to Menorca, where we have bought a delightful house in Mahón. The whole process of moving is bound to involve a bit of a bumpy ride, but what fun it will be when we get there. One of the great joys will be the Menorca Cricket Club, a thriving institution founded in about 1990 by Andrew Manners and David Sheffield, who have both become good friends. To a gentle extent, therefore, I shall be able to keep my eye on the ball in between frequent return visits to the UK for theatre tours, speeches and all the many other things Ralph Brünjes is constantly suggesting. And Roddy Bloomfield too, for he wants me to write another book and I am certainly up for that. I'm sure all our paths will cross again before too long.

ACKNOWLEDGEMENTS

I HONESTLY don't know where to begin. Everyone and anyone who has come into the *Test Match Special* box since 1972, when I began, would be a start. Then, of course, there are all those before that who showed us how it should be done, going as far back as Howard Marshall before the war.

I am going to name one or two at the risk of annoying those I leave out. I have to mention, with deep thanks for all the fun, laughter and the rest, the combined geniuses of John Arlott, Brian Johnston, Alan Gibson, CMJ, Vic Marks, Aggers, Tony Cozier, Jim Maxwell, Vaughany, Tuffers, Swanny, my stage partner, and, right at the end, Fazeer Mohammed, who covered the 2017 tour by the West Indies and, ipso facto, my last Test match as a TMS commentator. He was charming and delightful and gave me, rather too late I have to admit, a near-perfect object lesson in how to do the job.

The producers and their assistants – Peter Baxter and Shilpa Patel, and latterly Adam Mountford and Henry Moeran – have all bitten their lips with ever-increasing frequency and allowed me to carry on. The scorers: Bill Frindall for his bearded snorts and beautiful handwriting, as well as his immaculate scoring; Andrew Samson, certainly not for his beautiful handwriting, but for an amazing, also bearded, skill in coming up with remote, unlikely, interesting, relevant and entertaining facts and statistics before the bowler has even got back to the end of his run to bowl the next ball. He is undoubtedly the first among equals. Finally our irrepressible team of engineers, led always with skill by Andy Leslie and Brian Mack.

And now to the photographs. The Sage of Longparish, John Woodcock, famously of *The Times*, has dug fruitfully into his photograph albums of the many tours we covered together. Peter Baxter, our *TMS* producer for thirty-four years, has done the same. When it came to the stories I have told in this book, Peter kept me on the straight and narrow as best he could. Henry Moeran was the happy snapper at our party for *TMS* during the 2017 Oval Test. Philip Brown, a master cricket photographer, not only completed my hat-trick of beards, but also contributed some fine examples of his skill. My profound thanks to all of them.

Last but not least come the two who made it all possible. My agent, Ralph Brünjes – it is by the way pronounced 'Rafe', but is there any other way? – buoyed me throughout with his inexhaustible enthusiasm. From time to time, too, Ralph puts on his whites and bowls tripe, although he once had a benevolent Mark Ramprakash caught at long off.

Now we come to my great friend and publisher, Roddy Bloomfield, who has kept going in his trade for even longer

ACKNOWLEDGEMENTS

than I have in mine. Huge thanks to him for his eternal enthusiasm, too, and of course his friendliness, his avuncular know-how and impeccable judgement. He is, beyond doubt, another first among equals. This is the seventh book I have done with Roddy, and what fun it has been.

PHOTOGRAPHIC ACKNOWLEDGEMENTS

The author and publisher would like to thank the following for permission to reproduce photographs:

Hulton Archive/Stringer/Getty Images, Popperfoto/ Getty Images, Paul Popper/Popperfoto/ Getty Images, Central Press/Stringer/ Getty Images, Getty Images, Patrick Eagar/ Popperfoto/ Getty Images, Ken Kelly/Popperfoto/Getty Images, Bob Thomas Sports Photography/ Getty Images, Adrian Murrell/ Getty Images, Michael Ochs Archive/ Getty Images, Ben Radford/ Getty Images, Professional Sport/ Getty Images, Visionhaus/ Getty Images, Laurence Griffiths/ Getty Images, Julian Finney/ Getty Images, Philip Brown, Gareth Copley/ Getty Images.

All other photographs are from private collections.

Every reasonable effort has been made to trace the copyright holders, but if there are any errors or omissions, Hodder & Stoughton will be pleased to insert the appropriate acknowledgement in any subsequent printings or editions.

INDEX

INDEX

Wood, Graeme 141, 150
Wood, Mark 216
Woodcock, John 42, 119, 120, 122
Wooller, Wilf 108–9
Woolmer, Bob 81
World, Cup, Wembley 1966 101
World Cup cricket 115, 199
    England v West Indies (1999)
        167
    England v Australia (1979) 243
    India v Australia (1987) 135–6,
        185
    Pakistan v Australia (1996)
        134–5, 262
    West Indies v Australia (1975)
        78

World Series Cricket (WSC) 91,
    102–3, 208–9
    Australia v West Indies (1977)
        200–203
WorldTel 115
Worrell, Frank 166
Wrigley, Arthur 221
Wykes, Mr 14

Yallop, Neville 152
Yardley, Norman 165, 218
Yorkshire 267

Zamaan Park, Lahore 134–5
Zimbabwe 188